Behave
as a
Church

DR. CHRISTOPHER POWERS

WESTBOW
PRESS®
A DIVISION OF THOMAS NELSON
& ZONDERVAN

This book is a work of non-fiction. Unless otherwise noted, the author and the publisher make no explicit guarantees as to the accuracy of the information contained in this book and in some cases, names of people and places have been altered to protect their privacy.

WestBow Press books may be ordered through booksellers or by contacting:

WestBow Press
A Division of Thomas Nelson & Zondervan
1663 Liberty Drive
Bloomington, IN 47403
www.westbowpress.com
844-714-3454

Because of the dynamic nature of the Internet, any web addresses or links contained in this book may have changed since publication and may no longer be valid. The views expressed in this work are solely those of the author and do not necessarily reflect the views of the publisher, and the publisher hereby disclaims any responsibility for them.

Any people depicted in stock imagery provided by Getty Images are models, and such images are being used for illustrative purposes only. Certain stock imagery © Getty Images.

Scripture quotations marked (KJV) are taken from the King James Version, public domain.

Scripture quotations marked (NKJV) are taken from the New King James Version. Copyright © 1982 by Thomas Nelson, Inc. Used by permission. All rights reserved.

ISBN: 979-8-3850-1749-2 (sc)
ISBN: 979-8-3850-1750-8 (e)

Library of Congress Control Number: 2024901432

Print information available on the last page.

WestBow Press rev. date: 4/4/2024

To my Wife
Thanks for being there for me. Your support
and love have always been a blessing to me.

To Dad
Thanks for always being my pastor, taking me
to church, sharing the teachings of the Bible,
and being a godly example of a pastor.

To Mom
Thanks for always editing my books, for taking me
to church, and teaching me about the things of God.

CONTENTS

The Body of Christ

And let us consider one another in order to
stir up love and good works, not forsaking the
assembling of ourselves together, as is the manner
of some, but exhorting one another, and so much
the more as you see the Day approaching.
(Hebrews 10:24-25 NKJV)

Church, we have a problem. According to LifeWay Research, roughly 70 percent of young adults drop out of church (Stetzer, 2017) Church fights have been going on since the early church. However, could be part of the reason why so many young adults are leaving the church? Let me give you twenty-five examples of the silly church fights which has cast a black eye on the church. "1). Arguments over the appropriate length of the worship pastor's beard. 2). Fight over whether or not to build a children's playground or to use the land for a cemetery. 3). A deacon accusing another deacon of sending an anonymous letter, and deciding to settle the matter in the parking lot. 4). A church dispute of whether or not to install restroom stall dividers in the women's restroom. 5). A church argument and vote to decide if a clock in the worship center should be removed. 6). A 45-minute heated argument over the type of filing cabinet to purchase: black or brown; 2, 3, or 4 drawers. 7). A fight over which picture of Jesus to put in the foyer. 8). A petition to have all church staff clean shaven. 9). A dispute over whether the worship leader should have shoes on during the service. 10). The big church argument over the discover that the church budget was off $0.10. Someone finally gave a dime to settle the issue. 11). A dispute in the church because the Lord's Supper had cran-grape juice instead of grape juice. 12). Business meeting arguments about whether the church should purchase a weed eater or not. It took two business meetings to resolve. 13). Arguments over what type of green beans the church should serve. 14). Two different churches reported fights over the type of coffee. In one of the churches, they moved from Folgers to a stronger Starbucks brand. In the other church, they simply moved to a stronger blend. Members left the church in the latter example. 15). Major conflict when the youth borrowed a crockpot that had not been used for years. 16). An argument on whether the church should allow deviled eggs at the church meal. 17). An argument over who has the authority to buy postage stamps for the church. 18). A disagreement over using the term "potluck" instead of "pot blessing." 19). A church member was chastised because she brought vanilla syrup to the coffee server. It looked too much like liquor. 20). An argument in church over who has access to the copy machine. 21). Some church members left the church because one church member hid the vacuum cleaner from them. It resulted in a major fight and split. 22). An argument over whether to have gluten-free communion bread or not. 23). A dispute over whether the church should allow people to wear black t-shirts, since black is the color of the devil. 24). A fight over whether or not to sing "Happy Birthday" each week. 25). An argument over whether the fake, dusty plants should be removed from the podium." (Twenty Five things Church Members Fight Over, 2022) These arguments and fights are funny and illogical, however, the sad part about this is the fact that these arguments are a distraction from purpose and mission of the church.

The church, the bride of Christ, the body of Christ has a problem because the group of baptized believers are not behaving as a church. Well, whose is to blame for these problems? Who is to blame for a statistic of 70 percent of young adults dropping out of church? Is it the parents fault? How about college and young adult ministry could it be at fault? Maybe it is the kid's ministry? Or the youth ministry? I know, it's the pastor's fault, right? Listen, it would be a big mistake to see this statistic as an accusation and criticize the church.

The reasons for the problems in the church is because we are not behaving as church members using our spiritual gifts as we are supposed to. The problem of church growth stems from the fact that we are not behaving as fishers of men. The fault behind this statistic is the fact that we are not behaving as followers of Christ. The overall problem is we are not fulfilling all aspects of the great commission, which includes evangelism and discipleship. If you love Jesus, then you are going to love what Jesus loves; and Jesus loves the church! Therefore, never criticize the church, because when you criticize the church, you are criticizing the body of Christ here on earth. Overall, when you criticize the church, you are criticizing the Lord Jesus Christ. Sure, the church is not perfect, and stands in need of correcting from time to time. However, that does not mean we rebuke the church, accuse the church, or criticize the church. So, please be careful when you put down, talk about, or criticize the body of Christ in a negative way.

However, praise be to our Lord and Savior Jesus Christ! Not all hope is lost. We can still turn the world upside down. Let me just say, I believe that God's plans for the end of times and His timing of everything cannot be change or messed with. For He has those set-in stone, and He is the only one who knows when those events will take place. However, I do believe that the church can make a dent in the work we are called to do before we head home. That is if we can behave as a church. A New Testament church is to be a Spirit-filled, Bible-believing, Christ-honoring church. Therefore, I believe that God is still going to give the church one last surge of revival of all revivals before the terrible day of the Lord (Zeph.1:14-18). We are living in perilous times (2 Tim. 3:1), and I have the feeling that the world is going to look to the church one more time. Why? Because the world has tried everything; every form of government, every kind of leader, every excess of pleasure, everything that money can buy, and yet they still cannot fill their bellies and their purses have holes in them (Hag. 1:6). They are never satisfied, they are wanting more and more, and yet this still are left with a void they cannot fill. So, they turn to the church, and wonder one more time, do we have the answer? Certainly, the answer is yes! Jesus is the answer, He has always been the answer. But when they turn to the church, will they see the body of Christ that behaves as a church or will they see the body of Christ defeated, overcome with problems where failure has become a reality. I wonder what they are going to see, I wonder what they see now.

There was a philosopher by the name of Fredrick Nietzsche. Nietzsche was known for having a disciple by the name of Adolph Hitler. Nietzsche was a cynic, an atheist, an ungodly, lascivious man. He looked at the church, considered the church, and then made the statement; "I might believe in the Redeemer, if His followers looked more redeemed." (Friedrich Nietzsche, 2022) The world today is getting its idea of Jesus Christ not from the Word of God, because they do not read it, but from the body of Christ; the believers. Take for example the carnal church at Corinth. They were plagued with division (1 Cor. 1:10-13), believers not growing mature staying babies in Christ (1 Cor. 3:1-3), tolerant of immorality (1 Cor. 5:1-2); and yet they were still a spiritual congregation (1 Cor. 1:7). The reason they were so carnal, with a lot of problems, is because of the spiritual gifts. The problem at Corinth was not that they did not possess the spiritual gifts, it was because they wanted gifts they were not assigned by God. When God gives His spiritual gifts to a Christian, He does so in His own Sovereign will (1 Cor. 12:11, 18). The people of Corinth were stepping outside the boundaries laid down by the Lord and were trying to practice gifts they had not received. As a result, there was chaos and confusion in the church.

Because what was going on in the Corinthian church, Paul had to speak to this situation and tell them that they are guilty of coveting more than they were given. He says, "But earnestly desire the best gifts. And yet I show you a more excellent way" (1 Cor. 12:31 NKJV). Every believer is given a spiritual gift or gifts at their conversion, so they can behave as a church member. Which in turn when we behave as church members, we then begin to behave as a church. Those gifts are to be used for service and in 1 Corinthians 12:12-27 we see, that while we differ in our spiritual gifts, abilities, and our position in the body of Christ; we are nonetheless vital and important as we behave as a church. The church, not the building, but the redeemed of God, is an organism made up of many millions and billions of parts that is to function as one.

Your Placement in the Body

Just how does one go about getting in the body of Christ? It is simple, put your faith and trust upon the Lord Jesus Christ, His finished work on the cross, and His resurrection from the dead. Ask Jesus to come into your heart and save you from your sin (Rom. 10:13). The church is the mystical body of the Lord Jesus Christ, and He is the sovereign head of His body, which is the church. When did the church begin? Paul says, "For by one Spirit we were all baptized into one body whether Jews or Greeks, whether slaves or free; and have all been made to drink into one Spirit" (1 Cor. 12:13 NKJV). On the Day of Pentecost, the Holy Spirit baptized us into the Body of Christ. We were immersed into the Body of Christ at the moment we asked Jesus to come into our hearts. This baptism into the body of Christ is not something that is optional according to verse 13. In Luke 2, you have the story of the physical birth of Jesus. In Acts 2, you have the birth of Jesus's other body, His mystical body: the church. Both His physical body and mystical body are the result of the work of the Holy Spirit of God and both are supernatural. Therefore, baptism in the Bible is spoken both literally and figuratively. Literal baptism takes place in the water. But it is not the water baptism that puts you into the Body of Christ; it is the Holy Spirit's baptism that puts us in the Body of Christ (1 Cor. 12:13). Water baptism is a representation of the Spirit's baptism which places us into the Body of Christ. It is not something we seek, nor is it based on what we do, it is the Sovereign act of Almighty God.

Therefore, if by one Spirit we are baptized into one body, then that means that the church is not an organization; it is a family. The Holy Spirit of God puts us into the Body of Christ, and the Holy Spirit of God is in our hearts. The church is not an organization like Kiwanis or the Boy Scouts, the church is a family made up unique people placed there by the Holy Spirit who share the life of Christ. The Holy Spirit is the one Spirit within the heart of every believer, therefore, if we had the body without the Spirit, we would be a corpse. If we have the Spirit without the body, we be a ghost. But the church is a body indwelt by the Holy Spirit of God. The birthday of the church took place when the Holy Spirit on the Day of Pentecost took all those disciples and baptized them into one body. Ever since that time, every believer is added by the Holy Spirit into one body. Once a person has been baptized by the Holy Spirit, they are there to stay forever. The verb phrase "we were all baptized" (1 Cor. 12:13 NKJV) speaks of a one-time action that took place at some unspecified time in the past (Holman Illustrated Bible Dictionary, 2003) In other words, when you receive Jesus as your Savior, there is a one time, for all time, action that places you into the body of Christ. When you get in the body of Christ, you do not get out!

Your Place in the Body

According to Paul every believer is part of the whole. Paul writes, "For in fact the body is not one member but many" (1 Cor. 12:14 NKJV). There are hundreds and hundreds of believers that are in the body of Christ. While we are many, we have one agenda. Therefore, all members of the body of Christ are to behave as a church and be committed to fulfilling that one agenda. Because a healthy body is a body that is harmonize where the members learn to work together at the direction of the Head. Think of it this way; the human body has many parts just like an automobile has many parts. Every part is essential for the unit to properly function, and yet, the body or the car is thought of as one. This is true of the body of Christ as well. His body is formed of believers from all walks of life, all cultures, all sections of society, and all levels of wealth. His body is made up of people who have nothing else in common, except the fact they have received Jesus as their Savior. The body of Christ is a unified diversity and when every believer fills their purpose they are assigned by Jesus, then the body functions as it should and therefore glorifies Jesus and the work of the Great Commission is carried out.

Paul tells us that every believer is placed in the local body of Christ, the church, by God (1 Cor. 12:15-20). Just because these parts of the body do not get the attention, they think they deserve, they have no right to try and divorce themselves from the rest of the body. If every part were an eye, the body would be useless and only good for seeing. If every part were a foot, it would be good for nothing but a doorstop. What Paul is saying in 1 Corinthians 12:15-20 is, God has placed us in the body where He wants us to be. It may not be a high-profile position, it may not be glamorous, it may not even be what we want to do, but if it pleases the Lord then we are in the right place of the body. Therefore, no matter where you are to function within the church, remember you were placed in that exact office, position by the will of God. To me, there is no greater knowledge than to know you are walking in the will of God. If I fulfill my place in the body, then I am doing my part in helping the church to behave as a church. We need to surrender to our place in Jesus, even if we would like to be something else. God knows us and He knows where we can best function. When we submit to His will He is glorified and the ministry of the church is advanced in the world. After all, if we are behaving as a church that should be our primary goal (1 Cor. 10:31).

In the church, every believer plays an important role in the proper function of the entire body according to Paul (1 Cor. 12:21-24). The eye cannot tell the hand that it does not need it. If the eyes were disconnected from the hand, it would never be able to attain the object of its desire. The hand cannot tell the feet to get lost, for without them the hands have no method of locomotion. What Paul is saying is every part of the body needs ever other part to fully carry out the work of the body. The whole point of this section of Paul's letter to the church at Corinth, and to us, is to teach us that every member no matter how insignificant their office, position, or gift may appear is essential to behave as a church. No one should ever think they are not needed in the church. No one should ever say to or about another believer, "We do not need you." Every member is vital, every member is important.

Your Purpose in the Body

Paul says, "that there should be no schism in the body" (1 Cor. 12:25 NKJV). What that means is, as a church member you are to promote unity and harmony within the church. When every member does their part and submits to God by doing what they are called to do and gifted to do, then the church will function in absolute peace and unity. In our day, day there are too many feet who want to be hands and too many ears who want to be eyes. When this happens, the body is fractured and chaos is the results. God plan for His church is that we be united. (1 Cor. 1:10; Phil. 1:27). When we are not in unity, the body of Christ suffers (1 Cor. 1:10). Let me take this a little deeper. The writer of Hebrews says, "And let us consider one another in order to stir up love and good works, not forsaking the assembling of ourselves together as is the manner of some, but exhorting one another, and so much the more as you see the Day approaching" (Heb. 10:24-25 NKJV). In order for you to promote unity at church, in order to stir up love and good works you need to show up at church. The Greek word for "stir up" (NKJV) or "provoke" (KJV) means to contend (Holman Illustrated Bible Dictionary, 2003) The writer of Hebrews is talking about connecting deeply with one another so we cannot sit still as believers. We have to do something. Our affections for Christ are provoked so deeply when gathered together at church that we cannot help but to promote unity, harmony, love for one another, and good works.

Paul reminds us that we are to practice mutual care for one another. He writes, "but that the members should have the same care for one another. And if one member suffers, all the members suffer with it; or if one member is honored, all the members rejoice with it" (1 Cor. 25-26 NKJV). Paul reminds us that we are one unit, with each part having responsibilities to the other parts. When another believer is hurting, we need to respond to that need (Gal. 6:2). You may never take the time to think of you fingers, but just slam the car door on them and watch how the whole body gets involved responding to the crisis. The nerves will carry the message to the brain. The brain in turn sends a message to the feet who begin to hop around, the eyes receive the message and begin to water, the mouth hears about the message and hangs open in surprise, then the other hand finally receives the message who is now trying to find the door handle. When one of those less visible members gets into trouble, everything else responds to the need. This is what the writer of Hebrew is saying as well, when he writes, "exhorting one another" (Heb. 10:25 NKJV). The reason church members are to gather together is to encourage each other. When we hear the word encouragement, we tend to think that we should be positive around someone. Listen, God is not merely interested in the body of Christ thinking positive. The Greek word translated as "encouragement" means "to call alongside" (Holman Illustrated Bible Dictionary, 2003) This is the same action the Holy Spirit performs as a Helper. We encourage one another the same way the Holy Spirit encourages us. We are to practice mutual care that encompasses the whole body. Every member is called upon to look after the need of every other member, regardless of their place in the body of Christ.

When a member hurts, it affects the entire body. When one is exalted, the entire body should be blessed by it. The idea is this: when everything functions as it should, the body operates efficiently and accomplishes much. However, when parts do not function as they ought, then there are problems and nothing gets done as it should. Paul's goal is to get the church to see that we need one another. Together we are a complete body, individually, we are a small but vital component of a very important family. After you have learned how to *Behave as a Church Member*, now we can put together that knowledge and learn how to behave as a church. Here in this book, you are going to see the many ways the church, the Bride of Christ, God's children, should work together to fulfill the Great Commission (Matt. 28:18-20). It is my prayer that through this book the church, the Bride of Christ, can grow and continue the kingdom work.

CHAPTER ONE

Making Jesus Known

Therefore, let all the house of Israel know
assuredly that God has made this Jesus, whom
you crucified, both Lord and Christ.
(Acts 2:36 NKJV)

WHAT IS THE PURPOSE OF THE CHURCH? THERE ARE A LOT OF church members who do not even know the mission statement of their church. Let me suggest this mission statement to behave as a church: *To magnify Jesus Christ through worship and the Word, to move believers in Jesus Christ towards maturity and ministry, and to make Jesus Christ known to our neighbors and the nations.* This world needs to know Jesus. Your neighbors need to know Jesus. The church is to make Jesus known at home and abroad. There is a story about the legendary coach Vince Lombardi of the Green Bay Packers. In December 1960, the Green Bay Packers were playing the Philadelphia Eagles in the NFL championship game. The Packers played one of the most miserable games and lost that game in the last minutes. Come training camp in July 1961, they were still feeling the pain. Coach Lombardi brought them all in for skull practice. In other words, not on the field practice, but thinking practice. He wanted to get the thirty-eight players to get their head on straight, get things between their ears arranged in the right order. The legendary coach wanted to get the boys back to the fundamentals, back to the basics of the game. He reached in a bag and pulled out a football, and said, "Gentlemen, this is a football." (Maraniss, 1999) These were professional football players, they should know what a football looks like, however, what he was saying is that he wants them to get back to the basics.

"Ladies and Gentlemen, this is a Bible." I believe that is what the church of the Lord Jesus Christ needs to do today; get back to the very basic, fundamental, rudimentary elements of our faith. Let begin by looking at the first two chapter of the book of Acts at the early New Testament church. Let me give you a description of a New Testament church. The Bride of Christ is to be a Spirit-filled, Bible-believing, Christ-honoring church. This should be our prayer as church members that God would strengthen his children to behave as a church. Did the early church automatically know how to behave as a church, did every individual know how to behave as church members? No! It was not until the Holy Spirit anointed the first century church and gave them power from on high. Once we receive the same anointing, with the same power we are to make Jesus known to our neighbors and the nations. Let's start with the basics, and there are three things we find in the first two chapters of the book of Acts.

We Need to Recognize His Presence in Us

If we are going to behave as a church, then we are going to have to recognize the presence of Jesus in our hearts and the hearts of our brothers and sisters of God family. Now for the most part there are many church members who do not behave as though the Holy Spirit is living in their heart. If we could ever get this phenomenal thought that the Holy Spirit is present in our lives, then we too could turn our world upside down. Once we recognize the presence of Jesus in us, then we can continue what Jesus began to do. As matter of fact, did you know that the book of acts is not the story of the acts of the apostles? No! It is the story of the acts of Jesus Christ. "The former account I made, O Theophilus, of all that Jesus began both to do and teach" (Acts 1:1 NKJV).

Every good book has a hero, and the hero of the book of Acts is Jesus. If you look at your Bible, at the title for the book of Acts it will say, "The Acts of the Apostles." That title was put there by the publisher of your copy of the Bible. Luke begins this book by saying, "The former account I made" (vs. 1 NKJV). What is the former account that Dr. Luke wrote? Luke wrote the Gospel of Luke. So what Luke is saying in the first verse of the book of Acts is, "I have written the gospel of Luke, and this is what Jesus began to do. But now, I am going to write this book of Acts and this is what Jesus continues to do." In the Gospels, you find out what Jesus is doing in His human body, the body of His flesh. In the book of Acts, you find out what Jesus is doing in His mystical body, the church. You see, Jesus is still active and alive and well today in His mystical body. Paul calls this, "Christ in you" (Col. 1:27 NKJV). We are not here just imitating Jesus Christ; we are to let the Him work through us and continue the work which He began. The New Testament church is the body of Jesus. We are in Him and He is in us. If we could ever let the thought: Jesus Christ is in us and that He began a work in the Gospels and He continues that work today, then how powerful would the bride of Christ be here on earth (Gal. 2:20)?

For example, on the Day of Pentecost, Peter stood up and preached a simple and plain message. People accepted Jesus Christ into their hearts, and the church grew because they lifted up Jesus by making Jesus known to the world. Jesus said, "And I, if I am lifted up from the earth, will draw all peoples to Myself" (John 12:32 NKJV). No church is going to be a growing, vibrant church that does not exalt the Lord Jesus Christ by recognizing that Jesus is in us. To behave as a church, we need to make Jesus known, we need to magnify God the Father and God the Holy Spirit, but every service and every opportunity we must exalt the Lord Jesus Christ and make Him known. Why? Because He is the attracting power of the church. Notice what Peter said in his message.

"Men of Israel, hear these words: Jesus of Nazareth, a Man attested by God to you by miracles, wonders, and signs which God did through Him in your midst, as you yourselves also know" (Acts 2:22 NKJV). The life of Jesus has affected more people's lives than any armies, governments, philosophers, idealist, and celebrities put together. We behave as a church when we worship the King of kings and the Lord of lords, because Jesus Christ has affected our lives because He lives!

3

Peter goes on to say, "Him, being delivered by the determined purpose and foreknowledge of God, you have taken by lawless hands, have crucified, and put to death" (vs. 23 NKJV). What Peter is saying here is that Jesus Christ's death was not an accident; it was planned before the foundation of the earth. Nothing went wrong and God was not up in heaven wringing His hands as if something terrible had happen that was out of His control. The purpose of the cross is substitution; the Just for the unjust. Christ died for us and He took our place. He was sinless, lived a spotless life, and His vicarious death upon the cross paid our sin debt in full. If you were to take that message out of the Bible then the rest of the Bible would be useless. There is no gospel with the cross, there is no salvation without the cross, and there is no eternal life without the cross. All our hope would be gone, no joy, no happiness, no life if Jesus did not die on the cross.

Peter continues, "Whom God raised up, having loosed the pains of death, because it was not possible that He should be held by it" (vs. 24 NKJV). Death cannot keep his prey. There is no way possible for death to keep Jesus in the grave. Death says, "I will keep Him in. We will put Him there, and He will not rise." But up from the grave He arose! Jesus has conquered death, hell, and the grave for those how place their trust in Jesus Christ (Rom. 10:13). Jesus is alive! He lives forevermore! But just where is Jesus right now? Peter said in his message, "Therefore being exalted to the right hand of God, and having received from the Father the promise of the Holy Spirit, He poured out this which you now see and hear. For David did not ascend into the heavens, but he says himself: 'The Lord said to my Lord, "Sit at My right, till I make your enemies Your footstool."'" (Acts 2:33-35 NKJV). Jesus, right now, is sitting on the right hand of the Majesty on high, and He is waiting till the time when God gives the signal and He will step from His throne to come back down to this earth to rule and reign. Peter preached on the Day of Pentecost that Jesus is exalted, that He is Lord of lords and King of kings. Peter was making Jesus known, just as we are to behave as a church and make Jesus known to a lost and dying world. Listen, you may not be a believer, but one day you will confess that Jesus Christ is Lord. "That at the name of Jesus every knee should bow, of those in heaven, and those on earth, and of those under the earth, and that every tongue should confess that Jesus Christ is Lord, to the glory of God the Father" (Phil. 2:10-11 NKJV). If you do not know Jesus Christ as your Lord and Savior, then you need to stop and ask Him into your heart right now before it is everlasting to late.

We Need to Rely on His Promise to Us

Once we get saved, then what do we do? What is the promise of the Father? "And being assembled together with them, He commanded them not to depart from Jerusalem, but to wait for the Promise of the Father, "which," He said, "you have heard from Me; for John truly baptized you with water, but you shall be baptized with Holy Spirit not many days from now." Therefore, when they had come together, they asked Him, saying, "Lord, will you at this time restore the kingdom to Israel?" And He said to them, "It is not for you to know times or seasons which the Father has put in His own authority. But you shall receive power when the Holy Spirit has come upon you; and you shall be witnesses to Me in Jerusalem, and in all Judea and Samaria, and to the end of the earth."" (Acts 1:4-8 NKJV). The promise of the Father is one that Jesus had made earlier. In Luke 24:49 Jesus said, "Behold, I send the Promise of My Father upon you; but tarry in the city of Jerusalem until you are endued with power from on high" (NKJV). What Jesus wanted them to do is not go out and start any kind of ministry until they have received this promise from on high. The promise of the Father is the empowerment of the Holy Spirit. Again, we need to recognize that once we get saved, the moment we ask Jesus into our hearts is the moment the Holy Spirit comes in and takes up residence in our hearts and lives. His presence is forever with us and we need to rely on His promise to us. He has given us a job that we can do only as depend upon Him and behave as a church.

The people Luke was writing to were unlettered, uncivilized with no finances, no college education, no seminaries and Jesus tells us to go into all the world. Therefore, He did not leave them helpless. He sent the promise of the Father to equip the saints. He told them to wait in Jerusalem until then. They waited just like He told them to, and on the Day of Pentecost the promise came. Now, we are told not to tarry any more, because the Day of Pentecost has come, the promise has come and we do not need to keep on asking Jesus to send the Holy Spirit. He has already sent the Holy Spirit and we have "received power" (Acts 1:8 NKJV). If you want to behave as a church, learn this secret; you do not have to be an intellectual person in order to be used of God. As a matter of fact, I have been pastoring long enough to know that some of our brightest minds are our worst witnesses. There is nothing wrong with having intellect, but Jesus did not call you to be a lawyer; He called you to be a witness. A lawyer argues a case; a witness tells what he has seen and heard. But do you know why some of the church members do not witness? It is because they have not seen or heard anything. But a Christian who has had an experience with Jesus Christ is automatically a witness. He cannot help but witness. You do not have to know all the answers, however, when you go out to share the gospel and make Jesus known you can answer any question that is asked. Here is how to answer the questions that you think is too tough to answer, "I do not know." Isn't that a good answer? When you stop pretending you know things that you do not know, people will start believing you when you tell them what you do know. That is what a witness does. Just tell the fact of what you have seen and heard.

There was a preacher went into a department store. He went back to the back to where the sporting goods were. He was looking for some fishing tackle. When he got to the counter, He asked this question, "What is a good bass lure?" There was another customer that overheard the conversation and said, "Hey, let me tell you about a good bass lure," and he began to talk to the preacher and telling him everything there was about this bass lure. He even went on to talk about the best places to fish, the best time to fish, the best rods, and the best boats. The preacher finally said, "Well, thank you so very much for the information" and he buys one of the lures, and started walking out. The other customer just started following him all the way out to the car. All the way out to the parking lot, this customer was still talking about bass, and bass lures, and how to catch bass. Now, if there is one thing that can be said about that customer is the fact that there is little doubt that he was a bass fisherman. There was little doubt that he knew something about what he was talking about, and he was very interested in it. Now, I do not know whether the man that followed me to my truck knew Jesus or not, but probably, if that man were a member of a local church, and you asked him to testify, he'd say, "Well, I cannot do that." You want to know why he cannot testify? He was not interested in the subject, having not been filled with the subject. When Jesus is real to you, witnessing will be just as natural as talking about bass lures was for that bass fisherman. What is down in the well comes up in the bucket.

Not only will witnessing be easy when you rely on the promise, but you will want to know more and help other church members grow in the walk with Jesus. This is another possible reason why so many young adults are leaving the church because they have not been discipled. Here is how Peter put it in His message, "And they continued steadfastly in the apostles' doctrine and fellowship, in the breaking of bread, and in prayers" (Acts 2:42 NKJV). Once new believers are added to the flock, the family we are to take the time to make them disciples. We are not to baptize them and forget them. Here are just a few ways that you can begin discipling new believers.

First, plug them into a Bible study group. Wednesday night small groups is a great place to get them plugged into Bible study. The idea is to get the new believer excited about reading the Bible, meditating on the Bible, exploring the Bible, and developing a habit of going to the Bible. Sunday School is not school, but it is a Bible study class where believers discuss the Bible and ask questions about the Bible, ask questions about doctrine, and it is a great opportunity to get to know fellow brothers and sisters in Christ. If you are not plugged into some sort of Bible study at the church you attend then you are missing out on a major part of behaving as a follower of Christ, church member, worship, and growth. You may be thinking, "Well, Pastor, I just do not need it." Yes, you do! That Bible study group is how other church members are going to know your name. That is how they will know when you are sick, in need of prayer or a visit, or if you are in the hospital. It is how they are going to know if you need your yard worked on or have a need of something you have a need for. We behave as a church when we minister to one another through Bible study. We behave as a church when we disciple through Bible Study it creates opportunities to train.

Second, we can disciple new believers through fellowship. There are some church members who think fellowship is incidental, when in reality they are absolutely fundamental and intentional. The Bible never teaches a lone wolf Christianity or a lone ranger Christianity. Fellowship creates an atmosphere that show church members that we need one another. Fellowship is not all about a pot luck meal after church on a Sunday morning. Fellowship is also a time where mature believers can take the opportunity to mentor a babe in Christ. That is what it means to behave as a church. Fellowship is a time where we can be ourselves around fellow believers. Did you know that the mighty Apostle Paul had a need for fellowship with other believers? "And from there, when the brethren heard about us, they came to meet us as far as Appii Forum and Three Inns. When Paul saw them, he thanked God and took courage" (Acts 28:15 NKJV). Paul was on his way to Rome when he found some of the brethren (vs. 14). He stayed seven days with them and then headed towards Rome. As his group was traveling there came some of the brethren from Rome out to find Paul. When he saw them, he said, "Oh, thank you Lord" and he took courage. We need fellowship (Heb. 10:24-25). There reason so many young adults are leaving the church is because they are not being plugged in to a church family through fellowship. They need something tangible, they want somewhere they can belong, and one of the best way to behave as a church is through fellowship which aids in making disciples.

Another way to disciple new believers is to help them understand worship. New believers must be taught what it means to worship God. Jesus said, "God is Spirit and those who worship Him must worship in spirit and truth" (John 4:24 NKJV). The word "worship" translates from the Greek word meaning "to kiss towards" (Strong's Concordance, 1984) The word "worship" refers to giving someone their "worth" (Holman Illustrated Bible Dictionary, 2003) When we behave as a church and worship God and Jesus through the Holy Spirit, "it means we ascribe to God His worth." (Powers D. C., 2021)

We need to teach new believers that when we worship Jesus, we are affirming His deity, His love, and His glory. As a church we are to "humble ourselves and give glory, honor, reverence, awe, respect, and homage to God. It means we recognize His vastly superior standing, and we humble ourselves before Him and give glory to Him. Thus, worship is giving. Essentially, it is giving honor and respect to God. Hopefully, that is the reason we gather with other believers in a church setting." (Powers D. C., 2021) Real worship is us acknowledging Him to be our everything. We will discuss more about worship later in this book. But just know that young adults who do not see real worship in the lives of other believers, nor experience real worship themselves are typically going to become less interested in staying at that church.

Then let us talk about stewardship as a way to disciple new believers. Acts 2:44-45 says, "Now all who believed were together, and had all things in common, and sold their possessions and goods, and divided them among all, as anyone had need" (NKJV). God wants to use you to make Jesus know to our neighbors, and to the nations. We are to begin in Jerusalem (our communities), then in Judea (our state), then in Samaria (our country), and then the whole world (Acts 1:8). That is what the church exists for, to make Jesus known. The early church made Jesus known by being good stewards of what they had. None of them ever said, "What I have is mine." No, they shared it, by saying "Lord, if you want it, then you can have it." During the days of the early church there was a major crisis, a great emergency going on. There was persecution and oppression taking place. The point is, everything they owned was at the disposal of the Lord Jesus Christ. Is everything you own at the disposal of Jesus? What if He asked you for your last penny, would you give it to Him? Remember it all belongs to Him. This is one of the areas we do not often behave as a church, because the last thing we want to let go of is our finances, our material possessions. This is often how we feel as individuals. It all belongs to God, even the money in the church's general fund.

There was a church in Arkansas who learned this lesson the hard way. In a business meeting, they were discussing financial matters: should they spend money to paint the church, should they spend money to maintain their van, and should they spend money on new sound equipment. The church voted down all three. One church member said, "We do not need to spend this money on feverous things. It is God's money we need to take care of it." Over the next three months, God used His money of that church. There was a car that ran into the side of the church building; so, they had to paint the church after fixing the hole. The church van broke down while on a church trip; they had to get it fix. Someone broke into the church and stole the sound equipment, which was not covered under insurance, and the church had to buy new sound equipment. It all belongs to God. We behave as a church when we are good stewards of God's possessions and when there is a need we show Jesus to others by helping those in need.

Let me say something briefly about tithing. Do not get the idea that one-tenth belongs to God and the rest is yours for your pleasure and squandering. It all belongs to God. One-tenth is only a sign that it all belongs to God. There are so many church members who are afraid they are going to over-give. Listen, you cannot out give God. If you shovel it out, then He is going to shovel it in, and by the way, He has a bigger shovel. Plus, do not get the idea that one day belongs to God and six are for you. Every day belongs to God, and He is to be the Lord over it all. This kind of stewardship is what we are to be teaching to new believers.

We Need to Respond to His Program through Us

If we are going to behave as a church and make Jesus known, then what is His program through us? "But you shall receive power when the Holy Spirit has come upon you; and you shall be witnesses to Me in Jerusalem, and in all Judea, and Samaria, and to the end of the earth" (Acts 1:8 NKJV). Think about your neighbors, do they know Jesus Christ as their Savior and Lord? Do you know if they are saved or not? Do they know that you are a child of God? It does not matter how much Bible you know. It does not matter how much prophecy you know. It does not matter how much you give to your church. It does not matter if you are a Sunday School teacher, a deacon, or a preacher. If you do not witness for Christ and behave as a follower of Christ then they do not care. In Acts 1, the disciples aske Jesus if He was going to retore the kingdom of Israel (vs. 6). He basically tells them; it is none of their concern and it was for them to know. He just wanted them to go out and witness for Him (vs. 7-8). There was a man who had applied for missionary service. The man, in charge of the missionary program asked, "What are you doing in your neighborhood where you are right now?" while he looked over the application. The applicant said, "Well, not much." The interviewer said, "Well, please do not go across the ocean and do that. Because if you are not doing anything here, then you are not a candidate for missionary service anywhere." We need to recognize and fulfill His program and behave as a church here and now.

According to Acts 2:46-47, the early church was growing by leaps and bounds. Now, let me just say, there is nothing wrong with a small church, neither is there anything wrong with a big church. There is, however, something wrong with any church that is in an area where there are a lot of lost people, and the church is not growing. To behave as a church, we are to grow. The early church was a growing church. One theologian said that this church had a membership in excess of 65,000 members in the first six months. I believe they had somewhere around 250,000 members in the six months. Talk about going to a big church. Do you think God wants everybody to go to hell? Or, do you think God want people to be reached with the gospel? Now, you may not go to a church where 250,000 people can fit into your building, but you can build more building somewhere. We are to make Jesus known as He runs His program through us.

Do you know what evangelism is? Do you know what true salvation looks like? Do you know the steps involved in a true conversion? "Now when they heard this, they were cut to the heart, and said to Peter and the rest of the apostles, "Men and brethren, what shall we do?" Then Peter said to them, "Repent, and let every one of you be baptized in the name of Jesus Christ for the remission of sins; and you shall receive the gift of the Holy Spirit"" (Acts 2:37-38 NKJV). First, in true conversion is there has to be a conviction by the Lord. I have been a pastor long enough to know that there are services where there is no conviction. Often times when this happens, I begin to wonder "Lord is it me? Am I the one that has failed to pray and seek your face? Is there coldness in my life?" Let me ask you, have you been in a service where you just could not explain what happen? People begin to weep or tremble, and there is this moving of the Holy Spirit. Conviction means that there is a sense of guilt and shame leading to repentance. The Hebrew word for conviction means "to argue with, to prove, to correct" (Holman Illustrated Bible Dictionary, 2003) The Greek term for conviction means "to convict, to refute, to confute" (Holman Illustrated Bible Dictionary, 2003) We behave as a church as we evangelize the world by convicting (rebuking, refuting), just as Timothy and Titus had the responsibility of convicting those under their charge (1 Tim. 5:20; 2 Tim. 4:2; Titus 1:13; 2:15). The Holy Spirit is the One who convicts, and the object of conviction is the world. Conviction for sin is the result of the work of the Holy Spirit, who opens the eyes of humanity to a sense of guilt and judgment because of their sin and unbelief. Conviction is not a bad thing because with conviction comes hope and not despair.

Another step in true conversion is conversion to the Lord. Peter said "Repent" (Acts 2:38 NKJV). To repent means to "change your mind". But what are changing your mind about? For one thing, you are changing your mind about sin. Listen, you will never be saved nor have been saved if you have not changed you mind about sin. Jesus said, "I tell you, no; but unless you repent you will all likewise perish" (Luke 13:3 NKJV). Plus, you are to change your mind about self. You are now admitting that you do not have what it takes to overcome sin. You are admitting that you are a sinner in need of a savior. Something else you change your mind about is Jesus Christ. You are coming to the realization that Jesus is the only hope you have for salvation. That He is the only one that you must put your faith in for redemption. When you repent, you are turning away from sin and turning to Jesus Christ for salvation by faith.

The next step in true conversion is confession of the Lord. Paul writes, "That if you confess with your mouth the Lord Jesus and believe in your heart that God has raised Him from the dead, you will be saved. For with the heart one believes unto righteousness, and with the mouth confession is made unto salvation" (Rom. 10:9-10 NKJV). Confession is the admission of a changed mind and heart that has surrendered to the truth that Jesus is Lord and He died for your sins. "Then Peter said to them, "Repent, and let every one of you be baptized in the name of Jesus Christ for the remission of sins; and you shall receive the gift of the Holy Spirit" (Acts 2:38 NKJV). The question is does baptism save you? No, but if you repent, and you are truly saved, then you ought to be baptized. Baptism, by water, is the outer expression of what takes place on the inside, in your heart. Baptism, by water, represents the baptism of the Holy Spirit, by blood. I am not convinced that anybody is truly saved who says, "I know I ought to be baptized, but I am not going to." Jesus asked a good question when He said, "But why do you call me 'Lord, Lord,' and not do the things which I say?" (Luke 6:46 NKLJV). How can you say that Christ is your Lord, when He has commanded baptism, and you are nonchalant or oblivious to it? Do you know what the New Testament confession of Jesus Christ was in the early church? Not coming down the carpeted aisle and shaking hands with a preacher. (There is nothing wrong with that.) The early church confessed Jesus Christ by being baptized.

When you get baptized you are identifying with Jesus in the water of believer's baptism. Think about what baptism symbolizes, and there two statements being made through believer's baptism that you are identifying with. First, there you are standing in the water, which represents your old life. Then you are placed under the water, representing your death to self. When you come up out of the water, that represents your new life in Christ Jesus and being washed in the blood, which is the cleansing of all your sins. The second statement when you are baptized is when you are standing there in the water it represents the death of Christ on the cross. You are identifying with His death. Then you go under the water, representing His burial. When you come up out of the water, you are representing His resurrection. This is a confession of Christ that you are making when you are baptized. But what right do you have to claim that you are a disciple of Jesus if you have never been baptized? If you were baptized before you were saved, then that is like having your funeral before you die. The Bible says, "Be baptized and believe"; no, it always says, "Believe and be baptized" (Acts 18:8 NKJV).

Once true conversion is made, immediately after asking Jesus into your heart, that is when the Holy Spirit comes and takes up residence in your heart. The Holy Spirit then takes possession of the person who has been bought with the precious blood of Jesus Christ. Real salvation is not just to believe something, or to achieve something, but to receive Someone. The Holy Spirit of God come into your heart to stay forever. Real salvation is not just going to heaven when you die. It is not getting man out of earth into heaven; it is getting God out of heaven into man. Jesus did not call us to make decisions; He called us to make disciples (Matt. 28:18-20). In the early church notice what they were doing. "Then those who gladly received his word were baptized; and that day about three thousand souls were added to them. And they continued steadfastly in the apostles' doctrine and fellowship, in the breaking of bread, and in prayers" (Acts 2:41-42 NKJV). They continued steadfastly, as if there was a continuance with the Lord. They continued to evangelize and make disciples. That is why we behave as a church to preach the word, to teach the word. That is why we have faith, to evangelize and make disciples continuously.

There was man who was known as a great fisherman. He would come back with a ton of fish, a boatload of fish. One day, a stranger said, "Would you take me fishing with you?" The fisherman said, "Sure, come on." So, he and the stranger got out in the middle of the lake. The fisherman reached under his seat and got a stick of dynamite, and he lit the fuse, and threw it overboard. It sank to the bottom with a tremendous explosion, and hundreds of dead fish floated to the surface. The fisherman started picking them up. The stranger then reached into his pocket, pulled out his billfold with a badge, and said, "Sir, I'm the game warden. What you are doing is illegal. You are in serious trouble." The fisherman did not say a word. He just reached under his seat, and got another stick of dynamite, and lit it, and handed it the warden and said, "Are you just going to sit there and talk, or are you going to fish?" Let me ask you a question, what about you? Are going to go out and make

Jesus known or are you going to just sit there? There is no greater joy than to lead a soul to Jesus Christ. Recognize His presence in us. Rely on His power in us and remember His program for us. We are to be witnesses in Jerusalem, Judea, Samaria, and the uttermost part of the earth.

CHAPTER TWO

God's Vision for the Church

Therefore, brethren, having boldness to enter the Holiest
by the blood of Jesus, by a new and living way which
He consecrated for us, through the veil, that is His
flesh, and having a High Priest over the house of God,
let us dray near with a true heart in full assurance
of faith, having our hearts sprinkled from an evil
conscience and our bodies washed with pure water.
(Hebrews 10:19-22 NKJV)

THE YEAR WAS 2020, AND ALL IN THE WORLD WAS SHUT DOWN; nothing moved, for all the people of the world was quarantined. After a few weeks, here in the United States, it was deemed that only the essential personal could be out and about doing the essential service that they were called to do. Essentially, they then had to define who were the essential personal that could be out and about. Truck driver, policemen, nurses, doctors, EMTs, grocery workers were a part of the list of essential personal. But what about pastors? Shouldn't they be a part of the essential personal? Yes, after about a week or two it declared that pastors should be on the list of essential personal. But what about the church? Is the church an essential service that is being provided to the world?

In the book of Exodus, we see where God brought Israel out of Egypt into the wilderness, which we could look at as a type of quarantine. Because while they were in the wilderness, God protected them and provided for them in every aspect of life. He even was preparing them for when they would go into the Promised Land, claim it, settle down, and become an example to all other nations of God's love and grace. There in the wilderness, God showed them exactly how to worship Him, obey Him, and to put their trust in Him. He brought them to the edge of the Promised Land and gave them the commandments of all that He wanted them to do as they went in. We know that the first generation was punished for their unbelief and did not get to go in. So, the first generation, along with the next generation remained in quarantine until the first generation died off. The next generation was then brought to the edge of the Promised Land and then given the same commands as the first. The question is, as the next generation came out of quarantine, did the Israelites give their all to claim the Promised Land? Did they fulfill their mission and conquer the land with diligence and virtue?

The Covid Pandemic of 2020 should have been a wake-up call for the church. It should have prepared us to behave as a church doing the work God has called us to do, the Great Commission. After being quarantined the church should have been about the Father's business fulfilling the Great Commission with diligence and virtue (Luke 2:49). Instead, what we are seeing take place in churches across America, particularly in Southern Baptist churches, churches are struggling to get back to the numbers they had prior to the Covid Pandemic. I often hear pastors or other church leaders talk about the numbers they had before Covid and the numbers they had after Covid. Seldom do I hear them talk about what they are doing about how they are going about fulfilling the Great Commission, evangelizing, and making disciples. Yet, we wonder why the young adults are dropping from our attendance. Young adults and other people need something to believe, someone to love, something worthwhile to do. Jesus Christ is indeed the fulfillment of all three of those needs. Therefore, the church is the greatest organization by which the world can know more about the Lord Jesus Christ. Yes, the church should have been awakened, revived after the pandemic but sadly she has not. Church members will often say, "You are preaching to the choir, pastor." Listen, in psychology we call that deflecting from the problem. In theology, we call that the hardening of the heart to the truth. The fact that Christians do not want to deal with the problem, or the issue at hand tells me the world has become a greater impact upon the lives of church members, than the church has upon the world.

There are two restraining forces in the world that is restraining sin, holding back the wrath of God from being poured out upon the earth, the Second Coming of Jesus, and revealing of the Antichrist (2 Thess. 2:1-12). The first restraining force in the world is the church. So, if God was to pull back the cover of time to let the church see how she was doing, then what would it reveal. Since the early church, who it was said, "Turned the world upside down", what kind of impact has the church made upon the world? One of the characteristics of behaving as a follower of Christ is virtue. We are to behave as a church and fulfill the Great Commission with virtue. "Virtue (or excellence) is when anything in nature fulfills its purpose." (Powers, 2021) This means, that as a church we are to do everything for the glory of God. "Therefore, whether you eat or drink, or whatever you do, do all to the glory of God" (1 Cor. 10:31 NKJV). "A Christian is supposed to glorify God because he has God's nature with him. So, when he does "do all" (1 Cor. 10:31), he shows his excellence because he is fulfilling his purpose in life." (Powers, 2021) Furthermore, as church members, we are to behave as a church doing all we can to edify the church, (the bride of Christ), for God with excellence (1 Cor. 14:21). If we were looking at the world today and throughout time, then will we see that we have done all things with excellence?

The other restraining force in the world today is the Holy Spirit (2 Thess. 2:6-7; Gen. 6:3; John 16:7-11; 1 John 4:4). (Please note I do not to discuss all that Holy Spirit does in His restraining work in this book. But just mere pointing this out here.) Think about this, the Holy Spirit resides in the hearts of every believer. The Holy Spirit walks with us as we go out to fulfill the Great Commission (Matt. 28:18-20; Acts 1:8). Just like God expected Israel to depend on Him as they went out to claim the Promised Land with virtue. God expects His church to depend on God the Holy Spirit to evangelize and make disciples.

The Vision of the Dead Churches

In Ezekiel 37 we have the familiar passage of Scripture of Ezekiel's vision of the Valley of Dry Bones. From these Scriptures we are blessed to have that great children's song which teaches the kids where each bone is connected in the body. In addition, it teaches us to identify each bone. The most important part about that song is the fact that God is the Creator, and He is the one connecting the bones together. The vision and the message from God to Ezekiel is about the condition of Israel. However, in this passage of Scripture as well as the passage of Scripture found in Jeremiah 6:6-17 there are examples of churches for us to take a look at. Let me be clear, I do not believe in replacement theology. I believe Israel is God's chosen people and the church does not replace Israel.

CHURCH OF DRY BONES

The first church we come to is the church of dry bones. "The hand of the Lord came upon me and brought me out in the Spirit of the Lord, ands set me down in the midst of the valley; and it was full of bones. Then He caused me to pass by them all around, and behold, there were very many in the open valley; and indeed, they were very dry" (Ezek. 37:1-2 NKJV). Here we have a normal church, who would hold normal church services on Sunday and Wednesday. They have the normal Sunday morning service: Sunday School, a song service, prayer time, taking up the offering, and a message from the pastor. But what makes this church dry bones?

For the answer to that question we have to turn over to Ephesians 4:17-19 which says, "This I say, therefore, and testify in the Lord, that you should no longer walk as the rest of the Gentiles walk, in the futility of their mind, having their understanding darkened, being alienated from the life of God, because of the ignorance that is in them, because of the blindness of their heart; who, being past feeling, have given themselves over to lewdness, to work all uncleanness with greediness" (NKJV). The reason this is a church of dry bones is because they have given into the world's way of thinking. What is the world's way of thinking. Paul gives us three things that a church should not do, and the church of dry bones did and did not behave as a church.

First, Paul tells us that a church should not have futile way of thinking because it does a church no good. He says, "you should no longer walk as the rest of the Gentiles walk" (vs. 17 NKJV). The Gentiles in Ephesus were living sinful lives, as matter of fact Paul already stated they were "dead in trespasses and sin" (Eph. 2:1 NKJV). The church should not behave or imitate the life of a dead unsaved person. To behave as a church means that we live as thought we have been raised from the dead, giving eternal life through Jesus. The Gentiles of Ephesus were making the city of Ephesus a thriving city and had become the leading city of commerce and culture in the Roman Empire. Ephesus was a pagan city, especially as it was the home of the Temple of Diana, which was one of the seven wonders of the ancient world. The worship that was done at the Temple of Diana was the worst immorality of degrading pagan religion which influence the Gentiles to live a life of wickedness. Because of what was going on in Ephesus, and the fact that many of the Christians in the church of Ephesus came from that kind of background, Paul is making a plea for them not to live like the Gentiles.

Second, Paul implies that living like the Gentiles leads to having your understanding darkened, because they have turned their backs on God (Eph. 4:18). In the church of dry bones this is exactly what has happened. They started living like the world, turning their backs on God, and darkening their understanding and hardening their hearts. They basically shut themselves off from God. The world told them, "You can be religious, but you cannot bring your religion outside the four walls of your church building." So, they listened to man instead of God. The world's way of thinking comes from the knowledge given to them by Satan himself. The devil knows the fastest way to kill a church and make it a church of dry bones is to take away its evangelism ministry. If the evangelism is stopped in a church, then the church will cease to grow. When there is no growth, eventually the church will have to shut the doors. Christian lives and church bodies that live separated from God's holiness amounts to foolish living. Therefore, with that kind of living it does not please God, and the church is not behaving properly.

Third, Paul says that having a hard heart and darken mind will lead to ungodly life (vs. 19). The Gentiles had given themselves over to lewdness and were living as if they did not care about the consequences, neither were they taking responsibility of their actions. They were given into their fleshly appetites for pleasure and gave no thought for any other moral practices. However, the more they practiced such immorality, the more they had to have because such desire never satisfied them. Lust dominated their lives and because of this Paul said do not walk as the Gentiles because they do not behave as church members.

There are churches who are falling victim to Satan's attacks, because they do not want to take a stand and stand in the gap (Ezek. 22:30). Then they cry out, "Our bones are dry, our hope is lost, and we ourselves are cut off!" (Ezek. 37:11 NKJV). But praise God, there is hope for the church of dry bones. God asked Ezekiel a question about this church of dry bones. "And He said to me, "Son of man, can theses bones live?" So, I answered, "O Lord God, You know."" (Ezek. 37:3 NKJV). Then God tells Ezekiel to tell these bones to listen to what God has to say to them. Here is the hope God gives to the church of dry bones. "Thus says the Lord God to these bones: "Surely, I will cause breath to enter into you, and you shall live. I will put sinews on you and bring flesh upon you, cover you with skin and put breath in you; and you shall live. Then you shall know that I am the Lord"" (vs. 5-6 NKJV). If a church wants to quit being a church of dry bones, then the church needs to return to God. When the church does, they will begin to experience an awaking, a revival. This goes to show, that no one person can shut the doors of a church only God can do that (1 Sam. 4:17-22; Matt. 16:18).

THE CHURCH OF THE FLESH

The church of the flesh is similar to the church of dry bones. They have their Sunday and Wednesday services; the Sunday School, song service, prayer time, offering, and message. The difference between these two is the fact the church of the flesh has an out-reach ministry.

The church of flesh does a great job of evangelizing, they do invite and bring people to church. So, what is wrong with this church to make me call them the church of the flesh is the fact there is no breath of life in them. "So, I prophesied as I was commanded; an as I prophesied, there was a noise, and suddenly a rattling; and the bones came together, bone to bone. Indeed, as I looked, the sinews and the flesh came upon them, and the skin covered them over; but there was no breath in them" (Ezek. 37:7-8 NKJV). When a body has breath of life that is breathed from the mouth of God, it comes to life. The Lord is the only source of all life. It is He Who can rejuvenate those who are bowed down (Ps. 119:25). Ezekiel has already been asked to prophesy to mountains (Ezek. 6:2; 36:1) and to forest (20:47), and now God told him to prophesy to dead bones. The church of the flesh may have the truth of God's word being preached among the church members, because the Word of God is "living and powerful" (Heb. 4:12 NKJV) and it can impart life (1 Pet. 1:23). Jesus said, "It is the Spirit who gives life; the flesh profits nothing. The words that I speak to you are spirit and they are life" (John 6:63 NKJV). The bones were brought together, and the body was restored, however the essence of life was still gone. In the church of the flesh there is no breath of life.

Why was the Spirit of God not in them? It is because the church of the flesh is full of pride. Their pride overcame their ability to be humble, fruitful, and loving. They may have got people to church, but they were struggling to keep people in church. You see, a man may take up all the appearances of spiritual life, yet have none, therefore he is dead before God. This could be a reason young people are leaving the church.

The church of the flesh was a church who likes to point out the faults of other churches, the faults of people; instead of humbling themselves and asking forgiveness for their faults. This church behaved as though they were the only church that was right with God. This church loved to tell others what they have done as a church. For example, their giving to mission, ministry, charities, how much they are paying their pastors, their fancy buildings, etc. So, instead of bragging on what God had done, they went about telling others what they have done. They were basically pointing others to themselves, instead of pointing lost people towards Christ. Do you know what Jesus says about the church of the flesh? He says that a church that builds up a name for itself is spiritually dead (Rev. 3:1). The Church of the flesh reminds me of the time Jesus was hungry. He saw a fig tree that was full of leaves, by the road. When Jesus got to the fig tree, He found that the fig tree had no figs, no fruit on it. Therefore, He cursed the fig tree (Matt. 21:18-22). The church of the flesh is like the fig tree full of leaves. The leaves represent the outward appearance of religion, but it produces not fruit. The church of the flesh looks and acts like a church, but it is spiritually dead. Like the fig tree, Jesus will curse this church for not producing fruit, and the church will wither away and become like the church of dry bones (1 Sam. 4:17-22). Jesus even warns the church of the flesh, He says, "Remember therefore how you have received and heard; hold fast and repent. Therefore, if you will not watch, I will come upon you as a thief, and you will not know what hour I will come upon you" (Rev. 3:3 NKJV). There is hope for the church at Sardis and for any church today. "You have a few names even in Sardis who have not defiled their garments; and they shall walk with Me in white, for they are worthy. He who overcomes shall be clothed in white garments, and I will not blot out his name from the Book of Life; but I will confess his name before My Father and before His angels" (Rev. 3:4-5 NKJV). He is saying all a church must do, all church members must do, is turn from their prideful ways, then they would experience the breath of life, and have revival. Basically, He is saying, "If My people who are called by My name will humble themselves, and pray and seek My face, and turn from their wicked ways, then I will hear from heaven, and will forgive their sin and heal their land" (2 Chron. 7:14 NKJV).

THE SUGAR-COATED CHURCH

In Jeremiah 6:9-15 we find an example of the Sugar-Coated Church. The name of this church implies exactly what was taking place in this church. In Jeremiah's day Israel was not behaving as they should. The Babylonians were getting ready to attack Jerusalem and God was telling them what to do, why they were doing it, and exactly how to do it (Jer. 6:4-8). Jeremiah knew this was a critical time in history for Israel. Just like Israel, this is a critical time for the church for we are living in perilous times (2 Tim. 3:1). Jeremiah cried out to God because nobody was listening, just like the people who go to this sugar-coated church (Jer. 6:10). The people of Israel had not circumcised their hearts (4:4), and neither were their ears circumcised (6:10). Luke writes, "You stiff-necked and uncircumcised in heart and ears! You always resist the Holy Spirit; as your fathers did, so do you" (Acts 7:51 NKJV). Israel refused to hear God's Word.

In the sugar-coated church they would have all the normal church services. The only difference in this church is the fact that when God's Word is preached, they do not hear the Word of God. The pastors of this type of church preach messages as if they are too worried about what people might think of them. The church members are too worried what others might think if they showed any interest in the message. This could have been the reason why the priest in Jeremiah's day were "Saying, 'Peace, peace!' When there is no peace" (Jer. 6:14 NKJV). This is what Paul said would happen in the last day. "For the time will come when they will not endure sound doctrine, but according to their own desires, because they have itching ears, they will heap up for themselves teachers; and they will turn their ears away from the truth and be turned aside to fables" (2 Tim. 4:3-4 NKJV). The truth of the matter is the Word of God cannot speak to them because their hearts are hardened, and their ears are clogged. Pastors are to be the watchmen, the shepherds, monitoring and protecting the church from ravenous wolves in sheep's clothing (Matt. 7:15; Acts 20:29). In this church the pastors were not behaving as pastors; they were dealing falsely with the church members and had lost the trust of the member. If they were being true, then these pastors were not taking a stand because they were just letting the people continue to live in sin. They would not preach against their sins and the consequences of their sins. Basically, they were letting the members have their way, and flattering them with positive opinion that made the people feel good (Jer. 6:13-14).

The sugar-coated church was giving in to covetousness (Jer. 6:13). God purposes a question, "Were they ashamed when they had committed abomination? No! They were not at all ashamed; nor did they know how to blush. Therefore, they shall fall among those who fall; at the time I punish them, they shall be cast down," says the Lord" (vs. 15 NKJV). I believe that one of the reasons young adults are leaving the church today is Christians. They acknowledge Christ with their lips, then walk out through the doors of the church and deny Jesus by their lifestyle. What is fascinating about the sugar-coated church is the fact that the members are too busy to do anything for the glory of God (1 Cor. 10:31). No one wants to reach out in evangelism, no one wants to make disciples; one of their problems is they do not want people to persecute them or make fun of them. However, their biggest problem is they do not want to give up their worldly life (Luke 16:13). In Jeremiah's day, the people of Israel were unashamed and could not even blush for the sins they committed, same goes for the members of this church. Because of the hardness of their hearts, they were glorying in their wickedness, openly confronting those who point out their faults when it should have humbled them and brought about repentance. They wanted to blame God and everyone else for their sins, even going as far as to say that their pastor and deacons were not doing their job. Nobody in the sugar-coated church accepted responsibility for their own sins. This type of church reminds me of what Jesus said about the lukewarm church. "I know your works, that you are neither cold nor hot. I could wish you were cold or hot. So then, because you are lukewarm, and neither cold nor hot, I will vomit you out of My mouth" (Rev. 3:15-16 NKJV). The sugar-coated church is not a church that behaves as a church and therefore is not blessed of God.

The spiritual application of these three dead churches, or for any individual or ministry, is the need of new life from God. It seems that there are more dead churches in our world today than ever before. We are not behaving as a church because we are standing as an army, however we appear to have life, but there is no breath in us.

The Vision of the Living Church

Ezekiel is told by God to "Prophesy to the breath, prophesy, son of man, and say to the breath, "Thus says the Lord God: "Come from the four winds, O breath, and breathe on these slain, that they may live."'" (Ezek. 37:9 NKJV). Then after Ezekiel speaks to the breath, the Lord gives Ezekiel another message to speak. "Then He said to me, "Son of man, these bones are the whole house of Israel. They indeed say, 'Our bones are dry, our hope is lost, and we ourselves are cut off!' Therefore, prophesy and say to them, "Thus says the Lord God: "Behold, O My people, I will open your graves and cause you to come up from your graves and bring you into the land of Israel. Then you shall know that I am the Lord, when I have opened your graves, O My people, and brought you up from your graves. I will put My Spirit in you, and you shall live, and I will place you in your land. Then you shall know that I, the Lord, have spoken it and performed it," says the Lord'" (Ezek. 37:11-14 NKJV). In the Hebrew language, the word *ruah* can mean wind, breath, spirit, or Spirit. This should remind us of what Jesus told Nicodemus about the blowing wind and the new birth through the Holy Spirit (John 3:5-8). There is a reference here to the creation of Adam. Adam was lifeless when God created him, until God breathed into his nostrils and the breath of life entered into Adam (Gen. 2:7).

When Ezekiel spoke the living Word, that is when the breath of life entered the dead bodies and they stood to their feet. God explained to Ezekiel how these bones represented Israel and their hopeless state, but as "Jesus looked at them and said to them, "With men this is impossible, but with God all things are possible" (Matt. 19:26 NKJV). There is coming a day when the nation of Israel will come together, however the nation will not have spiritual life until they see their Messiah, believe in Him, and receive the Holy Spirit (Ezek. 39:29; Zech. 12:9-13:1).

The church of the living God is a church that did the normal church services and ministries, except for the fact that this church is not like the other three. The church of the living God is not like the church of dry bones, because this church does not give into worldly views. When it came time to take a stand, they stand for what is in line with God's truths. Jeremiah is told to stand in the way, to ask for the old paths where the good way is, to walk in them, to listen to the watchmen as he trumpets for the truth (Jer. 6:16-17). They proclaim

God throughout the world and Satan's attacks never can harm this church. Jesus said, "And I also say to you that you are Peter, and on this rock, I will build My church, and the gates of Hades shall not prevail against it" (Matt. 16:18 NKJV). The church of the living God is not like the church of the flesh, because this church is not prideful. This church was going out and evangelizing, pointing lost souls to Christ. When they had events, ministry opportunities, or special offerings they would give God all the glory and praise. Instead of finding faults in other churches, or other people, they are praying for them and asking for forgiveness of their own faults. In their worship, Jesus Christ is at the center of it, and everyone is focused on Him. This church was spiritually alive, on fire for the Lord, experiencing revival growth both spiritually and numerically. Oh, how we need churches to behave as a church of the living God today!

How does the breath of life come into a church? The answer is through the Holy Spirit using faithful preaching of God's Holy Word. Charles Spurgeon once said, "Decayed churches can most certainly be revived by the preaching of the Word, accompanied by the coming of the heavenly breath from the four winds." (Spurgeon, 1864) There are times when God responses to our prayers and He sends showers of blessings with a new breath of life in them. Therefore, let us consider how we are to behave as a church to be the church God blesses.

IT IS A HOUSE OF GOD

Over in 2 Chronicles 5, we can see that Solomon has assembled the leaders of the tribes of Israel and whoever of the citizens that could attend to the dedication of the temple at Jerusalem. But what made this costly building the house of God? It was not because God commanded it to be built. It is not because Solomon was chosen to build it, nor was it because God gave the plans to David and provided the wealth to construct it. Yes, those things are important, but the reason the temple was the house of God was because the presence of the Lord God was in the sanctuary. "So that the priest could not continue ministering because of the cloud; for the glory of the Lord filled the house of God" (2 Chron. 5:14 NKJV).

Before the Glory Cloud filled the temple, Solomon had the Ark of the Covenant brought in. He then had the priest place the Ark in the Holy of Holies. Remember, in the Holy of Holies is where Jehovah was enthroned between the cherubim (Ps. 80:1). The pagan nations had their temples, altars, priest, and sacrifices, but their temples were empty, and their sacrifices were done in vanity. The True and Living God dwelt in the temple and that is why Solomon felt the need for his first act as king was to dedicate the temple and have the Ark of the Covenant brought from the tabernacle to the temple. When the Ark was brought in, God's glory filled the temple, because the Ark was a symbol of the throne and presence of God. The presence of God is important when we are behaving as a church. As children of God, the Holy Spirit indwells in our hearts. He is to fill our hearts so much that there is no room for anything else. Jesus said, "For where two or three are gathered together in My name, I am there in the midst of them" (Matt. 18:20 NKJV).

IT IS A HOUSE OF PRAYER

"For Solomon had made a bronze platform five cubits long, five cubits wide, and three cubits high, and had set it in the midst of the court; and he stood on it, knelt down on his knees before all the assembly of Israel, and spread out his hands toward heaven" (2 Chron. 6:13 NKJV). Our traditional posture for prayer is to fold our hands and close our eyes, which this kind of posture would be very awkward to Jews. Their posture was to look up by faith towards God in heaven or towards the temple. They would lift their open hands towards the heaven to show their humbleness, poverty, and their expectancy as they waited on God to answer. This posture did carry over into the early church (1 Tim. 2:8). But what makes a church a house of prayer?

First, the church of the Living God should be a house of prayer because it is a consecrated place. This includes His people and the place they worship. In Isaiah 56:7, God said, "Even I will bring to My holy mountain, and make them joyful in My house of prayer. Their burnt offerings and their sacrifices will be accepted on My altar" (NKJV). Jesus reaffirmed this truth when He was running out the money changers. "And He said to them, "It is written, 'My house

28

shall be called a house of prayer,' but you have made it a 'den of thieves'" (Matt. 21:13 NKJV). Of all the ministries, events, programs, and business that is conducted at the church building, none touches even the hem of the garment of prayer. God's house must always be known as a place of prayer and His people as a people of prayer. God honors a praying people because praying honors God! How many services throughout the years of your church have ever been fully dedicated to just praying?

Second, it is a house of prayer because it is a place that cares. As Solomon prays, he asks the Lord to hear the supplications of God's people (2 Chron. 6:20-21). He wants the Lord's house to be a place where one can bring their cares and leave them before the Lord. When we behave as a church, the church is the best place to bring your burdens. Why? Because there is a God in heaven that cares for you! "Therefore, humble yourselves under the mighty hand of God, that He may exalt you in due time, casting all your care upon Him, for He cares for you" (1 Pet. 5:6-7 NKJV). Plus, when we behave as a church, within the church there are people, followers of Christ, who will get under the load, your burden, and carry it with you (Gal. 6:2). You do not have to fret and worry, you do not have to fear life's hills and valleys, learn that God has a place of prayer, and He invites you to come to Him. "Be anxious for nothing, but in everything by prayer and supplication with thanksgiving, let your request be made known to God; and the peace of God, which surpasses all understanding, will guard your hearts and minds through Christ Jesus" (Phil. 4:6-7 NKJV).

Next, the house of prayer should be a place for conflicts. In Solomon's prayer, he says that when there is trouble between two parties, the place to settle the issue is before the presence of the Lord in prayer (2 Chron. 6:22-23). When we behave as a church bringing your conflict to the church in prayer still works today! It is virtually impossible for you to hate someone and pray for them at the same time. I am convinced that there would be far less trouble and confusion in the church body if the Lord's people would learn to pray with and for one another, not to mention they would be able to work out their differences if they were on their knees praying together. It is God's will that you forgive and forget every time (Eph. 4:32)! You cannot worship the Lord Jesus Christ when you have bitterness in your heart towards someone else (Matt. 5:23).

Then, the house of prayer should be a place for casualties. Everyone has heart break, sorrow, depression, and struggles. Solomon prayed for God to hear the cry of the battle-weary believer (2 Chron. 6:24-25). Whether we understand it all or not, we all are engaged in a brutal conflict (Eph. 6:12). Often, we find ourselves engaged in intense spiritual warfare. Sometimes, while in these battles, there are those who get wounded by the enemy. The place to bring those wounds is to the house of prayer because that is where the weary soldier will find refreshment and help. At the church of the Living God, you will find a word from the Lord and place to lay your burdens down and leave them. It is here you will find strength to fight the battles that you will face tomorrow (Isa. 40:31).

Lastly, the house of prayer is a place for confession. Solomon leaves no stone unturned. He prays for the sins of the people (2 Chron. 6:26-30). By doing this, Solomon teaches us that prayer is the remedy for our sin problem. The Lord's house is the place to take your sin to and confess them before God. When there is evil in our lives, then the church cannot behave as a church (Ps. 66:18; Josh. 7). However, when we deal with our sins God's way, He will bless and will bless abundantly (Prov. 28:13). In fact, the Lord is looking for people who will confess their sins so He might abundantly forgive them (1 John 1:9). Do not allow your sins to stand between you and the Lord's blessing on you or the church!

When we pray, we ought to seek the Lord's face, seek His will, and seek His glory in our lives. There is no better place for us to make our vows unto the Lord than in His presence at His altar. What a blessing it is to see the people of the Lord bowing before Him in an altar of prayer calling out on His name and surrendering their lives to His will. The point here is that no matter what kind of help you need, you will find it in prayer before the Lord. While we can pray anywhere and at any time, there is something special about getting together with the Lord's people at His house and calling on His name for the things we need!

IT IS A PLACE OF PEOPLE

In the assembly that was present at the dedication of the Temple, there were people that were not part of God's covenant with Israel there. These people were welcomed to come to the Temple and call on the Lord. This should be a lesson for the modern church. As we gather in church to worship our Redeemer, we must never lose sight of the truth that Jesus came to redeem all those who were lost under sin. The doors of the church should always be open to the stranger who is seeking God. We may not agree with their lives, but we need to receive them, love them, and pray for them.

In ancient times, the Temple was the rallying point of the army of Israel, because the army depended upon the Lord as they went into the battle. Solomon's prayer is that the Lord will help His people when they go to battle in His name (2 Chron. 6:34-35). In our day, we have those in the church who are engaged in spiritual battle for the Lord! These Christian soldiers need the help and power of God to do battle for Him. The church should be a place where the battle-scarred and weary can come in and find refreshment for their souls and be equipped for the next battle. When we behave as a church and let it be a place for R&R for the soldiers of the Lord, then they will be able to walk out of the church doors and into battle and fight valiantly for the glory of the Lord Jesus. God will bless the church who provides a haven for the weary soldier.

Solomon asked the Lord to incline His ear to the prayer of the repentant soul (vs. 36-39). There will comes times of waywardness and rebellion in your life; and when those time come you can expect God to give us a spiritual spanking (Rev. 3:19). However, the church needs to be the kind of place where the Prodigal Christian can come and unburden his soul before the Lord in humble repentance. We must never become a place where those who have strayed are made to feel unwelcome. May God bless the church to be a place who receives the wayward back into the fold.

Before Solomon finishes praying, he takes a moment to lift his voice in exaltation and praise. He worships the Lord! We need to behave as a church where the saints of God can come in and find sanctuary from battles, storms, trials, and burdens of life. The church needs to be a place where followers of Christ can lose themselves in the presence and power of the Lord and be drawn away from the daily living and find themselves at the feet of Jesus. The church of the living God should be a place where the presence of God is felt, enjoyed, and cherished. The church should be a place where the saints are filled with praise and worship for our glorious God (Ps. 22:3).

As we reflect on these churches in this chapter, where do you see your church? Where do you want your church to be? What are you going to do about it? May we behave as a church of the living God.

CHAPTER THREE

A Place of Power

*When Solomon had finished praying, fire came down
from heaven and consumed the burnt offering and the
sacrifices; and the glory of the Lord filled the temple.
And the priest could not enter the house of the Lord,
because the glory of the Lord had filled the Lord's House.
(2 Chronicles 7:1-2 NKJV)*

WHEN WE BEHAVE AS A CHURCH, THE LORD WILL MANIFEST
Himself in a display of supernatural power among His people. When
Solomon finished praying, the fire of God fell from heaven and
consumed the sacrifice. That was a demonstration of Divine power
in the presence of His people. Today, God demonstrates His power
through the saving of souls, the testimony and praise of His people,
the power of the preached Word of God, and various other ways.
However, when a church is behaving as they should, God will show
His power in the midst of His people. This is something God's people
should never take for granted. After consuming the sacrifice, the glory
of the Lord filled the temple (2 Chron. 7:2). This was not something
they only heard about; it was something they experienced firsthand.
They could see what God was doing. When the Lord moves in the
church, there will be no question about Who has shown up. God will
manifest His presence and power among a people who approved by
Him. There are times when the atmosphere gets right in and around
the church house. That is when God goes to work and it will be seen

by His followers, because God does not do anything in a corner. He works where others can see and where He can receive the glory. When God shows up you are going to know it. He will manifest His power and even the sinners will know Who is doing the work.

So, at the dedication of the temple and God showed up, the priest could not enter in the temple for the presence of God was there (vs. 2). When God moves in a church, He will move in a matchless way. He will demonstrate His power through His people and to the lost. God has a way of doing things that leaves men shaking their heads in amazement at His power and glory. God deserves all the praise, honor, and glory! When a church is moving under the power and approval of the Lord, there is no force under heaven that can stand in her way (Matt. 16:18). Hell trembles before a church that is filled with the power and glory of God. Sinners get uncomfortable in the presence of the Lord's power.

The chairman reported that the church roll now stood at 120 members. They had not been able to obtain a building, so they were still meeting in a second-floor room they had been able to rent in the city. There had been a lot of discussion about how they should fill a leadership position, which had recently become vacant. Besides all of that, there was not a lot going on. The task of reaching their community seemed beyond them. There was very little money, very few people, a lot of fear, and outside of their meeting place was a culture who had very little room for their message. Now, whether you have experienced a church like this church; this was how it was in the only church in existence at the beginning of the book of Acts. When Jesus ascended to heaven, there were only 120 followers in Jerusalem (Acts 1:15). They believed Jesus died for their sins and rose again, but they had been focused essentially on themselves and their own internal organization. Nothing that was happening among them would make any sense to the world outside the doors of this church. However, Jesus had spoken about an event that was about to happen and what happen at that event would turn their world upside down. In a few days they would be baptized with the Holy Spirit (Acts 1:5). Then He said, "But you shall receive power when the Holy Spirit has come upon you; and you shall be witnesses to Me in Jerusalem, and in all Judea and Samaria, and to the end of the earth" (Acts 1:8 NKJV). They did not have to wait long, because ten days after Jesus ascended into heaven and fifty days after the resurrection, there was a festival called Pentecost.

Pentecost was the time of year when all Jews were to take part in a glorious time of celebration. Pentecost was a time when the Jews would come before God in celebration of the beginning of the harvest and of the occasion when God came down to Mount Sinai and gave the law to Moses. The term Pentecost means fifty and this celebration came fifty days after the Passover (Holman Illustrated Bible Dictionary, 2003) People from all over the known world would journey to Jerusalem to take part in this great celebration. Luke tells us that people had come "from every nation under heaven" (Acts 2:5 NKJV). Pentecost to the Jews is like Thanksgiving Day to the Americans. There would be many different languages spoken by people who have traveled many miles away to offer their sacrifices and offering to the Lord. There was a lot of excitement going on in Jerusalem. However, in Acts 2:1-13, not everyone is celebrating the Passover. There in an upper room is a small group of Christians. This group is unique because the Bible says they were all assembled in one place (vs. 1). The reason they are in one place is because ten days earlier, before Jesus ascended into heaven (Acts 1:14), He had told them to go to Jerusalem and wait for the Holy Spirit to come (Acts 1:4-5). During those ten days, they gathered in one place and spent their time in prayer, calling out to the Lord. It is possible that some of them laid prostrate before the Lord seeking His will, His way, and His Word. Can you imagine spending ten straight days doing nothing but praying? Think about those who had been with Jesus in the Garden of Gethsemane who could not remain awake a few hours while Jesus prayed. Yet this group was uniquely assembled in prayer. They wanted so much to be at one with Jesus, that they are willing to spend the time in continuous prayer. How much praying do we do as a church? Could we pray like this group in the upper room?

The upper room represents what happens when God's people get together and pray. Attending church is so important because it is the place where God has designated it as a place of corporate prayer, for the fellowship of the saints, and where God moves in extraordinary ways in the lives of His people (Matt. 18:20). This group of people, which we often refer to them as the early church, were all together in one place, praying and prostrating before God; and were there together in unity and harmony. This says something powerful about the early church. These words about this group of people go beyond just faithful church attendance. They needed the love and support they could only get from other believers as they waited on something to happen.

On the Day of Pentecost, the Holy Spirit was poured out on the first Christian believers. After that, things were never the same. The church should be a place a power because of the presence of God. The same Holy Spirit, which was poured out on Pentecost, is still available today. The same power the early church received, is still the same power that we have available to His followers, to help make us effective as His witnesses to a lost and dying world. The more we understand the power we have as followers of Jesus Christ, the better we can behave as a church. To be clear the most important part of any church and its ministry is the power of the Holy Spirit. The most important part of the ministry of the Holy Spirit is to glorify Christ in the life and witness of the believer.

The Lord Assumes Control

When the Holy Spirit showed up in that upper room something happened. Luke vividly describes how the Holy Spirit came to church by describing the authority of the Holy Spirit. "And suddenly there came a sound from heaven, as of a rushing mighty wind, and it filled the whole house where they were sitting" (Acts 2:2 NKJV). Jesus said, "The wind blows where it wishes, and you hear the sound of it, but cannot tell where it comes form and where it goes. So is everyone who is born of the Spirit" (John 3:8 NKJV). In other words, the wind blows wherever, however, and whenever it wants to blow. Therefore, the movement of the Holy Spirit is likened to the movement of the wind. When the Spirit of God shows up, and moves in, His movement cannot be predicted because He will move when, where, and how He chooses. The Holy Spirit is the irresistible force of the divine nature. When the Holy Spirit comes and show up in a church service, He will assume control and take over that service with authority.

How did the disciples know this was the Holy Spirit? Because if you think about it, the sound of wind is pretty much the same as the sound of breath; only it much louder and it last longer. In the ancient world, they thought the wind was like breath but on a larger scale. Perhaps that is why they used the same word for both (Holman Illustrated Bible Dictionary, 2003) Where have we seen the "breath" before? The first time we see it is in the very beginning, where God created man (Gen. 2). God shaped a lifeless corpse from the dust of the ground, and it just laid there. Then God breathed into this skeletal frame and gave Adam the kiss of life, and the first man became a living being. The second time we see the "breath" upon man was after the resurrection. "And when He had said this, He breathed on them, and said to them, "Receive the Holy Spirit" (John 20:22 NKJV). Jesus was explaining what would happen on the Day of Pentecost. He is teaching His disciples what it would be like. He explained that He would ascend to heaven and that He would breathe His life into them from above. Then He took a deep breath and blew it out towards them, and it sounded like the rushing of the wind. So, when the disciples heard a sound like the rushing wind a few weeks later, they would immediately associate it with the sound of Jesus breathing on them and recognize this was the fulfillment of what Jesus had promised.

CLARITY OF THE LANGUAGES

"And when this sound occurred, the multitude came together, and were confused, because everyone heard them speak in his own language" (Acts 2:6 NKJV). The Greek word translated "language" and the word "tongue" in Acts 2:8 is the same Greek word; *dialektos* (Strong's Concordance, 1984) The Greek word refers to a language or dialect of some country or district (Holman Illustrated Bible Dictionary, 2003) Therefore, unless we are instructed otherwise in Scripture, we must assume that when "speaking in tongues" is mentioned elsewhere in Acts, or in 1 Corinthians, it refers to believers praising God in the Spirit, in languages that are known. Most, if not all the confusion over the Day of Pentecost, stems from Acts 2:3-6. Those who misunderstand what took place say that when the Holy Spirit came, He delivered some type of "unknown" heavenly prayer language which enabled these people to pray in a mystical manner. However, to properly study the passage in its context, the miracle of the Day of Pentecost had nothing to do with what they said, but how they heard. In had nothing to do with their speaking, but their hearing. The Holy Spirit became the divine interpreter and allowed each person to hear, and understand a language, or tongue other than their own.

Why did God do this? What purpose could this serve? For one thing, Pentecost was a reversal of the judgment at the Tower of Babel when God confused man's language (Gen. 11:1-9). God's judgment at Babel scattered the people, but God's blessing at Pentecost united the believers in the Spirit. At Babel, the people were unable to understand each other, but at Pentecost men heard God's praises and understood what was being said. The Tower of Babel was a scheme designed to praise men and make a name for men, but Pentecost brought praise to God. The building of Babel was an act of rebellion, but Pentecost was a ministry of humble submission to God. Another reason could be the fact that at Pentecost there were people from "every nation under heaven" (Acts 2:5 NKJV). To be exact, there were seventeen nationalities of people present at Pentecost. However, again the miracle was "every man heard them speak in his own language" (vs. 6 NKJV). Peter stood up to preach in his native Greek, or Aramaic language; and the Holy Spirit interpreted the message, so every person heard and understood in their own language. The Holy Spirit came to church, and instead of problems there was peace; instead of turmoil there was tranquility; and instead of chaos there was clarity. God assumed control of the first early church and is still in control of every church. The Holy Spirit is the translator of God and can speak to someone who needs salvation, to another who needs healing, and to someone else who needs provisions all in the same breath at the same time. When God speaks there is clarity.

SMELLS LIKE FIRE

"Then there appeared to them divided tongues, as of fire, and one sat upon each of them" (Acts 2:3 NKJV). At the dedication of the temple, "When Solomon had finished prying, fire came down from heaven and consumed the burnt offering and the sacrifices; and the glory of the Lord filled the temple" (2 Chron. 7:1 NKJV). The glory of the Lord filled the house of God and because He did, the priests in their holy vestments were unable to enter the temple (vs. 2). In the Holy of Holies, the Lord was enthroned between the cherubim (Ps. 80:1). The ark was a symbol of the throne and presence of God; it was the actual presence of the Lord in His house that was important. When Solomon had the ark brought in and placed it in the Holy of Holies, God's glory came and filled the house of the Lord. The shekinah glory had guided Israel throughout the wilderness (Num. 9:15-23), now comes to dwell in the temple Solomon built.

The prophet Ezekiel had a vision of a chariot throne in Ezekiel 1, and then in Ezekiel 8-11 he has a second vision with the same chariot throne. In this second vision Ezekiel was in the temple and the glory of the Lord was present on the throne (the chariot throne). Then, "the glory of the God of Israel had gone up from the cherub, where it had been, to the threshold of the temple" (Ezek. 9:3 NKJV). The glory of the Lord moved from the throne to the threshold of the temple, in preparation for leaving the temple. Then in Ezekiel 10, Ezekiel sees the glory of the Lord leaves the threshold of the temple and moves to the east gate of the temple. When you get to Ezekiel 11, the chariot throne departs from the threshold of the east gate and rests over the Mount of Olives which is east of Jerusalem. Ezekiel could have written "Ichabod" over the east gate, for indeed, "the glory had departed" (1 Sam. 4:19-22). Ezekiel did not prophesy the destruction of the temple, which was destroyed in 586 BC. He did, however, see the glory of God return, this time to the new temple that will stand during the reign of Christ in His kingdom (Ezek. 43:1-5). After the temple was destroyed in 586 BC, the glory of the Lord disappeared from the earth and would not return until the birth of Christ in Bethlehem (Luke 2: 9, 32). Then wicked men would crucify the Lord of glory (1 Cor. 2:8), but He arose from the grave and then ascended back to heaven from the eastern slope of the Mount of Olives.

On the day of Pentecost, the Holy Spirit came like a rushing mighty wind and divided tongues of fire sat upon each believer that was present in the upper room (Acts. 2:3). Try to imagine yourself among these 120 people when this happened. What they saw at first must have looked terrifying. A great ball or a pillar of fire was coming right toward them and rested upon them. The astonishing thing is none of them got burnt. This fire on the Day of Pentecost reminds me of Moses and the burning bush. Particularly the part where it said that the bush appeared to be on fire bud did not burn up (Ex. 3:2). Moses realized he was in the immediate presence of God. The fire did not depend on the bush for fuel. It was self-sustaining fire. Fire normally depends on the fuel it consumes. When the fuel is burned up, the fire goes out. But fire did not depend on the bush to sustain it, that is why the bush did not burn up.

The fire in which God made His presence known was self-sustaining and it never went out. God has life in Himself. He depends on nothing and needs no one. When He revealed Himself to Moses, He chose to make Himself known through a fire which rested on a bush but did not consume it. On the Day of Pentecost, God gave the same sign of His immediate presence with the first disciples. It must have been awesome to see. When God appeared to Moses, he was a believing man whose life was going nowhere. He had built a successful life in Egypt and then, after some trouble, left the country and settled down in a kind of semi-retirement in the desert. His life was counting for little to nothing in advancing the purpose of God in the world. Before the Day of Pentecost, the church was like Moses in the desert, it consisted of a group of believing people who enjoyed their prayer meetings and spent a great deal of time discussing how to elect leaders. But nothing was happening through them to advance God's purpose in the world. Then God's fire came down. When the fire came to Moses, he was commissioned to advance God's purpose. Now, God is commissioning every believer to advance His purpose in the world. The presence of God and His power rest in you!

Yes, one day Jesus will return to the Mount of Olives (Zech. 14:4) to deliver His people and establish His kingdom. God's glory filled the temple and then left earth; Jesus the embodied glory of God came to earth then left earth; the Holy Spirit came and dwelt in believers, and both (believers and the Holy Spirit) will leave earth; and then finally Jesus will come back, and the glory will have returned! Until then behave as a church.

The Lord Administers Conviction

Shortly after the disaster of the Tower of Babel, God gave a wonderful promise to Abraham, "I will make you a great nation; I will bless you and make your name great; and you shall be a blessing. I will bless those who bless you, and I will curse him who curses you; and in you all the families of the earth shall be blessed" (Gen. 12:2-3 NKJV). God's judgment on the nations at Babel was not His final word. He determined that His blessings would come through Abraham to all the scattered peoples and language group of the world. On the Day of Pentecost, God's wind blew, and His fire fell on the 120 children of Abraham. God was filling these people with new life and anointing them for ministry. These found themselves speaking in languages they had never learned because God's purpose was to communicate the good news of Jesus to people from every language group on the face of the earth.

On the Day of Pentecost God gathered a vast crowd from every nation under heaven. When the crowds in the city heard the sound of the wind (Acts 2:6), they headed in the direction it had came from to see what was going on. When they arrived, they found the 120 believers declaring the great things God had done in different languages. God had determined that people from every nation and language group would hear the good news of Jesus Christ. Language would be no barrier to the gospel. Jesus had said when the Holy Spirit came, the disciples would be His witnesses in Jerusalem, Judea, Samaria, and to the ends of the earth (Acts 1:8). In an extraordinary way, that began on the first day.

In Acts 2:14-36, we find one of the greatest sermons ever preached. Peter stood up, obeyed the Spirit of God, and three thousand souls were saved, as a result. The sermon consisted of 431 words, 225 of which were devoted to the actual words of Scripture. The topic of the sermon was the Lord Jesus Christ, crucified, buried, and raised from the dead. When Peter finished preaching, we can see what happened, "Now when they heard this, they were cut to the heart, and said to Peter and the rest of the apostles, "Men and brethren, what shall we do?"" (Acts 2:37 NKJV). In other words, Peter stood up to preach, the Holy Spirit came to church, and He brought about conviction by the preached Word of God to the point where it cut these men to their hearts. Peter's point was not lost on the crowd. If Jesus was indeed the One God had promised for the beginning of time, and the people had killed Him, what were they to do? These people clearly believe what Peter had said about Jesus, so he told them what they should do in Acts 2:38-39. Three thousand people responded to Peter's invitation. They understood from the beginning this good news was for people from every nation. In the coming days the children of Abraham would return to their homes and take the good news of Jesus to people whose language they already knew. God took a church that was like a lifeless corpse and breathed new life into it. God's presence came and rested in all His people, as He commissioned them to advance His purpose in the world.

Activating the Power and Presence of Jesus

How do we activate the power and presence of Jesus in our lives? If the church is to be a place of power, then how do we behave as a church with the power of Christ in us? How does a dead church become a living, vibrant, thriving, revived church of the living God, under the power of the Holy Spirit in the presence of Jesus? Please understand revival is not a human work, it is the work of the Holy Spirit breathing upon His children. Revival can never be fully explained in terms of activity, organization, meetings, personalities, and preaching. These may or may not be involved in the work of revival, but they do not and cannot account for the effects produced. Revival is essentially a manifestation of the Holy Trinity. It can be difficult to understand revival fully because people have no control over when or how it occurs. Historically, people have often been caught by surprise when revival came, even when they had been fervently praying for it. When you go to church, do you expect to meet with other brothers and sisters in Christ with power and in the presence of Jesus? Or is it just another Sunday meeting at the church house? The church of today is trying to do the work of Christ without the power of Christ, without His presence, without His blessing, without His favor. So, again how do we activate the power of Christ? Let me suggest a few things.

BE DESPERATE FOR JESUS

As followers of Christ, we need to get desperate for Jesus if we are going to activate His power in our lives and in the church. For example, "behold, a woman in the city who was a sinner, when she knew that Jesus sat at the table in the Pharisee's house, brought an alabaster flask of fragrant oil, and stood at His feet behind Him weeping; and she began to wash His feet with her tears, and wiped them with the hair of her head; and she kissed His feet and anointed them with the fragrant oil" (Luke 7:37-38 NKJV). If you take in all that was going on this day, you discover just how desperate this was woman was for Jesus. In those days it was customary for outsiders to hang around during banquets and listen to the conversation of the important people at the banquet. Back then everything was open, and where they held this banquet was in an open area of the house, which means people could stop on the outside and look in and listen. As a matter of fact, it would have been very simple for outsiders to walk into the banquet and speak with the guest. This is probably how this woman got to Jesus even though women were not invited to banquets.

Jewish rabbis would never talk to women in public, little lone eat with them in public. A woman of this caliber would not even be considered nor welcomed in the house, especially the house of Simon the Pharisee. We do not know her sin, however, she was a woman of the street with a bad reputation. However, according to the harmony of the gospels before this event takes place Jesus gives out a gracious invitation. He said, "Come to Me, all you who labor and are heavy laden, and I will give you rest. Take My yoke upon you and learn from

Me, for I am gentle and lowly in heart, and you will find rest for your souls. For My yoke is easy and My burden is light" (Matt. 11:28-30 NKJV). This invitation is possibly what turned this woman from her sin to place her faith in a Savior. Therefore, she was desperate to get to Jesus because she was filled with worship and awe of what He had done for her. Her tears, her behavior, and her elaborate gift is proof that her life had been changed by Jesus.

You can plan to have as many so called "revival meetings" you want, but you cannot manipulate a move from God until we become desperate and repent of our sins. We are living in perilous times and the situation of the time is desperate, but it seems today that the bride of Christ is not desperate for the Groom. This woman was not invited to the banquet, but she had a holy desperation about her. She just had to get to Jesus! The moment you have been diagnosed with cancer is the moment you have become desperate. The moment you lose your job, and the bills begin to pile up is the moment you become desperate. This should be the same desperate behavior you use the moment you sin against God. This woman was a sinner, she knew it, but that did not stop her from getting to Jesus and seeing the power and presence of Jesus in her life.

So how do we get desperate for Jesus? Have you ever noticed a dog walking a path? A dog will usually walk the path its master is walking, only the dog is out in front. The dog will either have its nose to the ground or its head held up and tail wagging. Then suddenly, the dog will stop, and turn its head to see what it just heard or seen. It sees a squirrel and off the path the dog goes chasing after the squirrel. The dog does not catch the squirrel, but frantically searches for evidence of the squirrel. If it is during late spring to early fall, the dog will come back to its master with scratches, fleas, or ticks. We the followers of Christ often behave just like the dog in our Christian walk. We will be walking with our Master, Jesus Christ, and then we see or hear a squirrel (temptation); and off the path we go. When we depart, we go astray, we become wayward form our relationship with Jesus. Therefore, He must lovingly discipline us to get us right with Him. If we are experiencing God's discipline, then we must respond immediately with desperation by repenting of our sin. The longer we delay, searching for evidence of the squirrel (more temptations), then we get scratches, fleas, or ticks (mainly our hearts will get harden). That is when we need to cry out in repentance to Him for relief. He will invite us to repent and return to Him. "Yet from the days of your fathers you have gone away from My ordinances and have not kept them. Return to Me, and I will return to you," Says the Lord of Hosts" (Mal. 3:7 NKJV).

King Solomon understood that God's people would inevitably sin and depart from Him. As he dedicated the temple in Jerusalem, Solomon asked God if He would forgive His people when they cried out to Him (2 Chron. 6:24-39). Sin is always ultimately against God, and Solomon knew God could use drought, famine, plague, disease, mildew, insect plagues, military defeat, and captivity to discipline His people. His question was, if the Lord punished His people because of their sin and they return their hearts back to Him, will He forgive them? God's answer is a favorite revival verse that has been used for generations. God said, "When I shut up heaven and there is no rain, or command the locusts to devour the land, or send pestilence among My people, if My people who are called by My name will humble themselves, and pray and seek My face, and turn from their wicked ways, then I will hear from heaven, and will forgive their sin and heal their land" (2 Chron. 7:13-14 NKJV). Basically, God's answer was yes! Yes, if He punishes His people, and they return to Him, He will forgive and restore them. In God's reply to Solomon, we can identify four requirements that shows that we are desperate for Jesus. They are humility, prayer, seeking God's will, and repentance leading to a changed behavior. When people get desperate, with a holy desperation, God will respond by forgiving their sin and healing their land. We need to behave as a church and get desperate for Jesus. We cannot run to church, sing a few ditties, preach a sermonette, and call it church and go home. No! Life is too short, hell is too hot, and people are too lost, we need to get desperate for Jesus.

IGNORE CRITICISM

There are different types of criticism, and some are good, and some is bad. Take constructive criticism, it can help you learn, grow, and be alert to something the next time. Constructive criticism can be positive or negative depending on how you take it and handle it. This type of criticism is not the kind I'm talking about. The kind of criticism I am talking about is the kind that attacks you, puts you down, the kind that hurts your feelings. So, let me ask you this question: what kind of sinners do you want in church? Please, do not sit there and say the good kind, because the last time I checked we are all out of the good kind of sinners! All we have left is the bad kind of sinners. Just for the record, do not sit there being all pious either, because you were once one of those bad kind of sinners as well. Paul writes, "Do you not know that the unrighteous will not inherit the kingdom of God? Do not be deceived. Neither fornicators, nor idolaters, nor adulterers, nor homosexuals, nor sodomites, nor thieves, nor covetous, nor drunkards, nor revilers, nor extortioners will inherit the kingdom of God. And such were some of you. But you were washed, but you were sanctified, but you were justified in the name of the Lord Jesus and by the Spirit of our God" (1 Cor. 6:9-11 NKJV). The church was never designed to be a museum for saints, but a hospital for sinners.

"Now when the Pharisee who had invited Him saw this, he spoke to himself, saying, "This Man, if He were a prophet, would know who and what manner of woman this is who is touching Him, for she is a sinner"" (Luke 7:39 NKJV). Simon was a Pharisees, a religious leader, who knew the law and how to treat other people no matter their social standing; and he missed the miracle because he was too busy keeping score. Simon was embarrassed, both for himself and for his guest. People had been saying that Jesus was a great prophet (Luke 7:16), but according to Simon the Pharisee, Jesus was certainly not exhibiting much prophetic discernment if He allowed a sinful woman to anoint His feet. Simon's real problem was blindness, he could not see himself, the woman, or Jesus. It is easy to say, "She is a sinner," but it was impossible for him to say, "I am also a sinner." Jesus proved that He was indeed a prophet by reading Simon's thoughts and revealing his needs. Question: how much sin must a person commit to be considered a sinner? Understand, Simon and the woman were both sinners in the eyes of God. Simon was guilty of sins of the spirit, especially pride, while the woman was guilty of sins of the flesh.

Her sins were public knowledge, while Simon's sins were hidden to everyone except to God. Both were bankrupt and could not pay their sin debt to God. Simon was just as spiritually bankrupt as the woman, only he did not realize it. I believe we need to behave as a church that realizes that God loved the world: sinners, human beings, men, women, boys, and girls; and we are all candidates to be saved by His grace (Rom. 10:13).

When you are desperate for Jesus you are going to ignore the criticism, and this will be reflected in your repentance with a changed behavior. "If we confess our sins, He is faithful and just to forgive us our sins and to cleanse us from all unrighteousness" (1 John 1:9 NKJV). Because you have repented of your sins, you are going to have an adjusted attitude. There is going to be an alteration of your mind, this occurs when you agree wit God about the truth of sin. That is what we call confession, it is the affirming of what we have done is wrong. If we argue with God about whether we have sinned, we are not in a position to repent neither will we see the power and presence of Jesus in our lives. "If we say that we have not sinned, we make Him a liar, and His word is not in us" (vs. 10 NKJV). Something else also takes place when you repent, you will have a changed heart. Instead of enjoying your sinful ways, you must be grieved over your sins as the Father does. If our sin does not grieve us, we make a mockery of Christ's supreme sacrifice on the cross. One other thing that happens when you repent, you will have transformed your desires and your actions. There are too many Christians trying to walk as close to the world as possible without sinning. We flirt with temptation when we should be fleeing from it.

This woman that came into Simon's house realized her sins and she did not let the critics stop her from getting desperate and receiving power and presence of Jesus in her life. If you check through the harmony of the gospels, you will discover that just before this event Jesus had given the gracious invitation by saying, "Come to Me, all you who labor and are heavy laden, and I will give you rest. Take My yoke upon you and learn from Me, for I am gentle and lowly in heart, and you will find rest for your souls. For My yoke is easy and My burden is light" (Matt. 11:28-30 NKJV). Perhaps that is when the woman turned from her sin and trusted the Savior. Her tears, her humble behavior, and her expensive gift all spoke of a changed life. What speaks of your changed life in Jesus?

WORSHIP WITH PASSION

When you are in the presence of Jesus and the power of the Holy Spirit inside you is moving, Christians should worship Him with passion. Here are a few things worship does for a Christian. First, worship impacts your love for Jesus. After pouring from the alabaster flask, this woman, "stood at His feet behind Him weeping; and she began to wash His feet with her tears, and wiped them with her hair of her head; and she kissed His feet and anointed them with the fragrant oil" (Luke 7:38 NKJV). This woman was broken hearted over her sins and was weeping at the feet of Jesus. When you cry that is an emotion, and we should be weeping over ours sins we have committed against our Savior. But did you know that you can weep tears of joy? This woman was happy because she was in the presence of Jesus, therefore, she worshipped Him with her tears, and she worshipped Him with her kisses. When she kissed the feet of Jesus, she was showing affection, love for Jesus which is an emotion expressed through an action. When is the last time you were worshipping God with passion all because you were plugged into Jesus? When is the last time you have seen Him move in your life with power? When was the last time you got a hold of the altar of God and would not let go until God did move? When you get desperate for Jesus and you come to Him, and Him with passion it is going to be expressed through your emotions.

Worship impacts your giving. This woman and an expensive alabaster flask which contained perfume and she gives it to Jesus. Here is something to think about; perfume is an aromatic oil or substance that women use to entice men, and men use to entice women. In those days, prostitutes would use perfume to lure men into their beds. But here this woman gave her perfume to Jesus because that was what the enemy was using to keep this woman at bay, but Jesus used it to set her free. In the act of worship this woman gave all she had and poured it all out for Jesus. Not only did she give her perfume, but she gave her hair. Why did Luke point this out? According to Scripture, the hair of a woman is her glory (1 Cor. 11:15). She gave up her glory for His glory (1 Cor. 10:31). Our worship should never be me-centered, but Christ-centered. When you worship with passion it is going to be expressed through your giving.

Worship impacts your love for others. When you are plugged into worshipping Jesus, the church body becomes one heart and one soul. "Now the multitude of those who believe were of one heart and one soul; neither did anyone say that any of the things he possessed was his own, but they had all things in common" (Acts 4:32 NKJV). The early church was a congregation of one heart and one soul. What that means is, they did not live for themselves, but they lived for those around them. Because these church members were plugged into the power and presence of Jesus in their lives, they were driven by ministry to meet the needs of other believers (Acts 4:32, 34-37). Plus, they were consumed by the needs of the lost around them (vs. 33). What is amazing is not only were they concerned for the need of salvation that the lost people had, but they went out of their way to meet the physical need of the lost people. The early church possessed a servant's heart that was like the heart of Jesus (Phil 2:3-8). These church members lived out the will of the Savior. Remember Jesus said, "By this all will know that you are My disciples, if you have love for on another" (John 13:35 NKJV). Jesus later said, "That they all may be one, as You, Father, are in Me, and I in You; that they also may be one in Us, that the world may believe that You went Me" (John 17:21 NKJV). When we love one another as we should, and when we walk in unity and harmony as we should, it lets the world around us know that our profession of faith is real, and we truly belong to Christ. No other testimony we give preaches so loud and so clear as our love for one another.

We need to plug into His power of love. Not just love that talks, but love that says, "I love you." We need to put our money where our mouth is; (so to speak). We need to let our actions speak louder than words. We need to plug into love that acts. John writes, "My little children, let us not love in words or in tongue, but in deed and in truth" (1 John 3:18 NKJV). We need to plug into the power of love that puts others ahead of ourselves. We need His kind of love in our lives, because without His kind of love, everything we do is going to be in vain. Paul writes, "Though I speak with the tongues of men and of angels, but have not love, I have become sounding brass or a clanging cymbal. And though I have the gift of prophecy, and understand all mysteries and all knowledge, and though I have all faith, so that I could remove mountains, but have not love, I am nothing. And though I bestow all my goods to feed the poor, and though I give my body to be burned, but have not love, it profits me nothing" (1 Cor. 13:1-3 NKJV). When I love my fellow church member like I should, I will forgive him for the times he as hurt me (Eph. 4:32). When I love my fellow church member as I should, I will see his best interest ahead of my own. When I love my fellow church member like I should, I will treat him like I should (1 Cor. 13:4-8). When we Behave as a church in Christ power of love, it will produce the same kind of behavior and power that existed in the early church. Think about the characteristics of the early church's behavior. Love made them considerate of others, it makes people more important that possessions, and enable them to put away their differences (Acts 4:32). The early church was made up of people from all over the world. They were of different cultures and different backgrounds and the power of Christ's love helped them. Love produces a passion for the lost who live in the world around us (vs. 33). Love gives us the power we need to minister to others, without love we will lack the power of God we need to be effective in the day and age which we live.

The church should be a place of power because Christ through the Holy Spirit resides in each believer. The church is a place of power because Christ is there in the midst of the believers gathered in His name. When we behave as a church with the power and presence of Jesus Christ in us and with us, we are plugging into His power. We should always be plugging into His power, especially in the day and age in which we live in. When we plug into this power, we do so because of what He has done for us. Look at Jesus's response to the woman. "Then He said to her, "Your sins are forgiven."" (Luke 7:48 NKJV). Jesus forgave her. He will forgive the church. He will forgive you if will plug into His power. Behave as a church in His power.

CHAPTER FOUR

Praise and Worship

Oh come, let us sing to the Lord! Let us shout
joyfully to the Rock of our salvation. Let us come
before His presence with thanksgiving; Let us shout
joyfully to Him with psalms. For the Lord is the
great God, and the great King above all gods.
(Psalm 95:1-3 NKJV)

AT THE DEDICATION OF THE TEMPLE, PRAISE AND WORSHIP BROKE out among the people because of the power and presence of God. "When all the children of Israel saw how the fire came down, and the glory of the Lord on the temple, they bowed their faces to the ground on the pavement, and worshiped and praised the Lord, saying: "For He is good, for His mercy endures forever"" (2 Chron. 7:3 NKJV). The church building and the church people should be a place of praise and worship. When the people who had attended the dedication ceremony that day saw God's power and presence they reacted with praise and worship by bowing humbly before Him. They were praising the Lord for Who He is! This should be a lesson for the modern-day church. While God's house is to be a place of prayer, people, and power; it is also to be a place of praise. When we place our focus upon Jesus and see Him just as He is, when we become lost in the awe and wonder of God, there will arise out of the soul a praise that cannot be stifled, but a praise that must be expressed! Praise is pleasing to the Lord! "Whoever offers praise glorifies Me; and to him who orders his conduct aright I will show the salvation of God" (Ps. 50:23 NKJV). Not only were they praising the Lord that day, they also were worshipping Him. They fell before the Lord in humble adoration and exaltation. They gave Him the glory that was due His name. We behave as a church when we make the church house a place of praise and worship. They also lifted their voices, opened their mouths, and rendered praises to the Lord for all that He is and is doing! They praised the Lord vocally!

Sadly, praise seems to have fallen out of favor with church members in our present day. We should never come to a place where we neglect or fail to offer the sacrifice of praise to the Lord (Heb. 13:15). However, too often church members come to the house of the Lord with their minds on a million other things besides honoring the Lord. We then find it hard to focus on His glory, we have a difficulty falling before Him in worship. To behave as a church means we are known as a place of worship! As a place where people can lose themselves in the wonder of God and get so caught up in who He is that we find ourselves with nothing else on our minds but the praise and worship of the Lord! But what is worship? Genuine worship is all that I am responding in adoration for all that He is. Worship is rendering to God the glory He is due. It is ascribing worth to the Lord. This is an absent element in the modern church. We need to learn that it is still okay to praise the Name of the Lord Most High! God has not changed, and He is still seeking people to worship Him (John 4:23-24). But how do you maintain a place of praise and worship? How do you keep from giving half-hearted worship? Because it is sad to see a full church building of empty people trying to overflow. How do we behave as a church with praise and worship?

This was the same issue God had during Malachi's day in Malachi 1:6-14. The key verse in this passage is found there in verse 13. "You also say, 'Oh, what a weariness!' and you sneer at it," says the Lord of host. "And you bring the stolen, the lame, and the sick; thus, you bring an offering! Should I accept this from your hand?" Says the Lord" (Mal. 1:13 NKJV). Let me paraphrase this: You turn up your nose and say, "Oh, what a weariness it is! Are we really going to church again? Are we going to have to sit there and be bored again?" What happens when the joy, the awe, the wonder, the thrill, the enthusiasm goes out of your worship? What are we to do when we are behaving as though we are not excited about what we are doing for the Jesus? What do we do when church worship becomes humdrum, and we become weary of the services, and the joy goes out, and the love is gone? According to Malachi 1:6, he is talking to a priest. "A son honors his father, and a servant his master. If then I am the Father, where is My honor? And if I am a Master, where is My reverence? Says the Lord of hosts to you priest who despise My name. Yet you say, "In what way have we despised Your name?" (Mal. 1:6 NKJV). Now before you say, "Well, I am not a priest," you are! Peter said, "But you are a chosen generation, a royal priesthood, a holy nation, His own special people, that you may proclaim the praises of Him who called you out of darkness into His marvelous light" (1 Pet. 2:9 NKJV). According to Peter, not only are we priest we are royals; we are kings. Therefore, we are to offer sacrifices of praise to the Lord, day by day. We are to offer sacrifice of praise with enthusiasm, not weariness. The word "enthusiasm" means "in God" or "God in you" (Holman Illustrated Bible Dictionary, 2003) So now, let's answer the question how do we behave as a church with praise and worship?

Recognize the Nature of God

Malachi reminds us that God is our Father, and we are His sons, therefore fathers are to be honored (Mal. 1:6). The word "honor" comes from a word which means, "weight; giving weight to" the idea behind this word is "to take someone seriously" (Concise Oxford English Dictionary Eleventh Edition, 2004) When we behave as a church are we taking God seriously? Are we being serious about our worship? Look at this way, being lukewarm is the worst form of blasphemy. Jesus said to the church in Laodicea, "I know your works, that you are neither cold nor hot. I could wish you were cold or hot. So then, because you are lukewarm, and neither cold nor hot, I will vomit you out of My mouth" (Rev. 3:15-16 NKJV). Jesus would rather to have you cold than lukewarm. He would rather have you at odds with Him than lukewarm, because at least a person who is at odd with Jesus has enough respect for Him to be against Him. A lukewarm person might just be saying, "I believe in Jesus, but I am not that excited about Him. He just doesn't move me." We go to church, and we sometimes yawn in the face of God, while He is wondering where His honor is. When Jesus taught us to pray, "In this manner, therefore, pray: Our Father in heaven, hallowed be Your name" (Matt. 6:9 NKJV).

Not only is God a Father, but God is a Master (Mal. 1:6). Since God is our Father, then as our Master He deserves fear (reverence). I am afraid that we are amid a generation that does not know to fear God, raising a generation without God. Malachi uses the word servant here which implies the word bond-slave. This was someone who was bought in the marketplace. Children of God once were slaves of sin, however, after the price was paid with Christ's blood you became his bond-slave. Some people do not believe in a religion built on fear. Little do they know that all true religion is built on fear, just not a filthy fear. The Bible says, "The fear of the Lord is clean, enduring forever; the judgments of the Lord are true and righteous altogether" (Ps. 19:9 NKJV). This fear is not one of dread, not a cringing horror of God.

Then what is the fear that Malachi is referring to that we need to give to God? "And Moses said to the people, "Do not fear; for God has come to test you, and that His fear may be before you, so that you may not sin" (Ex. 20:20 NKJV). What Moses is saying, is there is one fear which removes all other fears. There is so many things going on these days, that could cause the bravest of hearts to fear or be scared: wars, famines, diseases, viruses, inflation, gas-prices, etc. There is no need to be afraid because there is one fear that removes all other fears. The fear of God is love on its knees and what we need in the world, America, and the church is old-fashioned reverence for God. There are church members who think we do not need loud music in church, they just want reverence. There are some who do not want people to do any handclapping, just reverence. Listen, if these people could understand how the early church praised God, we would probably get in trouble for being to quiet. Yes, in the Bible there are times the church needs to be quiet. "Be still, and know that I am God" (Ps. 46:10 NKJV). However, also in the Bible is drums, cymbals, leaping, dancing, praising God with all one's might, and shouting to the Lord. Those things do not mean you are irreverent; it means you are so full of joy that you cannot be still, you cannot be quiet because you recognize the nature of God.

Reverence the Name of God

In Malachi's day the priests despised the name of the Lord (Mal. 1:6). Later in this chapter Malachi had this to say, "For from the rising of the sun, even to its going down, My name shall be great among the Gentiles; in every place incense shall be offered to My name, and a pure offering; for My name shall be great among the nations," says the Lord of hosts. "But you profane it, in that you say, 'the table of the Lord is defiled; and its fruit, its food, is contemptible.'" (vs. 11-12 NKJV). How do we despise God's name, or profane His name? We despise His name or profane His name by half-hearted worship. "You offer defiled food on My altar, but say, 'In what way have we defiled You?' By saying, 'The table of the Lord is contemptible.' And when you offer the blind as a sacrifice, is it not evil? And when you offer the lame and sick, is it not evil? Offer then to your governor! Would he be pleased with you? Would he accept you favorably?" Says the Lord of hosts." (vs. 7-8 NKJV). Here is what going on in those day. When they would come to the temple for worship, they would offer animal sacrifice, according to the Law. However, they would go to their flocks and find a sheep that was crippled, oxen that was lame, an animal that was blind, something that was worthless, useless, something that had a scab, a scar, a blemish, or something perhaps that had even died in the field, and they would bring it and offer it to the Lord.

This totally goes against God's law. Over in Leviticus 22:17-24, the Law required that every sacrifice be presented as perfect. The reason why it was required to be perfect is because every one of those sacrifices represented God's perfect Lamb, Jesus. Peter said this about the Lamb of God, "Knowing that you were not redeemed with corruptible things, like silver or gold, from your aimless conduct received by tradition from your fathers, but with the precious blood of Christ, as of a lamb without blemish and without spot" (1 Pet. 1:18-19

NKJV). Jesus was the perfect offering, and all the Old Testament offerings were indeed a picture of the Lord Jesus Christ. Malachi is telling us that God does not want an offering that is wounded or weak or blind or sick or blemished (vs. 8). You would not want to give those kinds of offerings to your governor, would you? If you did, how would the governor respond? No, you would want to give your best to the governor, the king, the prince, whoever it is was to visit your home.

The question is do we give God less than we give the government? Do we treat the government with more respect than we do God? Do we respect society more than we do God? Do we care more about the social standard of doing things, and our position in society than we do God? Suppose when April 15 comes around and you write the IRS a letter that reads, "I really should pay my income tax, but I have had a bad year, and lately, financially speaking, I am not where I need to be. Therefore, I have decided not to pay my taxes this year." Let me ask you this question: Have you ever heard anybody talk that way about making an offering to the Lord? "Well, Jesus some things have happened in my life, and I have decided that I am not going to tithe until I get back on my feet." Or how about you try this one on your boss, "No, I did not come into work, I had company that came last night." Or tell your boss this, "I have been going so hard, I just decided I would sleep in today." Try those on your boss. Try this one on your spouse, "I bought myself a $300 suit, and I got you a $10 t-shirt from this yard sale down the road." But why is it that we eat the cake and give God the crumbs? Because that was what they were doing in Malachi's day. They were not offering the best to Jesus. God deserves our best, our very best, the best we have to offer (1 Cor. 10:31).

So, according to Malachi, we are giving to God things which we were willing to castaway, things we really did not want in the first place (Mal. 1:13). In some church, they have what is called a mission house. These mission houses take furniture that people do not want. It is broken, or bent, or scarred, or the cushion has a hole in it, or whatever. People will say, "You know what let's give this to the missionaries." These mission houses also take up food, or food offerings. How do we respond? We will look under the sink, and we will find that box of noodles, which has been sitting under a dripping pipe and give that. We will look in our cabinets, and say, "Well what don't we want, that we can take out." So, you find that 10-year-old can of sardines, and you give that. "What else can we give to the food pantry or mission house? What else is scabbed and blind scarred that we can get rid of, that we can give to God?" Listen, when we give, we should give our best to the Master. Let's not just give Him something we do not want anyway. This was what God inspired Malachi to write in Malachi 1:8. "And you shall be holy men to Me: you shall not eat meat torn by beasts in the field; you shall throw it to the dogs" (Ex. 22:31 NKJV). In other words, if you find a deer in the woods that has been killed by another animal, don't eat it give it to the dogs. Do you know what some folks are doing? They are giving God dog food. They are saying, "Here, it is not fit for us. We'll give it to God." This was what was going on in Malachi's day. The reason why their worship was weariness, or burdensome, or caused them to sneer and role their eyes at going to church to worship was because they were offering to God half-hearted, unworthy sacrifices. We need to behave as a church because church is a place of praise and worship. Therefore, when you bring your gift of praise and worship and offerings next Sunday to church, if it means little to you, it will mean little to Him. Give of your best to the master. Reverence the name of the Lord.

David, a man after God's own heart, knew how to praise God. In 2 Samuel 24, David comes to a man whose name is Araunah. Araunah had a piece of property that David thought would be a great place to put the Ark of the Covenant. David goes to Araunah, because he wishes to make a sacrifice to stop the plague that was going on at the time. Araunah, being a good man, tells the king that his plan was a wonderful plan. He then invites David to come and do what he desires to do, he even offers to give David his oxen to sacrifice with. Araunah offers David his farming instruments for wood, he is giving David all that he needs to make the sacrifice. However, David refused to let Araunah give him these things. "Then the king said to Araunah, "No, but I will surely buy it from you for a price; nor will I offer burnt offerings to the Lord my God with that which costs me nothing"" (2 Sam. 24:24 NKJV). Wow! What a statement! To behave as a church means that we are be a place of praise and it is sad that our giving, our praise makes no difference at all in our lifestyle. God forbid that I should offer to the Lord of that which does not cost me nothing. Did you know that God's name can be defiled by our sacrifice, that God's name can be defiled by our service. This was what Malachi, who was writing down what God said, pointed out to Israel and to us (Mal. 1:11-13). Notice that phrase in Malachi 1:12, "but you profane it" (NKJV). What do you think of when you hear the word profanity? You probably think of some bar room and the people there using swear words. Profanity is when you use the name of the Lord God and do not mean it. In other words, you are not enthused when you stand in a church service and sing, "Oh, how I love Jesus." You are not enthused, you are not thinking about your singing, because your mind is off somewhere in some business deal, or some situation that is going on in your life, or what you are going to eat after church and if you are going to be able to beat the crowds to the restaurants. The worst profanity happens in the house of God. We profane the name of the Lord when we offer up half-hearted worship. We are insulting God when praising Him with half-hearted praise. The same people who sit in church and say, "When will this service be over?" is the same people who get excited when a ballgame goes into overtime. Listen, we should behave as a church because we are in business for the King of kings, and we need to keep awe and wonder in our worship and praise.

A Church on Fire

Let me share an anecdote with you. The village atheist was not a bad man, he just did not believe. He was not interested in church and there was only one in this village. The church of this village was cold and dead for it had become more of a social club with no one ever making a decision to come to Christ. One day the church building caught on fire, and the whole village ran towards the church to help extinguish the flames, including the village atheist! Someone hollered out to the atheist, "Hey, this is something new for you. This is the first time we have ever seen you running to church!" Which he replied, "This is the first time I have ever seen the church on fire!" The early church is a great example of a church of praise and worship. The early church in Jerusalem was a church that was growing by leaps and bounds; a church where 3,000 souls are saved in one service and another 5,000 souls are saved in another service. They enjoyed miraculous display of the presence and power of God daily. Can you imagine being part of a church where the extraordinary is normal and miracles are a part of everyday life. Imagine being part of a church that is witnessing God answer prayer immediately, where all the church members love one another, where the power of God is in evidence and where Jesus is truly the centerpiece of everything that happens. But all wasn't sunshine and roses! When you go all out for Jesus, the lost and the religious are not going to like it very much. That is what we see happening in Acts 4.

After the lame man was healed at the Beautiful Gate of the temple (Acts 3:1-10), the people in Jerusalem really began to listen to the message of the apostles. When this happened, the religious elite arrested John and Peter, threw them in prison and then brought them before the Sanhedrin for trial (Acts 4:1-12). At this trial, John and Peter preached the Gospel and the Sanhedrin issued an order forbidding them from preaching the name of Jesus any longer and let them leave (vs. 13-22). When the meeting was over, the two disciples returned to the place where the church was gathered, to pray for their leaders. When John and Peter told the members what had transpired, instead of being upset and fearful, a praise and worship service breaks out. To behave as a church means that we are be a place where no matter what is going on in your life you praise and worship the Lord! Let's notice what happen during that worship and praise service.

THEY WERE WORSHIPPING

"So when they heard that, they raised their voice to God with one accord and said: "Lord, You are God, who made heaven and earth and the sea, and all that is in them"" (Acts 4:24 NKJV). As you read Acts 4, you notice the behavior of the early church members. One of the things you can see is their desire to be at church during the set aside church time. They were at church when it came time to worship. This is the way God would want us to behave as a church (Heb. 10:25). Of

59

course, there are times when it is necessary to miss church, however, there are some members who have gotten good enough to miss every service down at the church house. The problem for those who make excuses is most likely a heart problem. When your heart is not right with God then you will not be in the presence of God either. The big problem is the fact that we have personal sin that must be dealt with in order properly give praise and worship. "If My people who are called by my name will humble themselves, and pray and seek My face, and turn from their wicked ways, then I will hear from heaven, and will for their sin and heal their land" (2 Chron. 7:14 NKJV). "If we confess our sins, He is faithful and just to forgive us our sins and to cleanse us from all unrighteousness" (1 John 1:9 NKJV). When we acknowledge our sins, then we must repent of our sins and seek His forgiveness. There are a lot of church members who will acknowledge their sin, but they are not always broken over their sin. The reason why church members are leaving is because there is not any genuine praise and worship since no one has been broken over their sin. My sin is quenching the Holy Spirit, furthermore, how can i worship and praise Jesus, in His presence, with sin in my life?

When their worship service began it included the elements of praise. Their prayers began by calling upon the Lord and blessing His holy name. They praised God for Who He is (Acts 4:24). That should be a great reason to praise God. This should be a praise that never ceases from our lives. Every saint of God should take the time to praise God for Who He is and for the attributes that make Him God. Some of God's attributes include holiness, grace, mercy, goodness, love, presence, peace, power, glory, and hope. Have you ever noticed the reaction of the bride in Song of Solomon? In Song of Solomon 5:10-15, the bride tried to describe the love of her life. She finally concluded by saying, "Yes, he is altogether lovely" (Song 5:16 NKJV). Everything about him caused her to praise him. This is the same way the bride of Christ should be with Jesus. Everything about Him should drive the saints to praise Him.

In Acts 4:25-25, Luke recounts the hatred of the world towards Jesus and the sacrifice of Jesus on the cross for the sins of the world. Therefore, the early church praises God for His gift of salvation through Jesus Christ. It there was ever a valid reason to praise the Lord, it is the death of Jesus on the cross for our sins! The fact that He took our place, paid our debt, and set us free is a reason to offer Him praise that will never grow dim. When I think of how my sins have been washed away by the precious blood of Jesus, and that I have been forgiven! When I think about a prepared home in Heaven! When I think about God is my Father, Jesus is my elder Brother, and the Hoy Spirit is my indwelling Comforter! When I think of the price He paid, the love He showed, and the gift He gave, I cannot keep silent! I must praise the name of the Lord my God! Hallelujah! The church must not be silent, behave as a church praise His holy name!

The early church members also praised Jesus for His power and providence. "To do whatever Your hand and Your purpose determined before to be done" (vs. 28 NKJV). They were praising Him for His ability to exert supernatural power ant to accomplish His will by His hand. God has not changed; He is still the same today as He has ever been! He still has all power in heaven and in earth (Matt. 28:18). He is still the great "I Am" (Ex. 3:14). He is still a God who is "able to do exceedingly, abundantly above all that we can ask or think" (Eph. 3:20 NKJV). He is still Jehovah God! How many mountains has He moved for you? Shouldn't you praise Him? How many times have you seen God do the impossible in your life? Do you not believe you should praise Him for that? The early church praised Him for His power but also for His providence. They praised Him that in His death on the cross, things worked out just as God had planned before the creation of the world! They were praising Him for His control upon their life. If we really believe that God is control of everything, then why not praise Him?

Their worship was seen in their prayer time. After they praised Him, they being to pray and ask Him for some very specific things related to their situation. "Now, Lord, look on their threats, and grant Your servants that with all boldness they may speak Your word, by stretching out Your hand to heal, and the signs and wonders may be done through the name of your holy Servant Jesus" (Acts 4:29-30 NKJV). When they used the word "now" they were not commanding God to do something, they were requesting God to take notice of their situation. Of course, they believed that God already knew the situation (Heb. 4:13; Prov. 15:3), but they reminded Him, nonetheless. This is what the Lord wants us to do with the perplexing situations in our lives. He does not want us to worry, but He wants us to bring our matters to Him in prayer (Phil. 4:6-7). He already knows, our prayers are merely demonstrating the fact that we know He knows and that we believe He will take care of the matter for His people.

When you pray, pray for God's infilling of the Holy Spirit. The Holy Spirit is already dwelling inside His children, but what you are asking for to be so full of the Spirit you can worship His name by boldly proclaiming His message! The early church wanted the power of God in their lives, and because they did in their prayers, they took the place of "servants", basically slaves before God. They bowed humbly and asked God to take them and use them for His glory. This is the kind of praying we need in the church today! We need to be actively asking God to pour upon His church His supernatural power. We need His power to witness, to worship, to preach, to carry out the Gospel to the ends of the earth. We need Him to help us get the job done, because we cannot do it by ourselves (John 15:5; Phil. 4:13). We need to pray for God's power to be on His church and on His people! We need to be filled daily with a fresh power and a fresh anointing of God upon His church and on His people! Before we can do any ministry, we need to be filled with the Holy Spirit, because apart from Him we can do nothing.

These early church members ended their prayer by asking God to personally get involved in their situation. They want Him to demonstrate His approval of the church by manifesting His power through the church. They merely prayed that God would show up and show out among His people. This a valid object of prayer in our day and age as well. We need to pray that God will do the miraculous among His church once again. I am referring to an old fashion moving of the Holy Spirit among His people; where their hearts are stirred to love Him, their lives are changed and made holy, and the strings of their tongues are loosed to praise Him! We need His intervention in our day to help us behave as a church. Let us not be afraid to ask Him for it (Matt. 7:7-8; Jer. 33:3; Isa. 65:24).

After they finished praying, they began to worship Him in power. This was no ordinary church service! When they finished praying and started worshiping, they experienced an immediate answer to their prayers (Acts 4:31). The place where they were started to shake. When the Holy Spirit shows up, He cannot be hidden! He turned their worship meeting upside down! You are going to know when God is moving in a service and when He is not. When He is, things cannot remain calm and collected. When God shows up, and His Spirit begins to move through a place, that place will be shaken for the glory of the Lord. We need the Lord to shake us and awake us today! We need Him to move in our worship services so that our worship services are not just run of the mill, same old routine. When the Holy Spirit moved in this service those who were looking for something got something. Acts 4:31 says they were all filled with the Holy Spirit. Could you imagine what would happen in our homes and our community if every church member of every church was filled with the power of the Holy Spirit? Not only would we be shaken, but the world around us would be saturated with His praise.

THEY WERE WORKING

Did you know that when we behave as a church that our work, ministry, praises Jesus (1 Cor. 10:31)? "Now the multitude of those who believed were of one heart and one soul; neither did anyone say that any of the things he possessed was his own, but they had all things in common (Acts 4:32 NKJV). This verse gives us two reasons for what the early church did. First, it says they were of one heart. That means they had love for one another that could not be explained in human terms. However, Jesus said, "By this all will know that you are My disciples, if you have love for one another" (John 13:35 NKJV). The early church members worked on behalf of their brothers in Christ. Second, what made this possible is the within each of them was the same heart. They were of one soul. This means that one life filled each of them. They were not in this ministry alone and they knew it. They needed others and were needed by others! It is still the same today, when we accept Jesus as our personal Lord and Savior, the life of Christ comes into our hearts. The same life that lives in me lives in every child of God and we are one in the Lord. That is why when you have a need, another church member should have a concern about that need. When you hurt, other church members should hurt. When you are happy and rejoicing, the church should be happy and rejoicing with you. When you are blessed, others are blessed. This is what the Bible teaches (Rom. 12:15; Phil. 2:4; Gal. 6:2; 1 Cor. 13:5).

Because they were behaving with unselfish expressions of love for one another, they were demonstrating the proof of God's work in their lives and the in the church. Notice how their demonstration of love praised God. First, each one was willing to become a servant for others. They realized that the church was about more than them getting their way. They wanted the Lord's will to be done in the house of God. Churches begin to get in trouble when catering to man's desire rather than God's will for the church. When you get a few people who think they run the whole show and have the authority to call the shots, they will begin to try to tell the preacher how to preach. They will try to run the business and the affairs of the church. They will try to exert their will over everyone else. That is not praise, that is not God's will for His church. He never intended for any family or group to hold supreme power in His church. His desire is for the people of God to serve one another, as Christ served man when He came to die (Mark 10:45).

They also demonstrated selflessness by placing other's needs ahead of their own. They demonstrated the Spirit of Christ in that they were totally selfless in their love for one another. Did you know that this is part of God's plan for the church? We need to behave as a church where we stop thinking about how things affect us personally, and where we start thinking about how things affect the church as a whole and our brothers and sisters as individuals. Whether you are a pastor, deacon, worship leader, or a member without a position in church is not about you having your way, it is about bring praise to Jesus by doing the work He commanded us to do (Matt. 28:18-20). These people gave up things that were precious to them, so they could meet the needs of their brothers and sisters in Christ. May we behave as a church by sacrificing, being selfless, and serving others, whether it is through our time, our talents, our tithes, or other possessions.

THEY WERE WITNESSING

"And with great power the apostles gave witness to the resurrection of the Lord Jesus. And great grace was upon them all" (Acts 4:33 NKJV). When the disciples went out sharing the message of Jesus, they went in the power of God. He placed His power on them and enabled them to witness for His glory and praise. When we as individuals, and the church, are behaving as we should be then we will be able to count on the Holy Spirit's power in our witnessing as well. The reason thousands were coming to Christ was not because of the quality of their preaching or the glory of their services. Thousands were saved because they were operating in the power of God. We need that power today! We need to praise Jesus in that power today! It is available to us if we would only ask for it by faith (Acts 1:8; John 16:24).

Luke tells us that "great grace was upon them all" (Acts 4:33 NKJV). The word grace means "favor" (Holman Illustrated Bible Dictionary, 2003) The early church member found favor with God, and He blessed them accordingly. They went forth under the grace of God and were aided by the Holy Spirit as they witnessed and shared His plan of salvation. In other words, God helped them get the job done and through their actions they praised the holy name of Jesus. The early church was a church that was on fire for Jesus. Are we behaving as a church that is on fire for Jesus today?

CHAPTER FIVE

Experiencing the Joy of Jesus

These things I have spoken to you, that My joy may
remain in you, and that your joy may be full.
(John 15:11 NKJV)

TO BEHAVE AS A CHURCH, WE NEED TO BE EXPERIENCING THE JOY
of Jesus. Christianity is a joyful religion, but if you were to look at the
followers of Christ then your conclusion would be "Where is the joy?"
All too often we allow too many things to rob us of our joy we have
in Christ. We lose our joy when we do not get up on the right side of
the bed. We lose our joy when we don't get our way. We lose our joy
when we don't feel well. We lose our joy when someone we love gets
sick or dies. We lose our joy when we are abused or persecuted. We
lose our joy when we are misunderstood. We lose our joy when we
feel lonely or unwanted. We lose our joy when we feel pressured to get
something done for our job or school. We lose our joy over countless
other situations as well. This should never be the case for the bride of
Christ. It is Jesus's intent that Christians be joyful people. It is okay
to have joy in church. It is okay to laugh in church because laughter
is associated with joy.

Let me share with you something to laugh about. Here are some
bulletin bloopers that I have found throughout the year of ministry.
Some are from pastor friends, some are from the internet, and some
I have made when I did the bulletin at church. 1.) Don't let worry kill
you, let the church help. 2.) Remember in prayer the many who are sick

of our church and community. 3.) Tuesday at 4:00 p.m. there will be an ice cream social. All ladies giving milk please come early. 4.) This being Easter Sunday, we will ask Mrs. Smith to come forward and lay an egg on the altar. 5.) Thursday night, potluck supper. Prayer and medication to follow. 6.) At the evening service tonight, the sermon topic will be "What is Hell?" Come early and listen to our choir practice. 7.) Ladies don't forget the rummage sale. It is a chance to get rid of those things not worth keeping around the house. Don't forget your husbands. 8.) Next Sunday is the family hayride and bonfire at the Fowlers. Bring you hot dogs and guns. 9.) Barbara remains in the hospital and needs blood donors for more transfusions. She also is having trouble sleeping and request tapes of Pastor Chris's sermons. 10.) The pastor would appreciate if the ladies of the congregation would lend him their girdles for the pancake breakfast next Sunday morning. Please understand, it is okay to laugh in church. It is okay to have joy in church. It is okay to praise His name for the joy He bring in your life.

Did you know that we all respond to life in various ways. One of those ways is we laugh. But what does the body do when we laugh. When we laugh our body performs rhythmic, vocalized, expiratory, and involuntary actions. There are fifteen facial muscles that will contract and relax as you laugh, not to mention there is electrical stimulation of the zygomatic major muscles that are involved. Currents of varying intensity produce a wide range of facial responses. The respiratory system is upset by the epiglottis half-closing, so that air intake occurs in irregular gasps, rather than calm breaths. Under extreme circumstances, the tear ducts are activated, so that while the mouth is opening and closing there is a struggle for enough oxygen intake, the face becomes moist and often red. Noises often accompany this odd behavior ranging from controlled snickers, escaped chuckles, and spontaneous giggles, to ridiculous cackles, noisy hoots, and uproarious belly laugh. There is a great deal of benefits of laughter. Laughter aids in breathing by disrupting your normal respiration patterns and increasing your breathing rate. It can also even help clear mucus from your lungs. Hearty laughter is also cardio-protective! It is good for your heart. It increases circulation and improves the delivery of oxygen and nutrients to tissues throughout your body. Laughter stimulates your immune system to fight off disease. Laughter decreases epinephrine and cortisol (the stress hormones) levels. It is also good for allergies. Laughter helps control pain by raising the levels of your brain's natural endorphins, which are 50-100 times more potent than morphine itself. (Mayo Clinic Staff, 2021)

Furthermore, laughter is a natural stress reliever. Have you ever laughed so hard that you doubled over, fell off your chair, spit out your food, or wet your pants? When you laugh you have no control over you muscle tension. From a study done in Norway, laughter has been proven that people who laugh more live longer! (Rodriguez, 2016) There is a definite link between a cheerful outlook and longevity due to the release of cytokines! In comparison, melancholy people tend to have higher levels of stress hormones, in which these hormones effect melancholy people's ability to fight diseases. Laughter is just good medicine! There is a Yiddish proverb that says, "What soap is to the body, laughter is to the soul." Good, all-around, side shaking, sidesplitting laughter is healthy for everybody!

Two Thousand years ago, Jesus appeared on this planet and brought astonishing change in the quality of human life. He was unique, set apart, fascinating, and remarkable actions were attributed to Him! He had a universal appeal that made Him very special! This world has never forgotten Him, and His name is spoken every second of time! In fact, time is dated from His birth! Millions of follow Him today. However, He had a secret that spread throughout the entire New Testament. It is a secret that explains the grip that Jesus has had on His followers for over two thousand years. The secret of Jesus was and is His inner joy. The New Testament is loaded with passages showing us that while in our midst, Jesus had a cheerful and a merry heart that came from His Father.

The Source of His Joy

"These things I have spoken to you, that My joy may remain in you, and that your joy may be full" (John 15:11 NKJV). The you that you are to have in your life as a child of God is not your joy, but it is to be His joy in your life. It is to be a supernatural joy. It is to be the joy the Lord which is your strength. Your joy is not your strength, the joy of the Lord is your strength (Neh. 8:10), and His joy should remain in you. Why are so many followers of Christ living like they are defeated? It because we lack inward strength. We are to behave as a church full of His joy. Yes, it is easy to think that Jesus is a man of joy, but Jesus was also a man of sorrow. He was a man of sorrows and acquainted with grief. John tells us that Jesus had tears of sorrow over His friend Lazarus dying, "Jesus wept" (John 11:35 NKJV). Jesus was a man of sorrows acquainted with grief, but do not think of Jesus as a pale sanctimonious religious recluse because He also was a man of joy. As a matter of fact, John 2 tells us that He was the life of the party. Nobody had joy like Jesus did. Psalm 45:7 tells us, "You love righteousness and hate wickedness; therefore God, Your God, has anointed You with the oil of gladness more than Your companions" (NKJV). This prophetic Psalm tells us that God has anointed His Son, the Messiah with a joy that is above other humans. That means nobody ever had His kind of joy. His joy is greater than the sons of man.

Do you know one of the great proofs that Jesus was a man of joy? Little children wanted to come and sit on His lap. Little children loved Him because He was not negative, sour, and grumpy. He was warm, loving laughter, gentle, and a joy that cause other to want to be around Him. It is possible that Jesus's mother, Mary, had a role in the joy He had. After all, Mary's Hebrew name means "joyous, singing, and festive." (Strong's Concordance, 1984) However, Jesus had a more profound source to His joy, His heavenly Father. The joy of Jesus goes all the way back to eternity before creation. "You are worthy, O Lord, to receive glory and honor and power; for You created all things, and by Your will they exist and were created" (Rev. 4:11 NKJV). In the King James Version, it uses the word "pleasure" instead of "will" both imply the same. It was His will, pleasure, and joy to create all things. Deep within the heart of God is a joy expressing itself in His mighty acts of creation. He created us in is image and likeness, for His own pleasure and joy because He desired to do it. Not for power, not for glory but for His joy.

The Bible is very clear that God is infinite, eternal, immutable, unlimited, immortal, all-wise, all-knowing, all-goodness, spiritual, holy, sovereign, righteous, gracious, merciful, loving, true, and He is joy! When Jesus came to dwell on earth, He drew upon that joy in becoming our Redeemer, Savior, and friend. Jesus is a man of joy. Jesus wept and Jesus laughed. He was God and He was man. Laughter is a behavior of the kingdom of God. "For the kingdom of God is not eating and drinking, but righteousness and peace and joy in the Holy Spirit" (Rom 14:17 NKJV). Therefore, behave as a church that is full of the joy of Jesus.

The Sense of Humor of His Joy

The Joy of Jesus was evident by His great sense of humor! The gospels are full of evidence of His sense of humor. Here is a list of verses that point out His humor: Matt. 7:3-5; 8:22; 12:26-28; 23:24; Mark 10:25; Luke 6:39,44; 8:16; 11:39. In these verses, He described the teachers of the Jewish law as straining out a gnat and swallowing a camel. That's funny! He said that it was easier for a camel to go through the eye of a needle than for a rich man to enter the kingdom of heaven. Not to take away from the profound meaning of what He said, but when you read that it's funny. He described the care with which the religious leaders washed the outside of their cups before drinking from them, but left the inside soiled; how funny is that? He pointed out how ludicrous it was to claim He was casting out demons by the power of the head of demons himself. I mean what general shoots the solders of his own army, now that is funny. He talked about blind men attempting to lead blind men, about dead people burying dead people, about picking figs off a thistle, about hiding a lamp under a bed. He laughed at people who were quick to point out the speck of dirt in someone else's eye while they had a two-by-four plank in their own eye! Those are all funny.

If Jesus laughed a great deal, as the evidence shows, and if He is who He claims to be, then we cannot avoid the logical solution that there is laughter in the heart of God. Think about the way He summoned His disciples in Matthew 4:19. He visited some fishermen along the shore of the Sea of Galilee, "Then He said to them, "Follow Me, and I will make you fishers of men" (Matt. 4:19 NKJV). They wasted no time, dropped their nets, and took off after Him! What attracted them? Was it His commanding appearance? Was it His impressive voice of authority? Was it tempting prospects that He presented to them? Was it the poor conditions in the fishing industry? Was it something else? What was it that made Matthew the tax collector leave his booth and cash box and follow Jesus? Did he think Jesus was a rich man? There is only one answer to these questions. Jesus was a man of such gladness of Spirit, such freedom and openness and magnetism in His behavior, that He was irresistible! They wanted to be near Him, to catch His spirit, and to do what He was doing for other people.

Setting Forward of His Joy

Now remember, He and the disciples were in the upper room (John 13:1) and it was here He delivers to the disciples what we know as the Upper Room Discourse, although John 15:11 was given after they had left the upper room. The disciples were sad, worried, and scared. They knew that Jesus had enemies that wanted to have Him killed. They knew that Jesus had told them the He was going to leave them. In spite of all the sorrow the disciples were feeling at they walked towards the garden, Jesus tells them "These things I have spoken to you, that My joy may remain in you, and that your joy may be full" (John 15:11 NKJV). Jesus is the Great Physician, and what He is saying to His disciples is as if He is writing a prescription as He talks. In other words, "If you do what Jesus tells you to do, you will be joyful." Kind of like going to the doctor, the only way to become well is if you do what the doctor tells you and take the medicine the doctor prescribes.

So, what were some of the things that Jesus prescribed, that would help the disciples be joyful? For one, He told them to love one another. "A new commandment I give to you, that you love one another; as I have loved you, that you also love one another. By this all will know that you are My disciples, if you have love for one another" (John 13:34-35 NKJV). The disciples' responsibility is to love each other just as Jesus had love for them. These disciples would definitely need to obey this prescription once Jesus left them and Peter, who was the leader of the group, would fail Jesus and them. Furthermore, each of them would fail, and the only thing that would bring them together is their love for Jesus and each other. We need to behave as a church full of the joy of Jesus by loving one another. Another prescription that Jesus told them was to relax. You cannot be a joyful Christian if you are too uptight. Jesus said, "Let not your heart be troubled; you believe in God, believe also in Me" (John 14:1 NKJV). That word "troubled" is translated from the Greek word that also can mean "stirred up" (Strong's Concordance, 1984) Which means do get upset, bothered, annoyed, or sadden but believe in Jesus. Now, you know as well as I do, that it is very difficult not to get fretful, worried, bent out of shape, or uptight. How does Jesus expect us to avoid worry? Simply trust in Him just like we trust in God. But wait there is more! To help us not to be so uptight, the Lord Jesus has sent a special Helper to us (John 14:16-18). As we allow the Holy Spirit to control our lives, He produces the fruits of the Spirit in our lives which includes love, joy, peace, longsuffering, kindness, goodness, faithfulness, gentleness, and self-control (Gal. 5:22-23). The last prescription that Jesus gave His disciples was for them to obey. He said, "If you love Me, keep My commandments" (John 14:15 NKJV). When you love someone, you want to do everything to bring joy to their heart. Therefore, you do everything in your ability not to bring disappointment in their life. We need to behave as a church that obeys the commands of Jesus.

The Stableness of His Joy

Jesus wants His joy to remain in you (John 15:11). In other words, He wants His joy to be permanent. He is not saying that there will not be bumps in the road or trials along the way because there will. However, through the trials and bumps, He wants our joy in Jesus to remain. James writes, "My brethren, count it all joy when you fall into various trials, knowing that the testing of your faith produces patience. But let patience have its perfect work, that you may be perfect and complete, lacking nothing" (Jam. 1:2-4 NKJV). The only way we are going to behave as a church is to be joyful in Christ is if we are faithful to Christ no matter what the circumstances. "Blessed is the man who endures temptation; for when he has been approved, he will receive the crown of life which the Lord has promised to those who love Him" (vs. 12 NKJV). We know that when we get to heaven our joy will get even better when we see Jesus face to face. Therefore, if things are going to be so great in heaven, then shouldn't we have joy in the anticipation now? Think about this, every child of God knows somebody who needs the Lord Jesus Christ as their savior. What kind of commercial are you for Christ? The old saying is, "you are the only Bible some people read, then does your joy in Christ shine through despite difficult circumstances? If you are just as miserable as anyone else, then why should anyone want your Jesus?

The Specialness of His Joy

Jesus wants us to be so full of His joy, that there is no room for any sorrow. It was never His intent that He would have a bunch of grumpy old disciples. You cannot have the fullness of joy in your life without the fullness of the Holy Spirit in your life (Rom. 14:17, 15:13). Psalm 16:11 says, "You will show me the path of life; in Your presence is fullness of joy; at Your right hand are pleasures forevermore" (NKJV). The church is to be a place of joy. There should be joy when we worship the Lord in prayer and music. There should be joy as we listen to special music. There should be joy when we give our tithes and offering. There should be joy as we serve the church in the ministries of the church. There should be joy when we read the Bible and hear the Word of God preached. The behavior of the church fellowship should be one of joy!

But our joy should be personal as well. Each of us on the inside should have a sense of joy. We must learn to practice the presence of Jesus in our lives. Do you know why married couples have happy marriages? They stay close. Do you know how to remain joyful as a Christian? Stay close to Jesus, abide in Him, talk to Him, and let Him talk to you. Talk to Jesus about your problems and concerns, about your joys and sorrows; then sit still and listen to Jesus. Listen as He speaks through His Word. Strive to spend time with Jesus.

CHRISTIANS ARE BORN FOR GLORY

The more we spend time with Jesus the more we want to know Him, grow for Him, love Him, and be a special joy for Him. Why are the children of God as special joy for Jesus? Because of the death and resurrection of Jesus Christ, believers have been "begotten again" to a living hope, peace, and joy which includes the glory of God (1 Pet. 1:3). When you were born-again, you were born-again once and for all. You were born physically one time and you can only be born-again spiritually one time. We have never seen a human being born physically a second time; therefore, you will never see a child of God who is born twice spiritually. When you are saved by God's abundant mercy and you are begotten again it is a once for all time experience. Since we are begotten again, we are secured in the hands of God (John 10:28-29). Salvation is rooted in mercy and the child of God has received the nature of God, and it is all sealed, made a living hope in the resurrection of Jesus from the dead. I have this joy because Jesus is raised from the dead. "Therefore, He is also able to save to the uttermost those who come to God through Him, since He always lives to make intercession for them" (Heb. 7:25 NKJV).

But what do we mean by "the glory of God?" The glory of God means the total of all that God is and does. Glory is not a separate attribute or characteristic of God, such as His holiness, wisdom, or mercy, Everything God is and does is characterized by glory. He is glorious in wisdom and power, so that everything He thinks and does is marked by glory. He reveals His glory in creation (Ps. 19). He reveals His glory in His dealings with the people of Israel and in His plan of salvation for lost sinners. When we were born the first time physically, we were not born for glory. "Because "all flesh is as grass, and all the glory of man as the flower of the grass. The grass withers, and its flower falls away, but the word of the Lord endures forever"" (1 Pet. 1:24-25 NKJV). Whatever feeble glory man has will eventually fade and disappear; but the glory of the Lord is eternal. The joy of Jesus is eternal. The works of man done for the glory of God will last and one day be rewarded (1 John 2:17). But the selfish human achievements of sinners will one day vanish to be seen no more. Did you know that one of the reasons we have encyclopedias is so we can learn about the famous people who are now forgotten. Peter gave us two descriptions to help us better understand the specialness of the joy of Jesus and the truth about His glory.

First, he describes the Christian's birth. Peter writes to the "elect according to the foreknowledge of God the Father, in sanctification of the Spirit, for obedience and sprinkling of the blood of Jesus Christ: Grace to you and peace be multiplied" (1 Pet. 1:2 NKJV). This miracle of the Christian's birth all began with God determining how salvation would work. According to Paul we were chosen by the father (Eph. 1:3-4) and Peter calls it the elect. God chose/elected that "whoever calls upon the name of the Lord shall be saved" (Rom. 10:13 NKJV). God chose/elected to send His Son to die on the cross, to become sacrifice to atone for sin once and for all. Jesus completed that work on the cross of Calvary and was buried, then tree days later He arose up out of the grave. God chose/elected that anyone, any individual who place their faith in Jesus Christ as their personal Lord and Savior shall be receive eternal life, salvation, sanctification, justification, redemption, adoption, etc. The way of salvation was already predetermined by the foreknowledge of God in the deep counsels of eternity, and we knew nothing about it until it was revealed to us in the Word of God. This choosing/election was not based upon anything we had done, because we were not even on the scene. Nor was it based on anything God saw that we would be or do. God's choosing/election was based wholly on His grace and love. We may never understand all God's wisdom and knowledge (Rom. 11:33-36), but we can have joy in Him.

Second, Peter describes the Christian's "living hope through the resurrection of Jesus Christ from the dead to an inheritance incorruptible and undefiled and that does not fade away, reserved in heaven for you" (1 Pet. 1:3-4 NKJV). The joy and living hope we receive from Jesus is built upon the living Word of God (vs. 23; John 1:1) and made possible because Jesus rose from the grave. Therefore, this "living hope" comes from the One that has life in Him and then can pass His life on to us. The Christian life grows and becomes more joyous as time goes on because of Jesus and His promise to come back and get us (John 14:1-3). Peter called this joy, this hope, an inheritance (1 Pet. 1:4). As the children of the King, the bride of Christ shares

His inheritance in glory (Rom. 8:17-18; Eph. 1:9-12; John 17:22-24). However, this inheritance is unlike any earthly inheritance. Because the inheritance we receive from Jesus is incorruptible, which means that nothing can ruin it. It is also undefiled, which means it cannot be stained or cheapened in any way. It will never grow old because it is eternal; it cannot wear out, nor can it disappoint us in any way.

In 1 Peter 1:5 and in verse 9, this inheritance is called "salvation" (NKJV). The believer is already saved through faith in Christ Jesus (Eph. 2:8-9), but the completion of that salvation is awaiting the return of the Savior. When we get to heaven, we shall have new bodies and enter a new environment, much like the perfect environment of the Garden of Eden but it will be a heavenly city. In 1 Peter 1:7, Peter calls this joyous hope "the appearing of Jesus Christ" (NKJV). Paul calls this joyous hope "the blessed hope" (Titus 2:13 NKJV). How thrilling it is to know that we were born for glory, and we are a special joy of Jesus! When we are born again, we exchange the passing glory of man for the eternal glory of God!

CHRISTIANS ARE KEPT FOR GLORY

Peter writes, "Who are kept by the power of God through faith for salvation ready to be revealed in the last time" (1 Pet. 1:5 NKJV). Not only is this joyous glory being reserved for us, but we are being kept for the glory. On some of our vacations, Teresa and I have gone to a hotel or campground only to discover that our reservations have been confused or cancelled. This will not happen to us when we arrive in heaven, because our future home and inheritance are guaranteed and reserved by the power of Christ Jesus. The word "kept" is a military word that means "guarded, shielded" (Concise Oxford English Dictionary Eleventh Edition, 2004) When you understand the tense of the word "kept" it reveals that we are constantly being guarded by God, assuring us that we shall arrive safely in heaven. The word "kept" is the same word used to describe the soldiers guarding Damascus when Paul made his escape (2 Cor. 11:32). Believers are not kept by their own power but by the power of God. Our faith in Christ has so united us to Him that His power now guards us and guides us. We are not kept by our own strength, but by His faithfulness. How long will He guard us? Until Jesus Christ returns, and we will shine in the full revelation of His great salvation (1 Pet. 1:9).

CHRISTIANS ARE BEING PREPARED FOR GLORY

We must keep in mind that all God plans are performed through trials and tribulations in preparation for what He has instore for us in heaven. Peter and James say the same thing about these various trials that we are to have joy by rejoicing in them. Peter says, "In this you greatly rejoice, though now for a little while, if need be, you have been grieved by various trials, that the genuineness of your faith, being much more precious than gold that perishes, though it is tested by fire, may be found to praise, honor, and glory at the revelation of Jesus Christ" (1 Pet. 1:6-7 NKJV). James says, "My brethren, count it all joy when you fall into various trials, knowing that the testing of your faith produces patience. But let patience have its perfect work, that you may be perfect and complete, lacking nothing" (Jam. 1:2-4 NKJV). The reason why we can rejoice or have joy is because Jesus is preparing us for the life and service of things yet to come. Nobody yet knows all that is in store for us in the future nor knows of the things that God has for us in heaven. But this we do know, life today is a school in which God trains us for our future ministry in eternity. This explains the presence trials in our lives, they are some of God's tools and textbooks in the Christian walk. Thankfully Peter shares several facts about trials of life that aid in show us how to behave as a church full of joy.

First, Peter shows us that trials meet our needs. That phrase in 1 Peter 1:6 (NKJV), "if need be" indicates that there are special times when God knows that we need to go through a trial. Sometimes trials discipline us when we have disobeyed God's will (Ps. 119:67). At other times, trials prepare us for spiritual growth, or even help to prevent us from sinning (1 Cor. 12:1-9). We do not always know the need being met, but we can trust God to know and to do what is best. Next, Peter shows us that trials may vary. In this world we have our troubles, but this world is not our home and we are just passing through. We have a home that is laid up somewhere beyond the blue. While we are down here on planet earth we are going to go through many trials and troubles. "Man who is born of woman is of few days and full of trouble" (Job 14:1 NKJV). Living for Jesus does not mean that everything is going to be bed of roses without any thorns. Peter tells us that there is going to be many heartaches and tears (1 Pet. 1:6-7). But Peter also tells us that even though our trials may be many and though they are heavy, they are all under God's control. The is just simply working on you, for your good and for His special joy. Job said, "But He know the way that I take; when He has tested me, I shall come forth as gold" (Job 23:10 NKJV).

CHRISTIANS CAN ENJOY HIS JOY NOW

The reason we can behave as a church full of His joy, is because we can experience His joy right now. Peter says, "Whom have not seen you love. Though now you do not see Him, yet believing, you rejoice with joy inexpressible and full of glory" (1 Pet. 1:8 NKJV). I have never seen Jesus, however, that does not stop me from loving Jesus Christ with all my heart and soul. The love I have for Him is not based on sight but on a spiritual relationship with Him and through His Holy Word and what it has revealed about Jesus. Now, if Jesus was in the heart of Moscow, Russia I would be making plans to get there to see Him face to face. I have never seen Him, but I still rejoice with joy unspeakable and full of glory. One of these days, I am going to see my Jesus face to face. Peter then adds, "receiving the end of your faith; the salvation of your souls" (vs. 9 NKJV). The word "end" means "goal" (Concise Oxford English Dictionary Eleventh Edition, 2004) He is saying, "if you got the beginning, then you are going to get the end." The goal is when we get to see Jesus. You may not be able to rejoice in your trials and tribulations. However, you can rejoice while going through them by centering your heart and mind on Jesus. Every experience of trials is a new opportunity for us to learn something that God counted it worthy for us to learn and have joy in Jesus. Think about Abraham, he discovered new truths about God on Mount Moriah when he was told to go sacrifice his son (Gen. 22). Then there are the three Hebrew children who discovered Jesus as they were walking around in the fiery furnace (Dan. 3). Paul learned that God's grace is enough for his thorn in his flesh (2 Cor.

12). The specialness of the joy that Jesus produces is unspeakable and full of glory. His joy is so deep, so wonderful that we cannot put it into words because words fail us. Peter urged his readers to exercise love, faith, and rejoicing, so they might experience some of His joy amid suffering now.

The Simpleness of His Joy

Just what is the joy of Jesus? Joy is the enjoyment of God and the good things that come from His hand. If our freedom in Christ is like angel food cake, then Joy is the frosting that tops the cake! If the Bible gives the wounder words of life, then joy is the music! Joy is an attribute of God Himself. With comes pleasure, gladness, and delight. Joy is merriment, hilarity, and mirth. Joy radiates animation, sparkle, and buoyancy. It expresses itself in laughter and elation, yet it draws from a deep spring that keeps flowing long after the laughter has died, and the tears have come. In a world gone gray with grief and worry, joy remains cheerful! Notice the personal pronouns that Jesus uses with joy as recorded in John 15:11. "These things have I spoken to you, that My joy may remain in you, and that your joy may be full" (John 15:11 NKJV) There was joy at Jesus's resurrection and joy at His ascension. Over in the book of Acts, the disciples were filled with joy and with the Holy Spirit (Acts 13:52). On the day of Pentecost, after the Holy Spirit had come, the disciples were so full of joy and having a good time that people thought they were drunk (Acts 2:13)! When was the last time you were so joyful, so full of joy of the Lord, that people thought you were drunk? From Genesis to Revelation there 542 references to joy. There are 150 references in the book of Psalms alone. Chapter after chapter, psalm after psalm, proverb after proverb, and over and over in the Bible the message of salvation in Christ is a message of love bathed in joy!

Did you know that in many churches today hand-clapping is seldom practiced? In fact, there are some churches that would rather have the rivers and the trees do the clapping of praise for them. Isaiah says to put on the garment of praise, "To console those who mourn in Zion, to give them beauty for ashes, the oil of joy for mourning, the garment of praise for the spirit of heaviness; that they may be called trees of righteousness, the planting of the Lord that He may be glorified" (Isa. 61:3 NKJV). What is sad is that some people have turned their garment of praise inside out. Yet, there are some who cannot even find their garment of praise, and some would not put it on once they found it. Joyfulness, lightheartedness, and jubilation seems out of order in many churches and yet that is exactly how we should behave as a church.

Christianity is a joyful religion, but looking at the bride of Christ, His followers, you would not think so. All too often we allow to many things rob us of our joy. We lose our joy when we don't get up on the right side of the bed. We lose our joy when we don't get our way. We lose our joy when we don't feel well. We lose our joy when someone we love gets sick or dies. We lose our joy when we feel lonely or unwanted. We lose our joy over countless other situations. It is Jesus's intent that Christians be a joyful people. It is Jesus's intent that you be a joyful Christian. It is His intent that we be filled with His joy and that it remains. The lowly Christian is to have joy in the fact that he is exalted and included in the eternal plan of God (Jam. 1:9). The rich is to have joy in the fact that they are learning humility and dependence (Jam. 1:10). We need to behave as a church full of the joy of Christ.

CHAPTER SIX

The Secret of Effective Prayer

For of Him and through Him and to Him are
all things, to whom be glory forever. Amen
(Romans 11:36 NKJV)

DOWN IN THE ATLANTIC, THERE IS SOMETHING THAT IS CALLED the Bermuda Triangle. Some people like to call it the Devil's Triangle, because it is said that when airplanes and ships move into this area they disappear and are never seen again. There are those who want you to believe that it is a mystery; I however, believe it is nothing more than a myth or urban legend. I do not believe there is anything to this Bermuda Triangle. However, there is a triangle that I do believe is not a mystery, that it is real, powerful, and mighty. It is not a myth, it true. This triangle does not cause things to disappear, it brings things into being. This triangle is the divine triangle found in Romans 11:36 and all three God heads are present in this one verse: God the Father represented by the phrase "For of Him"; God the Son represented by the phrase "and through Him"; and God the Holy Spirit represent by the phrase "and to Him" (Rom. 11:36 NKJV). The Bible speaks of the sovereignty of Almighty God, who brought everything into being, who controls all things, and will consummate everything (vs. 36). For example, Genesis 1:1 begins like this, "In the beginning God," (NKJV). In the book of Revelation, Jesus said, "I am the Alpha and the Omega, the Beginning and the End," says the Lord, "who is and who was and who is to come, the Almighty"" (Rev. 1:8 NKJV). In Colossians, Paul talks about how the Lord Jesus Christ created everything, sustains everything, and how everything is going to culminate in Him. "For by Him all things were created that are in heaven and that are on earth, visible and invisible, whether thrones or dominions or principalities or powers. All things were created through Him and for Him. and He is before all things, and in Him all things consist" (Col. 1:16-17 NKJV). This is just a restatement of what Paul said in Romans 11:36. But notice that Paul said that through the Lord Jesu Christ everything came into being. That means Jesus is the power of creation. Where did everything come from? Through Jesus the power of creation, and furthermore, He is the preserver of creation, because it is of Him and through Him.

Paul said that by Jesus all things consist (Rom. 11:36; Col. 1:17) which means they all hang together. One way of looking at it is like this; Jesus is the glue of the galaxies; Jesus is the fuel that keeps the sun shining; Jesus veils the moon with beauty; and Jesus guides the planets and the stars in their orbits. I do not know if you ever think about the vastness of our universe, but when I was in school, I learned that light travels at 186,282 miles per second. I also learned that it takes eight and a half minutes for light to get from the sun to the earth, which is ninety-three million miles away. Jesus is the power of creation, preserver of creation, and the purpose of creation. Paul says, "For by Him all things were created" (Col. 1:16 NKJV), and the word "for" is a preposition which means, motion towards an object (Concise Oxford English Dictionary Eleventh Edition, 2004) People want to know what the world is coming to? The answer is simple, it is coming to Jesus for it was all created by Him.

Since this is true in the physical realm, then it is also true in the spiritual realm. As you think about salvation, ask this question, how does salvation work? Who thought up the idea of salvation? Simple God thought it. Who brought salvation about? Why did He do it? Jesus brought about salvation so we might know Him and come to Him, for of Him "we love Him because He first loved us" (1 John 4:19 NKJV). He sent His Son and through Him, Jesus suffered, bled, and died. It is to Him when we trust in Him; He draws us to Himself, and we will live with Him forever and give Him the glory forever and ever, Amen. God is involved in salvation, and He is involved in sanctification. How are you going to be more like Him? Well, God is the One Who energizes us to make us more like Him. Holiness is not the way to Christ; Christ is the way to holiness; for it is of Him and through Him and to Him. Not only is God involved in salvation and sanctification, but He is also involved in prayer.

The Origin of Prayer

What is the origin of prayer? Prayer is the purpose of God. The prayer that gets to heaven is the prayer that starts in heaven. What is the purpose of prayer? What did the Jesus teach us about prayer? Jesus said, "In this manner, therefore pray: Our Father in heaven, hallowed be your name. Your kingdom come. Your will be done on earth as it is in heaven. Give us this day our daily bread. And forgive us our debts, as we forgive our debtors. And do not lead us into temptation but deliver us from the evil one. For Yours is the kingdom and the power and the glory forever. Amen" (Matt. 6:9-13 NKJV). The disciples came to Jesus as He was praying, and desired to be taught about prayer. Evidently, they had seen something in the prayer life of Jesus that they wanted in their own prayer life. Their request is revealing for it was a two-fold request. First, they wanted to know how to pray and talk to God as Jesus Himself did. Secondly, they desired a burden to pray. They saw the priority prayer held in the Lord's life and they desired to be gripped by the same passion for communion with the heavenly Father.

When Jesus instructs His disciples how to pray, He gives them the framework for praying that accomplishes both of goals. This prayer is not a prayer to be memorized and quoted as many do, and there is nothing wrong with that. However, the Model Prayer is a framework which we are to use to build our own prayers. It is a pattern, or a template from which we can build the structure of our own prayers. Hence, it teaches us how to pray. The Jewish people had so many prayers they had learned to pray, and when they prayed to God, they had to figure which name of God they need to pray before they could even pray. So, when Jesus instructed His men in prayer, He told them to forget the formulas and the complicated names, but to just call on the Father. Prayer is not man's way of getting man's will done in heaven, it is God's way of getting His will done on earth. Why does God use prayer? Have you ever thought about the mystery of prayer? Did you know that prayer is mysterious? Why would God want us to tell Him what He already knows? Why would God want us to ask for what He already knows we need? I mean, He already knows what things you have need of before you ask, and He is a loving God, so why pray? Yes, it is true that God's house should be a house of prayer (Isa. 56:7, Matt. 21:13), and we need to behave as a church that prays both individually and corporately. God wants us to pray because He has given us the privilege of working with Him in the regulation and the administration of the universe. Paul said, "For we are God's fellow workers; you are God's field, you are God's building" (1 Cor. 3:9 NKJV) and when we are working together as a church body with God there is fellowship. For example: two friends take off in an airplane. One friend is a pilot and the other is a non-pilot. The pilot asks his friend, "Do you want to fly the plane?" The friend says "Yes." So, the non-pilot takes the controls of the plane and is now flying the plane. However, the pilot is still in the cockpit with him, then who is flying the plane? Yes, it is true that the non-pilot, who has a hold of the controls it the one flying the plane, but he is only flying the plane in cooperation with the pilot, under his instruction, with his encouragement, and with his background. Therefore, in a sense the pilot is flying the plane, but he has given his friend the privilege of flying alone with him. You see, God could do everything without you and me, and God could run this universe without us. However, you could not do it without Him, the non-pilot friend could not fly that plane without his friend the pilot, but what a joy it is to cooperate and to have that kind of fellowship. When there is that fellowship, then there is a bonding that takes place between two people: God and the person who is praying. Prayer is the way to bond you to God. God does not want you live your life independent of Him. Therefore, if He just gave you everything, then there would be no need to ask Him, or depend on Him, or trust Him, or look to Him for things we need. There would not be this bonding between you two.

Did you know prayer makes us disciples? Prayer makes us more like the Lord Jesus Christ. Have you ever prayed and asked God for something and the prayer was not answered? Or so we thought. If God told you no, wait, not yet, then He answered your prayer. You may have not got what you asked, and you said, "Well, why? Why didn't I get what I asked?" James says, "You ask and do not receive, because you ask amiss, that you may spend it on your pleasures" (Jam. 4:3 NKJV). The psalmist writes, "If I regard iniquity in my heart, the Lord will not hear" (Ps. 66:18 NKJV). In prayer, my life is being conformed more and more to the image of the Lord Jesus and I am to get my heart clean, and I am to get in fellowship with God, so I can have my prayers answered. Prayer is God's way of fellowshipping with us, bonding us to Him, discipling our lives, and whether you understand it or not, the Bible has commanded us to pray. That prayer that you pray is a prayer which began in the heart and mind of God. It begins with God, (for of Him), the purpose of God is the origin of prayer.

The Operation of Prayer

Something to we need to understand, God gives us the desire to pray, because your flesh has absolutely no desire to pray. Paul writes, "There is none that seeks after God" (Rom. 3:11 NKJV). Later he says, "Because the carnal mind is enmity against God; for it not subject to the law of God, nor indeed can be" (Rom. 8:7 NKJV). What does he mean? Your nature, your Adamic nature, your flesh, has about the same desire to pray as your dog has to go see the opera. The natural instinct in you does not have any desire to pray. As a matter of fact, your natural instinct is to shy away from God, like Adam and Eve running away and hiding from God in the Garden of Eden. We did not seek God, but God sought us. The Holy Spirit of God give us the desire to pray and commune with Him in fellowship.

How are we going to know what to pray for? It is through prayer that God give us the direction to pray as we should. The biggest problem most of us have when it comes to prayer is finding the will of God in prayer. John writes, "Now this is the confidence we have in Him, that if we ask anything according to His will, He hears us"

(1 John 5:14 NKJV). He hears us when it is the Holy Spirit of God in us that gives us that direction so we will know how to pray. Sure, the Bible says, "My God shall supply all your need according to His riches in glory by Christ Jesus" (Phil. 4:19 NKJV), but that doesn't settle it. I mean, it is true, but the problem many times is we want things we do not need! We church members think we should thank God for answering prayers, but maybe we should be thanking God for not giving us the things we want.

Do you know what is the dynamics of prayer? It is your faith! You cannot just make yourself believe God answers prayers, God gives you the dynamic prayer. Faith is the gift of God (Eph. 2:8-9). Faith cannot come out of a poor carnal heart, it has to come from God who put that faith into your heart, but you must abide and allow God to put that faith in you. "So then faith comes by hearing, and hearing by the word of God" (Rom. 10:17 NKJV). That does not mean just hearing somebody read the Word; it means hearing God speak to you out of the Word. Having God just take the spoken Word and just speaking to you through it.

The Objective of Prayer

The objective of prayer is the praise of God. Listen again to Romans 11:36, "For of Him and through Him and to Him are all things, to whom be glory forever. Amen" (NKJV). God is in the business of giving glory to Himself through us. The reason that so many of us do not get our prayer answered is we are not interested in the glory of God; we are trying to make God into Santa Claus or a bellhop. "Lord, I want you to do this for me, and that for me." Our prayers are not interested in the glory of God, but God is interested in giving glory to Himself. He is a jealous God and He will not share His glory with another. That why James is saying we have missed the point (Jam. 4:3). God will answer personal prayers, but not selfish prayers. So, when you pray ask yourself this question: "Is the desire of my heart to glorify God?" The cycle of prayer is that prayer originates with God, prayer operates through God, and prayers goes back to God to give God glory.

We need to behave as a church by being a church that prays. Prayer says, "Please"; while praise and worship says, "Thank You!" Prayer goes into God's presence to carry something away. Praise goes into God's presence to stay there forever and ever. The objective of prayer is not things, but God Himself, when your heart is consumed not with the gifts of God but with God for His glory. Jesus said, "And whatever you ask in My name, that I will do, that the Father may be glorified in the Son" (John 14:13 NKJV). When you ask in the name of Jesus, that does not mean that you have some little formula to put Jesus's name on at the end of your prayers and just because you tagged it on at the end of your prayer that He must answer it. No, Jesus wants you to ask in His name so the Father might be glorified in the Son. For of Him and through Him and to Him are all things, to who be glory. That is why you ask in the name of Jesus. You cannot pray anything in the name of Jesus that is not for the glory of God. Here is a definition of prayer: Powerful praying is the Holy Spirit finding a desire in the heart of the Father, then putting that desire into our heart, and then sending it back to heaven in the power of the cross, resulting in the glory of God. That is what powerful effective prayer is. There is a reason why so many churches are not behaving as a church because they are sitting on the shores of powerful effective prayer.

Pray with Serious Concentration

Prayer is important, but do you know how to show God that you are serious when you pray? Do you know how to fast and pray? Over in Daniel 9:3-19, Daniel had been reading Jeremiah, and Jeremiah had told how God was going to bring against His ancient people the Babylonians. Babylon, which is modern day Iraq, was going to take Judah captive. Judah would go through all this ordeal with the Babylonians, but God had a plan for them, God would bring them back again into the land and God would restore them. Now, right away we learn that God does bring judgment upon sin. Right away we learn that God has a plan, and His plan sometimes takes a long time to work out. It may look like God is allowing evil to succeed but it is only temporary.

The hour in which we live in is perilous and it is desperate. It is time for the bride of Christ, the family of God, the church of the Living God to behave as a church and be a house of prayer. The church needs to be serious about prayer because only believing, repenting prayer is going to hold back the floodtides of judgment and sin and release the cleansing power of the Lord Jesus Christ upon our personal lives and our nation. Our greatest resource, our greatest weapon prayer. Jesus is our only hope. We need a great awakening of God's people praying for revival. Pray for divine intervention. Pray that God would demonstrate His approval of His church, by manifesting His power through His church.

Daniel writes, "Then I set my face toward the Lord God to make request by prayer and supplication, with fasting, sackcloth, and ashes" (Dan. 9:3 NKJV). Have you ever set your face before God to pray? Ever said, "Dear God, I am going to pray with every inch, every ounce, every nerve, every sinew?" In church it seems like we do a lot of praying, but it also seems like much of our prayer has little effect. Why? Because it is not the number of our prayers; it is not the rhetoric of our prayers; it is not how eloquent our prayer is; it is not the geometry of our prayers; it is not how long or short our prayer is; it is not the emotion of our prayer, it is not how sweet our prayer is; it is not the logic of our prayer; nor is it how argumentative our prayer is. It is about the faith and fervency of our prayer that matters. When we talk about the nation, we must talk first about the house of God. "For the time has come for judgment to begin at the house of God; and if it begins with us first, what will be the end of those who do not obey the gospel of God?" (1 Pet. 4:17 NKJV). We as a church need to repent. There are churches across America that is playing church. We pray, but we pray without fasting; we witness, but without tears; we give, but without sacrifice. Is it any wonder that we sow, but without reaping? We need God in America again, and in every church; and prayer is the order of the day! But not just any prayer, prayer joined with fasting. Does that seem odd to you? Does that seem like somehow it is fanatical that we, in this twenty-first century, should go about fasting and praying? Well, Jesus said, "And when you pray, you shall not be like the hypocrites. For they love to pray standing in the synagogues and on the corners of the streets, that they may be seen of men. Assuredly, I say to you, they have their reward" (Matt. 6:5 NKJV). Notice it is "when you pray" not, "if you pray." When you do pray do not pray to be seen of men. Then Jesus says, "Moreover, when you fast, do not be like the hypocrites, with a sad countenance. For they disfigure their faces that they may appear to men to be fasting. Assuredly, I say to you, they have their reward" (vs. 16 NKJV). When you fast and pray do not parade yourself around in front of men, neither disfigure your face to gain the praise of men. I heard one preacher say, "The church has gone from its upper room with its fire to its supper room with its smoke." Now, I am not against fellowshipping around the table. Goodness knows how many Southern Baptist potlucks I have been to; Baptist love to eat. One day when we are gathered to the throne of God, we are going to come to the marriage supper of the Lamb for Jesus is constantly saying to His children, come and dine.

But we must never forget that fasting is mentioned in the Bible, and we need to fast and pray for the home, your church, for America, for your pastor(s), your deacons, for your brothers and sisters in Christ, and for all the lost sinners in the world today. But what is fasting? Fasting is not merely going without food. Fasting is going without food, water sometimes for a spiritual purpose. It is not dieting, it is not cutting down on our eating for health's sake, although we ought to do that. Fasting is giving up food, water, and certain pleasures for a spiritual purpose. It is like a spiritual string tied around your finger reminding you to pray. When you fast and you have a hunger pain that is a reminder that you should pray and seek the face of God at that very moment.

WHAT IS THE MOTIVATION FOR FASTING

Why should you fast? Well, when Daniel prayed his prayer, he prayed a concentrated prayer. It was a prayer with fasting in sackcloth and ashes. Sackcloth and ashes speak of being humble before God. Before we get into the motivation of fasting, did you know that you can fast for the wrong reason? One reason is you can fast in self-centeredness. Which means you want to boast about the fact that you are fasting. Jesus warned about giving money in public to be seen of men. Jesus warned about praying in public to be seen of men. He also warned about fasting to be seen of men. Jesus does not mean we cannot give in public, pray in public, or fast in public, because we take up a public offering at church, we pray together in services, and as a matter of fact, there were public fast called for in the Bible. Jesus does not want us to do these things to be seen of men. Don't be like the pharisee in the temple. He stuck out his chest, and began bragging about himself, and says "I fast twice a week." But the pharisee does not know anything about justice, mercy, and forgiveness. You should avoid exhibitionism, meaning do not have an extravagant behavior where you are drawing attention to yourself as you fast. Also, you want to avoid legalism, meaning do not treat fasting and praying as something that required to be spiritual. Christians will often treat fasting as a way to gain favor with God, Jesus was not giving a command to fast; He was just saying when you fast do not seek attention. Listen there is nothing we can do to earn favor with God. Our motivation for fasting and praying is to be serious and concentrated on seeking God's will and His glory. I know the devil has abused this thing of fasting and praying, maybe that is the reason we do not hear much about it in the modern church anymore. But when you fast it should be unto the Lord. He is our motivation.

WHAT CAN FASTING DO FOR YOU

Fasting and praying will strengthen your prayer life. When we pray, God bends His ear to hear us pray. However, when we fast and pray, we are giving heaven notice that we are serious; that we are seeking God with all our heart. Fasting causes you to be more focused on your praying, it also causes you to be more frequent with you praying. If you have a prayer life that is barely functional then commit to fasting and praying. Fasting strengthens your prayer life and because it does, it can hold back judgment. Preachers across America are telling us that America is ripe for the judgment of God. But if we fast and pray, God will hold back the judgment that we deserve. This is what happened to Nineveh in the days of Jonah. Remember, God told Jonah to go to Nineveh and preach to that great city that the judgment of God was about to fall upon them. When he went to Nineveh and preached God's message to the citizens, "the people of Nineveh believed God, proclaimed a fast, and put on sackcloth, from the greatest to the least of them" (Jon. 3:5 NKJV). The people of Nineveh humbled themselves before God and He stayed the judgment that Nineveh was due. Is it too late for America? Is it too late for the church? No, because God had rather show mercy than judgment. God wants to forgive and show mercy.

HOW SHOULD WE FAST

When you desire to get serious about doing a fasting and praying, the first thing you should do is examine your motivation. Why do you want to do it? You should also ask God if you should fast. Do not let your pastor, Sunday School teacher, or someone else tell you to fast. Pray and ask God, "Should I do a fast?" Then as you are praying about doing a fast, go ahead and ask God what you should fast, or do without to show that you are serious. Word of caution, avoid extremism, meaning do not say, "Well, I am going to fast without food and water for X number of days." Listen, if you are not accustomed to fasting this would not be good for you. Why not start out small at first? Try setting aside just one day to do a fast. Pick a day when your activities are light. Plan time when doing a fast. Maybe even do a partial fast, which by the way is okay to do. Partial fast is doing without a special certain pleasure. For example: maybe give up bacon for a week, or coffee, or pick a day and have a technology timeout where you do not get on social media, watch television, or radio and when you have those urges to get on technology then it is time to pray. If you are sick, or under medication, or you are pregnant then you should talk with a doctor before you fast without food and water. Again, do not strut around while fasting, neither brag to others that you are fasting. Do not be ashamed of the fact that you are fasting. What I am trying say is this: we are to pray with serious concentration. There are too many Christians who are not behaving as a follower of Christ when it comes to prayer. It seems as though they have this take-it-or-leave-it attitude towards prayer. Many rattles off their prayer and could not, an hour later, tell they prayed for. When you pray, it doesn't hurt to keep a prayer journal of your prayers. That way you can look back and see where God has answered or moved in your life and give Him thanks. The church often falls into routine in services and when it is time for prayer, we simply say the prayer and move on to the next part of the service. The church should behave as a church that prays with all sincereness and concentrated prayers.

We are to Pray with Steadfast Confidence

When Daniel prayed, he stated in his prayer that he believed in God. "And I prayed to the Lord my God, and made confession, and said, "O Lord, great and awesome God, who keeps His covenant and mercy with those who love Him, and with those who love Him and with those who keep His commandments" (Dan. 9:4 NKJV). Then He states it again, "To the Lord our God belong mercy and forgiveness, though we have rebelled against Him" (vs. 9 NKJV). The basis of our prayer should be the greatness of God and the mercy of God. It is impossible to see the greatness of God and the mercies of God and not pray with confidence. The basis of Daniel's prayer was the shed blood of Jesus. He says, "Now while I was speaking, praying, and confessing my sin and the sin of my people Israel, and presenting my supplication before the Lord my God for the holy mountain of my God, yes, while I was speaking in prayer, the man Gabriel, who I had seen in the vision at the beginning, being caused to fly swiftly, reached me about the time of the evening offering" (vs. 20-21 NKJV). In the KJV the phrase is "evening oblation" (vs. 21 KJV). What is the evening oblation? Also known as the evening offering, the evening oblation is when a sacrifice was made in the temple of God. When Daniel prayed this prayer, there had not been a temple for seventy years! The temple was destroyed, and yet, Daniel is looking back to a sacrifice that was made seventy years ago it was the time of evening offering. When was the evening offering? The evening offering was at the same time Jesus died upon the cross. The evening offering was from 3-4 p.m. In the New Testament, it was called the nineth hour. Daniel is looking back to a time of the evening oblation, looking back to a specific sacrifice. When we pray today, we are looking back to a bloody Calvary, because when Daniel prayed, not only was he looking backward he was also looking forward. Every Old Testament sacrifice was a picture and a prophecy of the Lord Jesus Christ, who would one day hang in agony and blood upon the cross. The plain message is this: because the blood of Jesus Christ, God's Son, cleanses us from all iniquity, then we should be able to pray with confidence.

We are to Pray with Sincere Confession

If sin brings judgment, then confession brings forgiveness. "And if prayed to the Lord my God and made confession..." (vs. 4 NKJV). "We have sinned and committed iniquity, we have don wickedly and rebelled, even by departing form Your precepts and Your judgments. Neither have we headed Your servants the prophets, who spoke in Your name to our kings and our princes, to our fathers and all the people of the land. O Lord, righteousness belongs to You, but to us shame of face..." (vs. 5-7 NKJV) "Now while I was speaking, praying, and confessing my sin and the sin of my people Israel, and presenting supplication before the Lord my God for the holy mountain of my God" (vs. 20 NKJV). Daniel confessed his personal sin, and he confessed the sin of the nation. We must confess our sins. "If we confess our sins, He is faithful and just to forgive us our sins and to cleanse us from all unrighteousness" (1 John 1:9 NKJV).

If you read the story of Daniel, you will not find one sin ever marked against him. However, just because God did not have it recorded in the Bible, does not mean Daniel never sinned. "If we say we that we have no sin, we deceive ourselves, and the truth is not in us" (vs. 8 NKJV). There is not a person on this planet that does not need to pray and confess his or her sin. Daniel prayed for forgiveness for personal sin, but he also prayed for the forgiveness of national sin. The national sin was not a sin that Daniel committed, but he identified with this sin to pray for it. I call this identification prayer. He identified himself with a nation and said, "O God, my nation has sinned. God have mercy on us" Listen, you can identify with America's sin or whatever nation you live in, because the sinful, wicked people of America are not going to pray for themselves. We need to pray with sincere confession.

We are to Pray with Spiritual Concern

After we have confessed our sin and the in of the nation and even the sin of the church for that matter; we need to ask God to remove the guilt. Daniel prayed, "O Lord, according to all Your righteousness, I pray, let Your anger and Your fury be turned away from Your city Jerusalem, Your holy mountain; because of our sins, and for the iniquities of our fathers, Jerusalem and Your people are a reproach to all those around us" (Dan. 9:16 NKJV). Our gracious Lord gives us what we do not deserve, and in His mercy does not give us what we do deserve. Daniel was asking God to remove His anger because of the guilt of himself and the nation. Daniel confessed the sins of Israel, including his, were the cause of the judgment and punishment upon the nation; however, he reminded God that He had promised to forgive His people who would repent and confess their sins. "...for we do not present our supplications before You because of our righteous deeds, but because of Your great mercies" (vs. 18 NKJV). We need to pray for America, our church, our brothers, and sisters in Christ, and for the Lost. We need to pray, "God, cleanse us, restore us, revive us, renew us, refresh us. O Lord, we need your divine intervention. Demonstrate Your approval of Your church, by manifesting Your power through Your church."

We need to pray with spiritual concern for the lost with the prayer of intercession. We need to pray more. Pastors need to pray more, deacons need to pray more, teachers, church members need to pray more. Paul said, "Brethren, my heart's desire and prayer to God for Israel is that they may be saved" (Rom. 10:1 NKJV). Prayer is so power and effective, because it is God's way of bringing lost souls to Him. We are to pray to the Lord, and bind the devil in prayer, and pray for soul winners, and pray for the church triumphant, that we might go out and win souls to Jesus!

We also need to pray with spiritual concern for God's glory. Daniel prayed, "Now therefore, our God, hear the prayer of Your servant, and his supplications, and for the Lord's sake cause Your face to shine on Your sanctuary, which is desolate." (Dan. 9:17 NKJV). He continues, "O Lord, hear! O Lord, forgive! O Lord, listen and act! Do not delay for Your own sake, my God, for Your city and Your people are called by Your name (vs. 19 NKJV). When you pray do you ever pray for God's glory? Do you know what most churches want? Churches want to have revival so we can return to our own way, so we can go back again, one more time, once God gets us out of this difficulty. Do you have a burning yearning in your heart for the glory of God? Daniel did, he desired that nation to be restored so God might be glorified. Remember the Jews were God's chosen people, and Jerusalem is the place God chose to put the temple; the longer God punished his people and the land the less glory He would receive. God did answer Daniel's prayer! The next year Cyrus permitted the Jews to return to their land, take the temple treasure with them, and allowed them to restore the temple. I want to see God's glory spread over this land. I want to see God do something again that cannot be explained by the pundits on television and social media. I want something that cannot be explained by technology, personality, propaganda, or persuasion. I want glory for God! The church should behave as a church that prays!

CHAPTER SEVEN

A Tale of Two Brothers, Part One

Then He said, "A certain man had two sons."
(Luke 15:11 NKJV)

AMNESIA IS A STRANGE CONDITION THAT INVOLVES A LOSS OF memory. There are cases on record in which the victim has forgotten his own name and address, the date of his birth, and his family relationship. These facts have been utterly blotted out of his mind. He has a mental block and cannot recall any significant events that occurred before he was afflicted. Even the most important milestones in the individual's life means nothing to him when he is told about them. What does this have to do with behaving as a church? Well, I am afraid that there are many Christians church members who are in this same shape. They have a form of spiritual amnesia. It seems that they have forgotten all that the Lord has done for them. They have forgotten His salvation and His blessings. They have forgotten the glory of being in a right relationship with the Father and other church members. They have forgotten how wonderful life is at the Father's house and what it is like to have a joyful fellowship within the family. Wayward church members have spiritual amnesia, and they seem to have no idea how to get back home. Church members, who see the wayward member come back to the church, have spiritual amnesia and has forgotten how to treat a wayward brother or sister. What we need to do is behave as a church that loves and cares.

In Luke 15 Jesus tells three parables and each one deals with lost things that are found by the owner. Luke 15:1-2 tells us what motivates Jesus to give these parables in the first place. The Pharisees and the scribe were criticizing Jesus because He received sinners. They are astounded that someone like Jesus would spend His time with "tax collectors and sinners" (vs. 1 NKJV). They were stunned the He would receive such wicked and evil people. These religious leaders had spiritual amnesia and had lost all understanding of what it meant to love thy neighbor. In response, Jesus tells them about these great stories in which each story is designed to teach the same great truth: "Every soul is precious to God, even your!" As Jesus moves through these stories, He places greater and greater emphasis upon the value of the thing lost. For example, in the parable of the lost sheep (vs. 3-7), there was one out of one hundred sheep missing. In the parable of the lost coin, there was one coin out of ten coins missing. In the parable of the prodigal son, there is one son out of two missing. In the first two parables, the objects missing were an animal and something material. In the parable of the prodigal son, the missing object is a human being. Each time the object lost grows in value and importance. Again, the great truth here is "Every soul is precious to God, even yours!"

However, there is more to the story of the prodigal son. There were two sons and each one can represent two different types of church members and they both teach us how to behave as a church towards members and lost people. The prodigal son shows us of a tale of a wasted life that learns how to go home. The prodigal's brother teaches us how to deal with a repentant brother or sister in Christ. In this chapter we are going to deal with the former and see, if we find ourselves in this situation, how to come home. Now, many times preachers will use this parable to preach to backsliders and there is plenty of application available to use it that way. The actual interpretation of this passage deals with lost things. Jesus is speaking about the salvation of lost souls; therefore we will incorporate both the wayward church member and the lost souls because every soul is precious to God, even yours!

Let me give a little background before we dive into this story. First, the original prodigal son is found in Deuteronomy 21:18-21. The only exception is the fact that the original prodigal son did not have to leave home to break the fifth commandment, which is: honor your mother and father. He did that by resisting the pleas, warnings, and chastisement of his parents every day. He refused to work, he stayed drunk, and did nothing at home or in the community. His sin was so terrible that Moses had it included in the curses that was read in the land of Canaan (Deut. 27:18; Ex. 21:17). In all actuality this was more than just a family concern because it also involved the peace and reputation of the community. The unity of the people of Israel, much like the unity and the harmony of the church, was important. The reason why is because the sin of one single person, family, city, or tribe could affect the whole nation (Josh. 7:1-15). This is also true of the church because we all belong to one body (1 Cor. 12), we belong to each other and therefore will affect each other (1 Cor. 5).

An Astonishing Request

The young son made a very cruel request. "And the younger of them said to his father, 'Father, give me the portion of goods that falls to me.' So, he divided to them his livelihood" (vs. 2 NKJV). This young man was requesting his share of the inheritance and he has every right to make such a request. According to Deuteronomy 21:17, he was entitled to one-third of his father's estate. His request was legal, since a man could divide his estate while he lived. However, when you start thinking about it, his request to us seem rude and cruel. When this young man asked for his father to divide the estate, he was saying in effect, "I wish you were dead and had no longer a say in my life! I am tired of you, and I want to be free from you and your control in my life." Few of us would ever say that to our parents! Furthermore, we are always heading for trouble whenever we value things more than people, pleasure more than duty, and distant scenes more than the blessings we have right at home. Jesus warned two brothers, who were arguing among themselves, "and He said to them, "Take heed and beware of covetousness, for one's life does not consist in the abundance of the things he possesses" (Luke 12:15 NKJV). Why? Because the covetous person can never be satisfied, no matter how much he acquires, and a dissatisfied heart leads to a disappointed life.

Now, right here we can see when the best time to come home for the Christian. It is when you realize that you have left the heavenly Father's house, or as soon as you feel that your love for Him has slipped away, or as soon as you realize you aren't as close as you once were, as soon as you see the signs of straying away from Him; that is the moment you should bow down before Him in repentance. This young man should have noticed the sign of behaving with a selfish behavior, notice he said "give me". His focus is on himself, he is wrapped up in what he wants. He cares for no one else but himself.

According to the Law of the Prodigal, the parents of the rebellious son were to take him to the local council at the gate, bear witness of his rebellion and stubbornness, and let the council decide. If the boy refused to change his ways, then the only verdict was death by stoning, with all the men of the community participating (Deut. 21:18-21). Why? To serve as a warning and put away evil in the family and community. The Lord and Moses believed that the public punishment of offenders could be a detriment to others sinning. Furthermore, the future of a family was at stake if the original prodigal son was allowed to continue in his sin. However, in the story that Jesus tells, the father responds with grace. He could have refused and kicked his son and drug him down to the gate, but he doesn't. He merely does what his son demands and gives his son his inheritance. He divided his life's savings. This father has poured his life into building his estate so that he might have something to pass down to his sons. This father gave his son the result and total of his life's work. The younger son wanted what the father could give, but he did not want the father!

The behavior of the prodigal son is a picture of a lost sinner! The lost person takes no thought for God but wants God to give them things. They want His air, His food, His water, His time, His world, etc. but they do not want Him involved in their lives! When God made man, He literally poured His life into man (Gen. 2:7). Every day that men live upon the earth, they consume resources which God created to sustain them, yet they do not acknowledge or want Him in their lives. They want what He can give them, but they do not want Him. No wonder the Bible says, "The fool has said in his heart, "There is no God." They are corrupt, they have done abominable works, there is none who does good" (Ps. 14:1 NKJV). If you want to live your life like there is no God, then He will allow you to do just that! If you want to take all that He can give you without acknowledging Him, then He will let you do that too. But you need to know that kind of life leads to an eternity in Hell. "There is a way that seems right to a man, but its end is the way of death" (Prov. 16:25 NKJV).

An Awful Reality

When a Christian begins to live like the world it is time for the wayward Christian to return home. "And not many days after, the younger son gathered all together, journeyed to a far country, and there wasted his possessions with prodigal living" (Luke 15:13 NKJV). When this young man left his father's house, he began a downward spiral. He takes his father's gracious provision, and he squanders it by living a wicked, self-indulgent life. He threw his possessions into the wind of sin and watched as they were all blown away. The words "prodigal living" refers to "a life totally given over to sinfulness and wickedness" (Wood, Marshall, & Millard, 1996) When this boy left home, he also left behind his moral restraints. He lived to gratify every whim and desire of the flesh. He thew it all away on things that were not sound investments. For example, drugs, alcohol, and harlots. We do not have any records of what he did, but this we know he did not have a house, nor any farm animals, nor anything to plant, he did not have any money to buy food. Did he have a good time squandering all his possessions? Oh yes! I will be so ridged as to try and tell you that there is not pleasure of sin (Heb. 11:25). In the KJV, the last phrase of that verse says that the pleasure of sin is for a season.

Just as the trees outside bloom and are full of promise, they will soon be wilted, and the leaves will die. The seasons of life change and when they do, everything that has brought you pleasure at one point in your life will bring you pain instead! A life lived in the bottle, a life lived indulging sexual sins, a life lived for fleshly pleasures, a life lived for self, all end up in the same place. Yes, pleasure may be found in these things for a short period of time, but for the lost sinner, is eternity without God in Hell worth the short time spent in the pleasure of sins embrace? But let's face it, there is a great deal of difference between the Christian and the world. "Therefore, if anyone is in Christ, he is a new creation; old things have passed away; behold all things have become new" (2 Cor. 5:17 NKJV). When the Christian sees that the line begins to blur, that is a good indicator that it is time to come home to the heavenly Father. Anytime we start to walk, talk, act, look, think, or do anything else like the world around us, then we need to wake up and see the danger we are heading into. You cannot be right with God and live like the world!

When you lose the Father's blessings the reality is sin has a price. "But when he had spent all, there arose a severe famine in that land, and he began to be in want" (Luke 15:14 NKJV). Since the young man had thrown all the blessings of his father away, he was left with nothing. Evidently, when the money ran out, his friends also ran out! The far country, a place where he thought that it was a place of wine, women, and song, turned out to be a land of weeping, worry, and sorrow. He found out too late that sin carries a high price tag. Here is what happens when you allow sin in your life. Sin will take your peace, your assurance of salvation making you feel as though you lost your salvation. Sin will rob your joy, destroy your prayer life, your devotional life, your witness, and your testimony. It will take everything of value and leave you spiritually bankrupt and destitute. When these things begin to be stripped from the Christian's life that is a good sign that you need to return home.

Sin brings separation. This boy found himself broke, alone, and miles away from a father who had nothing but love for him. By his own actions, he finds himself separated from the father by a wide gulf of sin, pride, and ignorance. Sin also brings sorrow. The young man began to be in want because his life had been turned upside down. When the music stopped, the friends left and when the money was all gone, he found out that he had needs that he could not meet. His sin had robbed him of everything of value and it left him hopeless and helpless in the far country. This is how sin treats all its victims!

It will promise you the world, but it can only deliver hopelessness, desolation, and death (Rom. 6:23 Jam. 1:14-15). We say, "It pays to live for God!" Yes, it does! But did you know that it also pays to live for the devil? It pays dividends that you cannot imagine! Broken lives, ruined marriages, shattered dreams, damaged trust, health problems, hopelessness, depression, defeat, and death are all part of the pay package the pleasure of sin. Someone once said, "Sin will take you farther than you want to go, keep you longer that you want to stay and cost you more than you want to pay" (Unknown, 2015) Do not worry sin always pays off, "Do not be deceived, God is not mocked; for whatever a man sows, that he will also reap. For he who sows to his flesh will of the flesh reap corruption, but he who sows to the Spirit will of the Spirit reap everlasting life" (Gal. 6:7-8 NKJV).

Because of his reckless decisions, this boy found himself in a mess. "Then he went and joined himself to a citizen of that country, and he sent him into his fields to feed swine. And he would gladly have filled his stomach with the pods that the swine ate, and no one gave him anything" (Luke 15:15-16 NKJV). This young man found himself flat broke, working as a swine feeder, watching the hogs eat and wanting their food because he had none for himself. For a Jewish man to stoop to this level would mean that he had reached the very bottom of the barrel of life! He must have been filled with shame. This gives us an idea of what the consequences of sin can do to our lives. When sin comes in, it separates you from those you love, it sends you away from God, and it literally strips you of everything and leaves you broken starving to death. This is how it was for this young man. He had no home, no help, and no one cared for him at all. He is starving because of the choices he has made. No one around him cared whether he lives or dies. He is alone, hungry, and broken. What a sad shape to be in, but for this young man, it was the first step in getting him home.

"Good understanding gains favor, but the way of the unfaithful is hard" (Prov. 13:15 NKJV). A man in Georgia got mad at the church and refused to go for a year. His six year old son begged him to go to church with the family, but this man refused, often getting verbally abusive with the child. One Sunday morning as the father was reading his paper on the front porch, his son came and asked his father to go to church. The father responded hatefully with the boy and told him to never ask him that again. The little boy began to play in the yard, tossing a little ball into the air. After a time, he dropped the ball, and it rolled across the highway. He ran after it and was hit by a car and thrown into the air. The father witnessed the whole thing and immediately ran to the boy and picked him up. Just before he died, the boy said to his father, "Daddy, will you go to church with me?" This broke the father's heart and there, holding the broken body of his little boy, he bowed his head and asked for forgiveness from God. He came home, but it cost him his son. What will your sin cost you?

An Altered Return

"But when he came to himself, he said, 'How many of my father's hired servants have bread enough and to spare, and I perish with hunger" (Luke 15:17 NKJV). The entire time this young man has been in the far country was a time of insanity. He had not been thinking clearly! Now, suddenly, he comes to himself, the fog lifts, and he remembers how good it had been at home with the father. He remembers that even his father's servants were in better shape than he is. Seeing where you are, is always the first step in getting to some other place. The first step in getting out of sin is to realize that you are in sin (Rom. 3:23). When that is settled, you will begin to see that God's servants are happy, they have hope, and they are not trapped in the same bondage you are in and you will want to be set free. That is the first step in getting out.

After coming to his senses, he makes up his mind to go home. "I will arise and go to my father, and will say to him, "Father, I have sinned against heaven and before you, and I am no longer worthy to be called your son. Make me like one of your hired servants" (Luke 15:18-19 NKJV). Repentance is a one hundred eighty turnaround from the direction you are going. You are returning to Jesus. This young man longed for fellowship with the father. He wants to go where he can be loved, fed, and care for. He wants to go home. Even as he makes up his mind to go home, he realizes what he has done. He sees his own unworthiness and he is willing to go home under any circumstances. He just wants to be back in the father's house.

Just as he had left his father in the beginning, now he leaves everything else behind to go back home. Now this young man is going to confess his sins and place himself under the authority of his father. Notice he left home saying, "Give Me!" He returns home saying, "Make me!" Before, he did not want to be under the father's authority. Now, he is willing to be a slave. If you have strayed from the Father's house, you need to come, but you will have to do it on His terms! He will receive you, but you have to repent of your sins (1 John 1:9). When we become willing to admit our wrongdoing and confess our sin to the Lord, He is more than willing to hear us and forgive us. We can never have that right fellowship with God until we first repent of our sins. However, you must decide for yourself just what being back in the heavenly Father's house and under His blessings means to you. This is where every lost sinner has to come to before they will ever be saved. God does the conviction. He sends the Holy Spirit to reveal the sin in the lost sinner's life and reveals their impeding judgment (John 16:7-11). The Holy Spirit shows us where we are; He shows us what we are, and He takes the blinders off and lets the lost sinner see their condition, then He points them to Jesus. No man is saved apart from the convicting ministry of the Holy Spirit (John 6:44).

This young man was willing to humble himself to the father. Before, he stood defiantly before the father and demanded his own way. Now, he is willing to be a servant before his father. Oh, wayward child of God, remember when you were saved. Did you feel humble before Him? It felt as though God were so great and you were so small. Listen, that is how it is going to feel when you make up your mind to return to God from a straying life. God will accept your humble heart. "Humble yourselves in the sight of the Lord, and He will lift you up" (Jam. 4:10 NKJV). "Therefore, humble yourselves under the mighty hand of God, that He may exalt you in due time" (1 Pet. 5:6 NKJV). A humble sprit realizes that it deserves nothing but judgment and punishment. It demands nothing for the Lord, but it comes before Him will to be and do whatever God demands. A humble spirit just wants to be back in the heavenly Father's house.

An Awesome Reunion

So, the young son gets up and heads home. He does not know what will happen when he gets there. He may be rejected, humiliated, or may even be put to death. At this point, he does not care! He is tired of the far country, and he is going home! That is what conviction does for you! The Holy Spirit will make the pain and penalty of sin real, therefore, the salvation Jesus offers so glorious, so sweet, that you will do anything to get to Him. "And he arose and came to his father. But when he was still a great way off, his father saw him and had compassion, and ran and fell on his neck and kissed him. And the son said to him, 'Father, I have sinned against heaven and in your sight, and am no longer worthy to be called your son'" (Luke 15:20-21 NKJV). As this young man headed home, he did not know what he might find there. But what he did find was something he never experienced in the far country. He found a father who had been longing, looking, and living for his son's return. He found a father filled with love, compassion, and grace. He found someone who received him and loved him back into the fellowship! We need to behave as a church following the example of what this father did for his wayward son. The church needs to be welcoming, loving, and responding in grace to another brother or sister who has come home.

This father was waiting and watching for his son and when he saw him, he was moved with compassion. He was overwhelmed with joy that he ran out to meet him and greet him with hugs and kisses. It was considered undignified for a man of his age to run in that culture. The "law of the prodigal" helps us understand this aspect of Jesus's parable (Deut. 21:18-21). In the East, it wasn't customary for old men to run. So, why did this father run? One obvious reason was his love compelled him to make haste and go meet his son and show him that love. But there is something else involved. This wayward son had brought disgrace to his family and village and news of his wicked behavior in the far country had drifted back to his hometown. The law-abiding men of that village knew he had disgraced their city and according to the law he should be stoned to death. Seeing the boy approach, the elders at the gate might be tempted to refuse him entrance into the city or in their anger they might have picked up stones to stone him. However, the father ran to meet the son and embraces him and kisses him, now if the elders throw stones, they might hit the father instead of the son. God runs to meet the sinner to quickly extend mercy and put away danger! What a picture of Jesus, where He took our punishment for us that He might be able to welcome us home. He literally placed Himself between us and His wrath (1 John 2:2).

Something else the church needs to be reminded of, and that is of the father's actions. This father who had compassion upon his son as he saw the shape his son was it. He probably looked terrible and filthy. That did not stop him for running out to meet him. The son probably even smelled rotten, but that did not stop the father from kissing his son. That word "kissed" is in the present tense (Wood, Marshall, & Millard, 1996) The father did not just give one kiss, but he gave a continual of kisses. Despite the smell, in spite of the filth, in spite of the hurt, the pain, and the loss, the father kissed the son! This was the ultimate sign of acceptance by the father. When we return home, the Father kisses us back into the family (1 John 1:9). The law demanded death, but grace extended the kiss of love and reconciliation! Because of forgiving grace, there was a feast instead of a funeral!

When the young son came home, he had everything he threw away restored by the good grace of the father. "But the father said to his servants, 'bring out the best robe and put it on him and put a ring on his hand and sandals on his feet'" (Luke 15:22 NKJV). The young son stood there in the rags of his sin. He does not look like a child of this father. But the father orders the best of his robes to be brought and to be put on the son. The robe would cover all the stains and dirt of the pig pen. The robe would make him look like the father. Anyone who saw this boy dressed in his father's robe might have mistaken him for the father! The robe erased all the visible signs of this boy's sinful past. When a sinner comes home, they receive a robe from the heavenly father (Isa. 61:10; Rev. 7:9-14). When a wayward Christian comes home, the robe of righteousness cleansed and made white as snow. The robe of righteousness is the righteousness of Jesus imputed to all those who receive Him by faith (Phil. 3:9) and it can never be taken away! When we are clothed in righteousness of Christ, all the pain and the stain of our past are forever washed away!

After the robe, the father placed a ring on the younger son's hand. The ring was a symbol of sonship and authority. The one with the ring could speak for the father! The one with the ring had access to all that belonged to the father! The one with the father's ring was in a position of great privilege! When a lost sinner repents of their sins and comes home, they are given the privilege of being recognized as His sons (1 John 3:1-2). When a way Christian comes home, he is still a child of the heavenly Father. The way this father treated his son is the way our heavenly Father treats His children when they come home. That is the way we should behave as a church towards those who come home. Then the father calls for shoes to be placed on his son's feet. Think about this, only slaves went barefoot, sons wore shoes! This boy returned home desiring to be a mere servant, but the father is determined to recognize his position as a son. In the boy's eyes, he did not even deserve anything from the father. The father looked at him and said, "This is my son!" The father alone determines the position and worth of his children. Think about this very carefully, you are not a nobody, your life matters. If you are saved, then you are saved by grace (Eph. 2:8-10). If you are a lost sinner, then you are loved (John 3:16). When you are saved, you became a child of God. He no longer sees you as a slave to sin or as a sinner, but He sees you as His precious child, whom He loves like He loves His Son Jesus. What I am saying is this: "Do not let the devil, the flesh, or the world keep you down by telling you, you are a not worthy to be a child of God." If you are truly saved, you have been accepted by the Father in heaven and He has called you, His child. Sounds to me like you are in a special place of privilege.

When this young son came home, he found rejoicing. The father said, "and bring the fatted calf here and kill it and let us eat and be merry; for this my son was dead and is alive again; he was lost and is found.' And they began to be merry" (Luke 15:23-24 NKJV). The fatted calf was kept for special occasions. Bringing out the fatted calf was the father's way of sharing his joy with everyone around. Instead of a wasted life, the father was celebrating a life redeemed and restored. When this son returned home, laughter filled a house that had been silenced by grief. When a believer is out of fellowship with the Lord, there is a breakdown in their joy. Everything that was missing in the pig pen was given to the young son when he returned home. When a lost sinner returns home to God, when a wayward Christian returns home to the father there should be rejoicing in the house of God. We need to behave as a church by rejoicing over the sinner that was once lost but now is found. We need to behave as a church by rejoicing over the wayward Christian that has come home.

CHAPTER EIGHT

A Tale of Two Brothers, Part Two

Then He said: "A certain man had two sons."
(Luke 15:11 NKJV)

THIS EXTENDED PARABLE IN LUKE 15 IS INTENDED TO TEACH THE truth that God loves sinners. He loves the lost enough to go after them in their lost condition, as we can see the evidence in the three parables in Jesus told in Luke 15. He loves the self-righteous sinner enough to tell them about their condition, which is why He told the parable of the Prodigal Son. Let me point out, that when Luke 15 is preached, you hear about the lost sheep, the lost coin, and the prodigal son, but it is rare that you ever hear anything about the brother. Why is that? I think preachers avoid this story because they focus more on the emotional reunion between the father and the prodigal son. I also think preachers avoid the brother because it hits a little too close to home. I can see that there is a little or maybe a lot in how this brother reacted to his brothers return in church member when a wayward brother or sister in Christ comes home.

As Jesus reaches the end of this parable, He is still dealing with lost things, but we must remember who it is He is talking with. He is talking with the Pharisees and the Scribes and their bad behavior towards lost sinners (vs. 1-2). The elder brother in this text pictures two types of people in the church. The first is a church member who is involved in the things of God, but he is fleshly and does not care for the wayward Christian. The second is a person who is involved in the things of God but has no real relationship with God. This type of person is in the Father's house but is lost and is in the far country in his heart. The message of this section of the parable is designed to speak to two classes of people. The primary message is to those who are in the far country in their heart. You might be religious, you might be a church member, you might be a good moral person, but you have never been saved. The secondary part of the message speaks to those who are saved but have the same spirit and bad behavior as the elder brother. It speaks to people who are upset when God bless His people. The story of Jonah comes to mind here (Jon. 4). The message speaks to people who do not like it when the prodigal son comes home. It speaks to people who refuse to rejoice over what God is doing because it is not being done their way. It speaks to the entire church not to behave as the elder brother. We need to behave as a church rejoicing that prodigal Christian has come home. So, let's examine the prodigal's brother and see what areas we need to work on.

The Brother's Respectability

The prodigal's brother is the oldest son in the family. Because he is the elder brother, he is entitled to two-thirds of his father's possessions (Deut. 21:17). Since the younger brother has already received his part of the inheritance (Luke 15:12), everything now belongs to the elder brother. When the father dies, not only will the elder brother receive his father's possessions, but he will become the legal and religious head of the family. Much has been given to the elder brother already and more is on the way. He has indeed been blessed.

When we first meet this man, he is in the fields. "Now his older son was in the field. And as he came and drew near to the house, he heard music and dancing" (Luke 15:25 NKJV). Since he was busy doing his father's business, we can conclude that the elder brother was a hard worker. While his younger brother was off in the far country living it up, this brother stayed home and worked. It seems that all is well in the relationship between the elder son and the father. There is a good fellowship between them. The elder son is a picture of the religious elite and a picture of the faithful church members. The religious elite in Jesus's day were in a place of privilege. They had God's law and it appeared, at least outwardly, that they were walking in the law. They looked good to others, but there was a real problem in their hearts. The problem was hidden from human view, but God could see it. They were religious, but they were lost. This could be said of faithful church members. You are a moral person; you come to church, you don't cuss, drink, steal, or cheat. You don't smoke, you don't chew, and you don't kiss girls who do. You have been baptized and belong to the church. By all appearances, you are as good, or better, than anyone around you. The Lord knows your true condition. You can fool others, but you cannot fool God (1 Sam. 16:7).

The religious leaders of Jesus's day were truly lost and today there are some church members who are lost. This is what Jesus was saying in His parable about the wheat and tares (Matt. 13:24-30, 36-43). I am not trying to make you doubt your salvation. I am simply saying that religion does not equal salvation. Church membership does not equal conversion. Being close to the things of God does not equal being saved by the grace of God. Being in a church building does not make you a Christian any more than sleeping in a garage make you a car, neither does climbing a tree make you a squirrel. You must not depend on who you are or some kind of work for your salvation. Salvation only comes by being born again (John 3:3, 7). Salvation is by grace through faith (Eph. 2:8-10). Let me also point out, there are some Christians church members who have hardened their hearts and when a wayward Christian comes home, they get upset and complain. I have heard it said that there are hard hearted Christians in church that are always complaining and getting upset and even if Jesus physically walked through the doors of their church and sat down with them, they would still be complaining and upset. Don't behave as the religious elite of Jesus's day, behave as a church with loving kindness.

The Brother's Resentment

Heading home after a hard day in the fields, the elder brother hears sounds of celebrating as he nears the house (Luke 15:25). He is confused, as far as he knows, there is no reason for celebrating at the father's house. He has lived there all his life and he has never seen a reason to celebrate. He calls a servant and asks for the meaning of all the noise. The servant tells him of his lost brother's return and about the father killing the fatted calf and throwing a party (vs. 26-27). When he hears this, he becomes angry (vs. 28). The word angry means "to become red-faced" (Dictionary, 1828) It speaks of a person clenching their fists and becoming red with anger. In his actions here, his resentment towards the father and his brother can be clearly seen. His actions teach us a great deal about his character that can be troubling as you consider this elder brother. Think about it, he did not love his younger brother. As the older brother, he had the responsibility of looking after his younger brother and he did not go after his brother when the younger brother left for the far country. A matter of fact according to the passage of Scripture in Luke 15:11-32, he did not even show up to say goodbye. His actions indicate that did not care what happened to his younger brother. He did not care that his brother had come home. The elder brother had already written off his younger brother and did not care what happened to him. He also did not love the father either. He was disrespectful to the father. He was resentful to the father's open love for the younger son. He was self-serving, hateful, and condescending. He might have been living at home and laboring for the father, but he did not love the old man.

When this brother hears why there is a celebration, in his anger he refuses to go in. His father comes out and gently pleads with him to come in (Luke 15:28). His reply to his father is very telling of the elder brother's heart. "So, he answered and said to his father, 'Lo, these many years I have been serving you; I never transgressed your commandment at any time; and yet you never gave me a young goat, that I might make merry with my friends'" (vs. 29 NKJV). The elder brother is reminding the father of his faithful service and complains that he has never been giving a feast for what he has done. The bottom line here is this: he did not care that the lost brother had come home, and he did not care about that which pleased the father. This is the same behavior that can be seen in the church. There are some in the church that will not rejoice when sinners are saved, because they feel threatened. They have the same behavior as Jonah had in Jonah 4. These are the same people who cannot get excited when the church is growing spiritually and physically, because they feel their hold of power slipping away. There are those in the church that do not care about God's will being done in the church; especially if runs against their personal agenda. These are the people that want all the accolades, all the pats on the back and all the glory. Their service in the church is not about God, it is about them. Some people go through the motions on the outside, serving the Lord for what they think they will gain from it. When you see this kind of behavior on display, either you have a lost person masquerading as a saved person, or you have a Christian who is out of God's will.

The elder son went on to say, "But as soon as this son of yours came, who has devoured your livelihood with harlots, you killed the fatted calf for him" (vs. 30 NKJV). When you listen to this son talk to the father, you quickly realize that he is proud, disrespectful, arrogant, and angry. There is obviously something wrong with his attitude about this situation. He should have been overjoyed! His brother had returned safely from the far country. He should be rejoicing in the fact the father has received a lost son that has come home. All he can do is whine, pout, and complain. Do you know what his real problem is? The answer is here in verse 30. Who told the elder brother that the younger brother had spent his money on prostitutes? He hasn't talked to the father, until now, or to his brother. The real problem this brother has is the fact that he is jealous! He may be at home in the body, but he is in the far country in his heart! He is as far away from the father as was the other son when he went away. All the elder brother wants to do is, live it up like his brother! He would not go, nor did he do it, because his pride would not let him. So instead, he gets mad at the one who did the very things he wants to do in his heart. This is what was wrong with the Pharisees. They kept the letter of the law outwardly, but in their hearts, they lusted, they hated, and they longed for sin. You do not have to be drunk to be out of God's will! You do not have to be an adulterer to be in the far country spiritually. You can serve your church, sing in the choir, preach the Word, or anything else you want to name and still be out of God's will! You may look as good as anyone else, but you can have a heart that is filled with lust, evil thoughts, desires for sin, etc. You can pretend to be anything you wish outwardly, but it is the condition of the heart that matters. The elder brother was jealous, the Pharisees were in some way jealous, and in some way so was Jonah.

Jonah

The prophet Isaiah has this to say about the mysterious ways of the Lord. "For My thoughts are not your thoughts, nor are your ways My ways," says the Lord. "For as the heavens are higher than the earth, so are My ways higher than your ways, and My thoughts than your thoughts" (Isa. 55:8-9 NKJV). The sooner the bride of Christ realizes this, the better off we will be! Of course, even though we can read this truth and know it to be right, the ways of God are sometimes still hard to stomach. This was the case for Jonah. In Jonah 3:10-4:11, Jonah watched the Lord work His sovereign will in the city of Nineveh and Jonah did not like God's way at all! "Then God saw their works, that they returned from their evil way; and God relented from the disaster that He had said He would bring upon them, and He did not do it" (Jon. 3:10 NKJV). The book of Jonah records what may be the greatest revival in the history of the world. An entire city repented of sin and got right with God. This revival did not happen by itself! There were a few things involved in bringing this revival to the people of Nineveh.

First, it involved a man by the name of Jonah. In the first three chapters we are told of the details of Jonah's call to service, his disobedience, and his restoration. We are told how the Lord used this prophet to bring the word of God to a lost people. Second, it involved a message. According to Jonah 3:4, Jonah walks into Nineveh with a simple eight-word message from the Lord. When this message is preached, God uses the word to pierce the hearts of the Ninevites and revival begins to be poured out and spread through the city. Third, it involved a miracle. The miracle lies in the fact that a whole town turned to God (Jon. 3:5-9)! There have been great revivals throughout history, but this is the only instance of a town of this size, filled with such wicked people, being converted, and delivered from sin. It is a great miracle when revival comes, and lives are changed. But it is always a miracle when a soul hears the gospel and puts their faith in Jesus (Rom. 1:16, John 1:12). The last thing that was involved in bringing revival to Nineveh is it involved mercy (Jon. 3:10). When the people of Nineveh repented of their sins and turned to the Lord, God reacted to their faith in grace. When they turned to Him, He saved their souls by grace. Their conversion was part of His perfect plan! Salvation always works this way. God loves the sinner, has a plan to save his soul, He sends the Word that reveals the sinners lost condition, and then invites them to put their faith in Him. When the sinner chooses to repent of his sin, God saves him by grace through faith (Eph. 2:8-10).

JONAH'S REACTION

"But it displeased Jonah exceedingly, and he became angry" (Jon. 4:1 NKJV). When the Lord takes the message of Jonah and saves a city, Jonah reacts in a very bad way. Here is a prophet that becomes angry with God. He was hopping mad because God did not kill the people of Nineveh. Why was he so mad? There are several reasons why he was mad. First, remember that one of the marks of a true prophet of the Lord is that his prophecies always came 100% true (Deut. 18:20-22). Jonah had said that the Ninevites would be overthrown (Jon. 3:4). If this did not happen, then Jonah would be looked upon as a false prophet. Second, He was afraid that his fellow Jews would be angry with him for preaching a message that brought salvation to their enemies and see him as a traitor. Third, Jonah hated the people of Nineveh, and nothing would have pleased him more than seeing them all destroyed by God. But before we get too hard on old Jonah, maybe we need to look at our own lives and examine how we have responded to the Lord working out His will in your life and in the life of others. How have you reacted when a wayward Christian comes home? How have you reacted when God did something that went against your plans? Perhaps we need to be reminded of God's counsel from the Bible. "A man's heart plans his way, but the Lord directs his steps" (Prov. 16:9 NKJV). "The steps of a good man are ordered by the Lord, and He delights in his way" (Ps. 37:23 NKJV).

After seeing this take place Jonah prays to God. "So, he prayed to the Lord, and said, "Ah, Lord, was not this what I said when I was still in my country? Therefore, I fled previously to Tarshis; for I know that You are a gracious and merciful God, slow to anger and abundant in lovingkindness, One who relents from doing harm. Therefore now, O Lord, please take my life from me, for it is better for me to die than to live" (Jon. 4:2-3 NKJV). Jonah begins to pout and complain to God. There is rejoicing in heaven when a sinner gets saved, and here Jonah is down on earth pouting and complaining. Jonah tells the Lord that he knew that this is the way it was going to turn out. That is the reason he ran away in the first place. What you see here is a man throwing a first-class pity party! Jonah did not get his way and he wants God to know that he is upset. His hurt and anger is so deep that he even attempts to take it out on the Lord. Just in case you do not know this; your arms are too short to box with God! Just because He does not order life like we think it should be ordered, does not give us cause to line up against Him.

Jonah was not the first person to pray and ask God to kill him. Moses and Elijah both prayed for the same thing (Num. 11:15; 1 Kings. 19:4). Because he did not get his way and because he had to endure embarrassment, he wanted to give up on life itself. We need to behave as a church that reacts like the father in the parable of the prodigal son. Because how many people have put their testimony to death and have given up on serving God, all because He did not give them what they wanted? Obedience to what the Lord brings our way is better than anything else you can give Him (1 Sam. 15:22; Rom. 12:1-2). Jonah was concerned about his reputation among his fellow countrymen. His fellow Jews wanted to see all the Assyrians destroyed, not just the people of Nineveh which is in Assyria. Jonah was a narrow-mined patriot who saw Assyria as a dangerous enemy to be destroyed, not a people group to be brought to the Lord. When your reputation becomes more important than your behavior and your friends more important than pleasing God, then we are behaving like Jonah and the elder brother, and you are living to defend your prejudices instead of fulfilling your spiritual responsibilities. God's tender response was to ask Jonah to examine his heart and find out why he was angry in the first place (Jon. 4:4).

After being confronted with his anger, Jonah does not change his mind. Instead, he climbs a hill outside the city, folds his arms and sits down to wait (vs.5). He is probably hoping the Lord will change His mind. Jonah does not get his way about Nineveh, and he does not get his way about dying so he just starts pouting. There are a lot of people like Jonah in the church. For some reason life has not gone as they had planned. Their response is not humble submission to the will of the Lord. Instead, all they do is just quit on Him. That does not say much about your love for Him or for your devotion to His will when your disappointments translate into disobedience and desertion on your part. If you decide to go against God over His will for your life, then He is going to win that battle every time.

GOD'S RESPONSE

According to Jonah 4:6, the Lord extended grace to Jonah, even when his heart was obviously not right with God. "And the Lord God prepared a plant and made it come up over Jonah, that it might be shade for his head to deliver him from his misery. So, Jonah was very grateful for the plant" (Jon. 4:6 NKJV). Isn't it a blessing to know that even though we may walk outside of the will of the Lord, the Lord will still look after us and bless us? How many times has He continued to bless and use you even when you were out of His will? Praise God for His grace (Rom. 5:20). Notice what the father of the elder son did for his son. "But he was angry and would not go in. Therefore, his father came out and pleaded with him" (Luke 15:28 NKJV). "And he said to him, 'Son, you are always with me, and all that I have is yours. It was right that we should make merry and be glad, for your brother was dead and is alive again, and was lost and is found'" (vs. 31-32 NKJV). The father went out to the elder son and pleaded with his son to come into the feast. The father came alongside his son to comfort him, to beg him, to console him, and to encourage him. This is the same thing the "Comforter" does (John 16:13), which is another name for the Holy Spirit. This father loved him and came outside to encourage his son to come to the feast, to celebrate the return of his lost brother. However, the elder brother did not even call him father, but the father called him son. The father went to the son in the right spirit, but he was rejected. There are times when the Lord speaks to us as well. If we are saved, He will speak to us to encourage us, or to confront the sin in our lives. There are times when he calls us to behave as this father did towards another brother or sister in Christ. In those times we are being called to behave as a church with loving kindness to lift one another up. We should not behave like the elder brother and behave as a church that does not care.

While Jonah sat under the plant, cooling himself in the heat of the day; God caused a worm to come and damage the plant to the point that the plant withered up. God also caused an east wind to blow and blew the plant over so that Jonah was now exposed to the sun. This caused Jonah to faint, and he wished he was dead (Jon. 4:7-8). Because Jonah was angry, he was getting a tiny taste of the horrors of the judgment the Ninevites were headed to before they repented of their sins. So, God, set the record straight! "Then God said to Jonah, "Is it right for you to be angry about the plant?" And he said, "It is right for men to be angry, even to death!" But the Lord said, "You have had pity on the plant for the plant for which you have not labored, nor made it grow, which came up in a night and perished in a night. And should I not pity Nineveh, that great city, in which are more than one hundred and twenty thousand persons who cannot discern between their right hand and their left; and much livestock" (Jon. 4:9-11 NKJV). God reminds Jonah that Jonah cared more about a vine than he did for the souls of the people of Nineveh. People made in the image of God and people who would have perished had God not intervened! Every time I read this I get under conviction. Why? Because I see the same behavior in myself from time to time. We tend to get upset about things that simply do not matter. Think about the last time you that made you mad maybe it was because the waitress did not bring your food to the table fast enough, or maybe you got mad because you were stuck in traffic for a long time, or maybe they did not have the shirt in stock you wanted to buy. Those are just some of the things we get mad at that are not in our control. Now, ask yourself this question: "What will it matter in one hundred years?" The only thing that really matters as we pass through life is finding God's will for your life and walking in that will with all your might. There are people going to hell and you are upset because a wayward Christian came home? Our priorities need to be refocused and narrowed until they only want what He wants in our lives.

The elder brother's father praised him for his efforts and reminded him that everything was already his (Luke 15:31)! In effect, this father was saying, "I value you and our relationship far more than I value your works." Jonah, being a prophet of God, should have realized that all God wanted him to do was go and preach God's message and leave the results up to God; and essentially continuing to build on his relationship with God and enjoying that fellowship. The elder son could have enjoyed fellowship with the father anytime he wanted, but apparently, he was too wrapped up in his own legalism and narrow-mindedness to realize it. When are we going to realize that we need to behave as a church and do what God has asked us to do and leave the rest, that is out of our control, up to God? We cannot control who can and cannot get saved, we cannot control who repents and who doesn't, we cannot control when a wayward Christian comes home, we are to behave as a church and welcome a brother or a sister who was lost but now is found. In the parable of the dragnet, Jesus said, "Again, the kingdom of heaven is like a dragnet that was cast into the sea and gathered some of every kind, which, when it was full, they drew to shore; and they sat down and gathered the good into the vessels but threw the bad away. So, it will be at the end of the age. The angels will come forth, separate the wicked from among the just, and cast them into the furnace of fire. There will be wailing and gnashing of teeth" (Matt. 13:47-50 NKJV). In other words, you go catch them, I'll clean them and sort them out later. We need to behave as a church by going out and catching them and leave the rest up to God.

Jonah wanted just the Jews to succeed and no one else. He wanted to serve God, but only if he approved to whom he served God for. The elder brother wants what the father had, but he did not want the father, just like the younger brother (Luke 15:12). Even though he did not want the father, he did not want anyone else to have the father either. What a tragedy. The same is true in the behavior of the church today. People want the church and to feel better about themselves. They want a fire insurance policy and get out of hell free card. But they do not want that close intimate fellowship with Jesus. Then when a wayward Christian comes home and commits to a close walk with Jesus, they resent them. Listen, you can have as much fellowship with Jesus as you want to have, and you can have more if you want it. The question is do you want it? The father told the elder brother that it was right that they should have a celebration. To the father, the return of the lost son was a cause for celebration. The father was passionate about the younger son's return. Perhaps more importantly, a father's love and faith had been vindicated and the family name restored. There was much cause for rejoicing. The father wanted the elder brother to learn the truth that everything is not about him and about him getting his own way. There are bigger issues at stake, and they should take priority!

We should behave as a church with much celebration over a lost person being saved or wayward Christian coming home. Nothing is more important than the glory of God. That is why God does all He does. He seeks to glorify His name in the universe, and those who love Him have that as their goal as well. Instead of getting upset when God doesn't do things our way, we should learn to thank Him for what He is doing! Instead of pouting, Jonah could have gone and told the Ninevites the good news that God stayed His judgement and there would probably been a time of thanksgiving celebration. Instead of pouting, the elder brother could have been partying, and so could we. But just take notice of what is going on in Luke 15 and how Jonah 4 ends. In Luke 15, everyone is happy but the elder brother. The shepherd is happy. His friends are happy. The woman is happy. Her friends are happy. The father is happy. The prodigal son is happy. The servants are happy. The residents of heaven are happy. The only person not happy in Luke 15 is the elder brother. Jonah 4 ends with Jonah not happy. Both Jonah and the elder son are miserable because they refuse to be happy. The feast is there for the elder brother, there could have been a feast for Jonah. All this elder brother had to do was go inside the house. All Jonah had to do is go back and share the good news. Instead, both are standing outside pouting because they did not get their way. What a tragedy!

Have you noticed that the story of Jonah and the tale of two brothers are open-ended stories? Did the elder brother ever come into the feast? Did Jonah learn his lesson and go and tell the Ninevites the good news? We don't know! I think they are left this way for a reason. Here is that reason: "Every individual must write his or her own ending to this story." For example, the Ninevites repented of their sins and God withheld his judgment. Jonah's message of hope was the one chance they would get. Because when you get to the book of Nahum, Nahum's prophecy gives us a gory metaphor of the destruction of Nineveh. In the New Testament, the emphasis is more focused on the repentance of Nineveh than its destruction. Jesus said, "The men of Nineveh will rise up in the judgment with this generation and condemn it, because they repented at the preaching of Jonah; and indeed, a greater than Jonah is here" (Matt. 12:41 NKJV; see also Luke 11:32). What is unique is the book of Jonah and Nahum is the only two books in the Bible that end with questions and deal with the city of Nineveh. Nahum ends with the question about the city's destruction (Nah. 3:19), and Jonah ends with the question about God's mercy for Nineveh. This is a strange way to end these two books, especially Jonah with all the drama that unfolds in the book. For the rest of the story for the prophet Jonah; we know that the book began with God speaking first (Jon. 1:1-2). It is also God who has the last word in Jonah 4:11, which as previously stated is a question. How did Jonah answer God's final question? Hopefully Jonah surrendered to God's inquiry and did like the Ninevites, repenting and seeking God's face (2 Chron. 7:14). Some theologians believed that he came to himself and left the east gate of Nineveh and headed back to Gath Hepher and went back to his father's house; he returned home.

God was willing to spare Nineveh, but to do that, God could not spare His own son. Somebody had to die for their sins, or they would die in their sins. "He who did not spare His own Son, but delivered Him up for us all, how shall He not with Him also freely give us all things" (Rom. 8:32 NKJV)? Jesus used the ministry of Jonah to Nineveh to show the Jews how guilty they were for rejecting His witness (Matt. 12:41). For Israel, the story ended badly. The Lord Jesus Christ presented Himself to the nation as their long-awaited Messiah. He came to them as the fulfillment of all the ancient prophecies. They knew who He claimed to be, but they refused to receive Him

121

as their Messiah, as their Lord, or as their Savior. In the story of the two brothers, the elder brother represents the religious leaders of Israel. They refused to come to the feast, and in the end, they killed the father. They murdered Him because they would not have Him rule over them. When Israel crucified their King, they murdered the father and wrote their own ending to the story. When we behave as a church and see wayward Christians coming home, we need to welcome them with open arms and strengthen them. However, if we behave as a church just like the elder brother did or like Jonah then we are guilty of killing the Father. Behave as a church, don't stay outside listening to the celebration.

CHAPTER NINE

Lessons from the Lord's Vineyard

Behold, how good and how pleasant it is for
brethren to dwell together in unity!
(Psalm 133:1 NKJV)

THERE WAS THIS OLD COUPLE WHO BOTH HAD TROUBLE remembering common day-to-day routines. So, to help each other, they both decided to write down the requests the other made to try to avoid forgetting. One evening the wife asked the husband would he like anything. He replied, "Yes, I'd like a large ice cream sundae with chocolate ice cream, whipped cream, and a cherry on top." The wife started off for the kitchen and the husband shouted, "Aren't you going to write it down?" "Don't be silly" she hollered back, "I'm going to fix it right now. I won't forget." She was gone for quite some time. When she finally returned, she set down in from of her husband a large plate of hash browns, eggs, bacon, and a glass of orange juice. He looked and said, "I knew you should have written it down! You forgot the toast!"

What does a philosopher, a traveling saleslady, a former fortuneteller, and a prison guard have in common? They are all members of the church at Philippi and bonded together by the Holy Spirit. They had the same experience of salvation, being saved by the grace of God; and even though they came from vastly divergent backgrounds they have all placed their faith in the Lord Jesus Christ. Did you know that there is nothing like a church, a true New Testament church? You are blessed if you are a church member of a

New Testament church. What a fellowship! What a joy divine! What do you think when you hear the word fellowship? Let me give you some examples of how some use this word fellowship. "How about coming over to the house for some fellowship?" "What an awesome round of golf? Man, did we ever have some great fellowship!" "The fellowship at the evangelism conference was just terrific!" The word fellowship seems to mean many different things to many different people. The word fellowship has come a long way from the time of Moses. Particularly when God implanted the fellowship offering. The fellowship offering, also known as the peace offering, was a time to celebrate peace with God; it was a feast of joy, love, and communion with God and your fellow man (Lev. 3:1-17; 7:11-34). David wrote, "Behold how good and how pleasant it is for brethren to dwell together in unity" (Ps. 133:1 NKJV).

Jesus said, "And then many will be offended, will betray one another, and will hate one another. Then many false prophets will rise up and deceive many. And because lawlessness will abound, the love of many will grow cold" (Matt. 24:10-12 NKJV). We are living in perilous times where iniquity is flourishing, and love is dwindling. One psychiatrist said what people in this world needs more than anything else is the ability to love and to be loved. Somebody else said what the world needs now is love, sweet love. Every family, every organization, and every movement struggle with the problem of internal divisions. Not only are there divisions on the outside, but there are divisions on the inside. Many internal conflicts result from a struggle over control; however, the root of those struggles began with resentment and jealousy as we have seen in the life of Jonah and the elder brother. If we are going to behave as a church that loves one another then we need to learn to love as Christ loved us. Jesus said, "A new commandment I give to you, that you love one another; as I have loved you, that you also love one another. By this all will know that you are My disciples if you have love for one another" (John 13:34-35 NKJV). If everyone would learn to give the Lord Jesus Christ control for whatever they are responsible for, then many of the internal division can be eliminated. Because without Jesus leading the church, there will always be divisions.

In John 14:31, we see Jesus and His disciples getting up from the table, which is inside the upper room and where they observed the Passover meal, and they are heading towards the Garden of Gethsemane to pray. We know that while he was there, He prayed His great High Priestly prayer and then later He would be arrested by the mob led by Judas. As John 15 opens, Jesus and His disciples are walking though the dark streets of the city and on through the gates and into the surrounding countryside. As they walked towards the Garden of Gethsemane, Jesus began to talk to His men about vines, vinedressers, and fruit. What prompted His teaching? There are several possibilities. No doubt they would have passed near the temple which had grape vines carved into the doors. They may have passed through the Golden Gate which also had grape vines carved into it. Possibly, the fact that it was April which meant the grape vines were beginning to bloom and blossom with the promise of a fresh harvest. As Jesus walked with His disciples, perhaps He reached out and took a vine in His hand and used it to teach an object lesson to His men.

Why did Jesus give them this teaching now? The answer is simple: they needed it! These men had just been informed that Jesus is going away, but His work is going to continue and that it would continue through them and their lives (John 14:12). If they were going to carry on the work of Jesus, then they need to know how to produce the right kind of fruit in their lives, which includes: love for one another, unity, and harmony. Jesus wants them to know that the only way they can be fruitful for the glory of God is for them to abide in Him, the True Vine. Today, we are some 2,000 years removed from that night, but the work of the Lord Jesus continues. God is still working through His followers to accomplish His work and will in the world. There are several lessons we can draw upon from His teaching about the vine that will aid in helping us to behave as a church that loves one another.

A Lesson about Relationships

"I am the true vine, and My Father is the vinedresser. Every branch in Me that does not bear fruit He takes away, and every branch that bears fruit He prunes, that it may bear more fruit" (John 15:1-2 NKJV). The development of vineyards was important to Israel's economy. When Jesus was teaching this object lesson, He was not introducing anything new it was all familiar to every Jew. There are three different vines that are found in the Bible. The first one is the past vine which speaks of Israel (Ps. 80:8-19; Isa. 5:1-7; Jer. 2:21; Ezek. 19:10-14; and Hos. 10:1). Through God's grace He transplanted Israel into the Promised Land of Canaan and abundantly blessed them. God said, "What more could have been done to My vineyard that I have not done in it? Why then, when I expected it to bring forth good grapes, did you bring forth wild grapes" (Isa. 5:4 NKJV)? Israel is the only nation that had everything it ever needed to succeed. However, because they produced wild grapes God had to punish Israel. The nation practiced oppression instead of justice; unrighteousness instead of walking with God which brought about the cries of the sufferers. Regardless of what God's message was spoken to them by the prophets they rejected it. As a matter of fact, God sent His own Son to the vineyard, and they cast Him out and killed Him (Matt. 21:33-46).

The second vine is the future vine, which refers to the vine of the earth (Rev. 14:14-20). This vine is the Gentile world system that is ripe for God's judgment now. So as Jesus says, "I am the vine, you are the branches. He who abides in Me, and I in Him, bears much fruit; for without Me you can do nothing" (John 15:5 NKJV). Believers in Christ are the branches in the True Vine, Jesus Christ. Unbelievers are those who are in the vine of the earth. The unsaved rely on the world to sustain them, while believers depend on Jesus to provide for their needs (Phil. 4:13, 19). The vine of the earth will be cut out and destroyed with fire, just like the tares (Matt. 13:24-30) and the parable of the dragnet (Matt. 13:47-50).

The third vine is the present vine, which represents the Lord Jesus Christ and includes the branches. In Luke 15:2, Jesus uses the phrase "in Me." He is telling us that He is speaking to people who are in a vital life-giving relationship with Him. He is speaking to those who are saved. No one can be considered a branch in the Lord's vine unless there is a vital connection to Him. No one can bear fruit for the glory of the Lord unless they are attached to the Vine. How does a person get to be in Jesus? The only way this can happen is for the new birth to take place. This occurs when a person comes to see themselves as a sinner. At which point they become convicted of their sins and sense the Lord's calling them to come to Him. They respond to His call by faith, receive the finished work of Jesus at Calvary as the payment for their sins, and confess Him to be the Savior of their souls. This is God's plan of salvation (Rom. 10:9-10, 13; Acts 16:31). No can be a fruitful branch for the glory of God until they have a vital, life-giving connection to the Vine. Without that vital connection, the sap of life cannot flow in and through you. Before you can have anything else, from God or with God, you must have the relationship to God. Before you can have a hope of heaven, or forgiveness of sin, you must have a relationship with Him. Can you pinpoint a time in your life when that relationship with Jesus started? If not, you can be grafted in today, if you will come to the Lord Jesus Christ by faith and call upon Him for your soul's salvation. He will not turn you away (John 6:37).

A Lesson about Reproduction

A vine has one distinct purpose that is bearing fruit. But if you will notice the vine itself does not bear fruit. The vine delegates the bearing of fruit to the branches. The Vine has fruit, but its fruit is the branches! Jesus came to this world to die on the cross for the sin of fallen mankind (Mark 10:45; Luke 19:10; John 18:37). His fruit is the souls saved by grace. His fruit is believers. His fruit is those branches that been grafted into Him by grace. His fruit is the members of His bride, the church and anyone who places their faith in Him. Therefore, He has delegated the bearing of fruit to you and me.

Of itself, a branch is weak and useless. It is good for either building a fire or producing fruit (Ezek. 15). The branch cannot produce life by itself and must draw life from the vine. It is our relationship with Jesus, because of the indwelling Holy Spirit, that gives us the strength to produce fruit. The psalmist says, "He who dwells in the secret place of the Most High shall abide under the shadow of the Almighty" (Ps. 91:1 NKJV). Later he adds, "Because you have made the Lord who is my refuge, even the Most High, your dwelling place" (vs. 9 NKJV).

The children of God are to abide in Christ and have fellowship with Him. That does not mean we can avoid the struggles of life; however, we can escape the evil consequences. When the branches abide in the True Vine, walking with Christ, we can avoid a deal of trouble. Furthermore, it is better to suffer in the will of God than it is to disobey God's will (1 Pet. 2:18-25). Jesus is our refuge and strength, the True Vine, (Ps. 46:1). He invites us to bring our labors to Him for a rest (Matt. 11:28), He wants us to cast all our care upon Him (1 Pet. 5:7), then He sends us back out in the struggles of life much stronger than we were (Ps. 27:5; 31:19-20; 32:7; 73:27-28; Deut. 32:37). The safest place in the world it to abide in Christ, under the shadow of the Almighty.

According to John 15 verses 2 and 8, Jesus expects us to bear fruit, and not only that but to bear even more fruit each time as we grow in Christ. In verse 2, notice the words "bears not fruit", "fruit", and "more fruit" (NKJV). Then in verse 8, notice that He expects "much fruit". Jesus expects us to always be growing as we abide in Him, but also expects us to grow fruit in the process. We need to behave as a church that is growing and producing fruit. There are those who think that growth must be a result that is happening quickly, and they are often looking for results. The word results it the word that gets throwed around among Christian leaders, however, it is not a Biblical concept. Think about it, computers produce results, but it is the living organism that produces fruit. It takes time and cultivation to produce fruit; a good crop does not come overnight. The fruit you bear, or do not bear, says much about your life.

There are several different kinds of spiritual fruit that we can bear that are mentioned throughout the Bible. Of course, the first fruit that we tend to think is that of winning souls for Christ (Rom. 1:13). We are to behave as a church that harvests the fields (John 4:35-38). In chapter two of my book *Behave as a Fisher of Men*, I discuss how Jesus taught His disciples about planting the gospel and harvesting the souls (Powers, 2021) As we grow in our walk with Christ, by abiding in Him, we are to be about bearing for fruit for the Kingdom of God (Rom. 6:22). Paul considers us to be fruit that is dedicated to Him (Rom. 15:28). Paul also goes through a list of the fruits of the Spirit in Galatians 5:22-23. The fruit of the Spirit is the kind of Christian behavior that glorifies

God and makes Christ real to others. Your spiritual gift, which I discuss in my book *Behave as a Church Member* (Powers D. C., 2023), coupled with your good works and service to Jesus comes from abiding in Him (Col. 1:10). When you praise and worship God that comes from a heart that is abiding with Christ and is shown from our lips and actions, this is fruit that brings glory to God (Heb. 13:15). With all these different kinds of spiritual fruit that we are to produce we need to keep in mind that real spiritual fruit has a seed. That seed is planted to produce much fruit. Man-made results have no seed and cannot produce any fruit. A true branch will abide in the vine and will always bear fruit. Jesus says, "By this My Father is glorified, that you bear much fruit; so, you will be My disciples" (John 15:8 NKJV).

A Lesson about Responsibility

"If anyone does not abide in Me, he is cast out as a branch and is withered; and they gather them and throw them into the fire, and they are burned. If you abide in Me, and My words abide in you, you will ask what you desire, and it shall be done for you" (vs. 6-7 NKJV). When believers start thinking about bearing fruit, they often want to shy away from it because they think it is hard and they cannot do it. There are those who think that bearing fruit is for the "super saint," or for those who are in the place of leadership within the church. In truth, bearing fruit is not difficult at all! According to Jesus, "For My yoke is easy and My burden is light" (Matt. 11:30 NKJV). Bearing fruit is one the simplest things any believer can do if you will do one thing. What is that one thing? Jesus mentions that one thing seven times in John 15:1-11. The one thing required for branches to bear fruit is that they abide in Jesus the True Vine. If the branches will continue to abide (vs. 9) and remain abiding (vs. 11) in Jesus, the branches will bear fruit for the glory of God. The Lord wants the branches to rest in Him and draw their life strength from Him.

How does a person abide in Jesus? What does it mean to abide in Christ? First, you must be a child of God to be "in" Jesus. To put it simply, you must be saved! After that, to abide in Christ means that you keep in fellowship with Him through prayer, studying His Word, meditating upon Him and His Word (John 15:4), worship and praise, and being totally surrendered unto Him (Rom. 12:1-2). As you abide in Christ, His life will work in and through us to produce fruit. If we are going to abide in Christ, then we must draw our life from Him. We must yield to His commands and obey His will for our lives. We must come to the realization that apart from Him, we can do nothing. We must make a conscience effort to avoid sin and be quick to confess sin so that nothing hinders our fellowship and relationship with Him (John 15:3). How can we tell when we are abiding in Christ? Is there a special feeling? No, but there is special evidence that appear, and they are very clear. Of course, when you are abiding in Christ you are going to bear fruit (vs. 2). The quality of that fruit is not my responsibility, we are simply to abide in Him. He will bring that kind of fruit through me that pleases Him. The quantity of that fruit is not my responsibility. My duty is to abide in Him. He will produce the quantity of fruit from my life that pleases Him. Another evidence of abiding in Christ is the pruning experience that is done by the Father (vs. 2). The believer who is always abiding in Christ will have his prayers answered (vs. 7), will grow deeper and deeper in love with Jesus (vs. 9, 12-13), and will be full of joy (vs. 11). If we could hold fast to the truth that being a faithful Christian is about abiding, then it would make a world of difference in our lives.

A Lesson about the Formation of the Philippian Church

As you study Paul's letter to the church in Philippi, Paul seems to be talking about the same thing Jesus does. Paul writes about joy, love, abiding and communing with God and brothers and sisters in Christ. But have you ever wondered how the church in Philippi started? In Acts 16, we can find how the Philippian church was formed.

THE RESTRAINT OF THE SPIRIT

"Now when they had gone through Phrygia and the region of Galatia, they were forbidden by the Holy Spirit to preach the word in Asia. After they had come to Mysia, they tried to God into Bithynia, but the Spirit did not permit them" (Acts 16:6-7 NKJV). After visiting the churches, he had founded, Paul wanted to go into new territory for the Lord by traveling east into Asia Minor and Bithynia, but the Holy Spirit quickly closed that door. Think about it, Paul and his group discussed going into this territory, they started to go, desired to go, and they planned to go; but "nope" the Holy Spirit would not allow them to go. Can you imagine how disappointed Paul is? Everything had been going good on his second missionary journey, that these closed doors must have come as a surprise. Now, that tells us a couple things very clearly and plainly: first, we do not choose the place of our service the Holy Spirit does that for us. Second, the apostles were not always clear as to God's will for their ministries. David writes, "The steps of a good man are ordered by the Lord, and He delights in his way" (Ps. 37:23 NKJV). That also means that the stops of a good man are ordered by the Lord also. A good man knows how to step, and he knows how to stop. The reason why so many churches are not behaving as a church is because they do not want the restraint of the Holy Spirit in their lives, therefore God cannot use them.

This sad fact is seen Jesus's teaching of the vine dresser. Not all branches bear fruit at the same level. However, the Vine Dresser deals with every single branch in His vineyard. Notice what Jesus says, "Every branch in Me that does not bear fruit He takes away, and every branch that bears fruit He prunes, that it may bear more fruit" (John 15:2 NKJV). That phrase "takes away" means "to lift up or to raise higher" (Strong's Concordance, 1984) This is a picture of a branch that has fallen into the dirt, it pictures a church member that has fallen away into the world. This branch's leaves are dirty and covered causing the branch the inability to absorb light and if cannot absorb light, the branch cannot bear fruit. The Gardener sees the branch in this condition, and He lifts it back up, cleanses it, and puts it in a position where it can receive light and rain and where it can grow as it should. On a personal level, this means that when we get to a place in our Christian lives where we are unfruitful and barren, the Lord will reach into our lives; He will disturb our slumber and He will lift us up in an effort to challenge us and shock us to growth. He does the same for the church as well, and often we call this revival. However, I will say this, when Jesus removes something from our Christian life, it should remain removed. We need to quit behaving as though we are trying to reattach that which He personally removed! Jesus has removed that which was toxic in our lives, those things that keeps us from producing fruit, therefore quit trying to hang on to things He has gotten rid of for us! It might have been that He moved other church members to another church, loss of job, health, or death. Maybe He did it through giving you a promotion and you do not need that other position or brought you to another church where you can be fed and grow in you walk with Him. There are several ways He can prune your life or church to help you behave as a church.

THE RELEASE OF THE SPIRIT

How did Paul get to Philippi? In His sovereign grace, God led Paul west into Europe, not east into Asia. It is interesting to think what would have happen to in world history and how things might have been different had Paul been sent to Asia instead of Europe. But God the Holy Spirit led him west into Europe, for God had a plan for Asia to receive the gospel message another time (Acts 18:19-19:1). At Troas, Paul was called to Macedonia, by a man whom he saw in a night vision and Paul was quick to respond to the vision (Acts 16:9). Luke, the author of the book of Acts, joined Paul and his group at Troas (vs. 10). Luke devoted a good space of his writings to Paul's ministry. Acts 17:1 gives us the suggestion that Luke remained in Philippi to pastor the church after Paul left. There are some theologians who think it is possible that Luke was the man that Paul saw in the vision.

Now, the trip from Troas to Neapolis, which is a port of Philippi is about 150 miles and would have taken about two days to travel. Later we learn that on the trip back from Neapolis to Troas it would take about five days to travel, possibly because of the winds (Acts 20:6). Philippi was ten miles from the port and according to Luke, he was proud to be a citizen of that city. Philippi is a Roman colony organized by the emperor by giving the command to Roman citizens, retired soldiers to live in select places to ensure that there would be pro-Roman cities. They were expected to be loyal to Rome and obey the laws of Rome and give tribute to the emperor. In return they would receive political privileges and be exempted from taxes if they would leave Italy and live in foreign places.

Paul is led by the Holy Spirit to Philippi (Acts 16:11-12). Paul had a close enough walked with God that he could hear God tell him no and then tell him go. If Paul could find the restraint of the Holy Spirit, then he also could find the release of the Holy Spirit. God did not let him do what he wanted to do at first, however, God had something better in mind. If God does not give you what you want, He will give you something better because that is the kind of God we serve.

THE RESULTS OF THE SPIRIT

"On the Sabbath day we went out of the city to the riverside, where prayer was customarily made; and we sat down and spoke to the women who met there. Now a certain woman named Lydia heard us. She was a seller of purple from the city of Thyatira, who worshiped God. The Lord opened her heart to heed the things spoken by Paul. And when she and her household were baptized, she begged us, saying, "If you have judged me to be faithful to the Lord, come to my house and stay." So, she persuaded us" (Acts 16:13-15 NKJV). Please understand soul winning will take on a new dimension when you and I learn to obey the Holy Spirit of God, when we can hear Him tell us no and then tell us to go. You cannot read these verses without seeing the hidden hand of God, as God obviously started work at Philippi. There were saints at Philippi, and God the Holy Spirit was leading Paul there. God was already there at Philippi working on the heart of Lydia and He opened her heart. When God opened heart hear, He also opened her home and her purse. But not only was Lydia saved, a demon-possessed girl was liberated from the power of the devil (vs. 16-18).

What we need to realize is that when you are moving in the power of the Holy Spirit, iron gates will yield, and there will be miracle after miracle as our Lord and Savior Jesus Christ is gaining the victory. When there is the restraint of the Spirit, and when there is the release of the Spirit, there will be the results of the Spirit. What we are seeing beyond the shadow of any doubt is what God is doing. But did you notice that after she got saved, she invited them back to her house for a time of fellowship. This is huge, think about what is going on in this time of fellowship. With the Jewish population in Philippi being so small, it is possible that there was not a synagogue there, therefore there was only a place of prayer down by the river outside the city. Paul may have seen a vision of a man while he was at Troas, but here in Philippi he is ministering to a group of women (Acts 16:13). According to the rabbis of that time, it would have been better to burn the words of the Law than teach them to a woman. This was no longer what Paul believed and taught. He was going to be obedient to the Lord and he is on his second missionary journey preparing the way.

Lydia was a successful businesswoman from Thyatira, which is city known for selling purple dye. There is the possibility that she had to move to Philippi because she was managing a branch office there, in which case she became a citizen of Philippi. God brought her all the way to Greece in order that she may hear the gospel and be saved. Again, she opens her home to celebrate her salvation. She is a Gentile fellowshipping with a group of Jews, and they are worshipping together in her home. God opens her heart to the truth, she believes and is saved, she gets baptized so she can identify with Christ, and then all of household is converted. The results here is clear God just gave Paul the opportunity to teach the Word and establish the local church. We know later a jailer got saved, took Paul to his home and all his household got saved, and they had fellowship in that Roman jailer's home (vs. 25-31). So, again what does a philosopher like Paul, and a traveling saleslady, and a former fortuneteller, and a hardened jailer have in common? Jesus! The grace of God. The formation of the church was supernatural and there is only two kinds of churches: the supernatural and the superficial. Anything that is not of the grace of God is superficial and anything that is of the grace of God is supernatural. Jesus said, "And I also say to you that you are Peter, and on this rock, I will build My church, and the gates of Hades shall not prevail against it" (Matt. 16:18 NKJV).

A Lesson about the Fellowship of the Church

This brings us to this word fellowship. After the amazing conversions that were taking place, the church of Philippi continued the concept of worship and fellowship. The word "fellowship" means, "communion, sharing in common, partnership, fellow partaker" (Holman Illustrated Bible Dictionary, 2003) It implies in some instances that of breaking bread together, which is a close friendship. After a few years had gone by Paul writes to the church of Philippi and he opens his letter by saying this, "I thank my God upon every remembrance of you, always in every prayer of mine making request for you all with joy, for your fellowship in the gospel from the first day until now" (Phil. 1:3-5 NKJV). You see, you cannot have this kind of fellowship unless you have something in common. What did the members of the church at Philippi have in common as he prayed for their fellowship in the gospel? They had a common life, a common Lord, a common love. Having a sweet fellowship is what it is going to take for us to behave as a church. We are to have the same love of Jesus, have the same Holy Spirit in your heart and in mine, and have a common Lord. Let me show you how this works out in the church.

FELLOWSHIP OF SERVICE

"Being confident of this very thing, that He who has begun a good work in you will complete it until the day of Jesus Christ" (vs. 6 NKJV). These members were working together because the Holy Spirit had begun the work in them. They were fellowshipping through serving one another. Please do not think that fellowship is just huddling around some table reading the minutes of the last meeting and having Kool-Aid and cookies. When you break bread together and serve one another there is a growing fondness and bonding being built upon. For instance, do you want to have some friends, do you want somebody you really know, somebody that you can have fellowship with? Then what you need to do is find a fellow believer, follower of Christ and the two of you get together and go out into the community knocking on doors. Find a third person who is lost and win them to Jesus Christ. From then on the two of you will start getting closer the rest of your life. Because you let two men, two women, two any bodies go and serve the Lord Jesus Christ together, bringing souls to the Lord Jesus Christ, doing this service side-by-side; you will be one in the bond of love like you have never been before. You have something in common: winning somebody to Jesus.

FELLOWSHIP OF SUPPLICATION

When you begin to pray for somebody or when you pray together with somebody that is fellowship. Paul said, "Just as it is right for me to think this of you all, because I have you in my heart, inasmuch as both in my chains and in the defense and confirmation of the gospel, you all are partakers with me of grace" (vs. 7 NKJV). Now, if you are just a Sunday morning benchwarmer meaning that you just go to church, sit through the worship service, listen to the preaching, and then go home; well, you do not know anything about the fellowship of the church you attend. What you need to do is find someone in the church, get down on your knees with them, and pray and seek the face of Jesus together. Two people who are getting in tune with God on their knees will find themselves in tune with one another when they get up. Did you know that you cannot pray with a person without loving them? If there is somebody you would like to get close to in your church, there is nothing like going up to them and asking "Hey, let's pray to together." When you get down with that person, and the two of you get right with God, you are going to get up right with one another just as surely as night follows day, it cannot fail.

FELLOWSHIP OF SUFFERING

Since Paul was under house arrest in Rome, he sent this letter to the church at Philippi to explain his situation (Phil. 1:12-26). Plus, Paul wanted to give thanks for their financial support (Phil. 4:10-20) and to address the threat of disunity and heresy that threatened the church. Since the church at Philippi had sent Epaphroditus to help Paul, and since the church learned that Epaphroditus had become ill, Paul wanted to ease their minds about Epaphroditus. Paul encouraged the church to work at having great fellowship by building on the unity and harmony within the church (Phil. 1:27-2:18). The church at Rome was now divided and feeling the effects of disunity from within the church. Paul knew and heard the report from Epaphroditus that disunity was creeping into the church. Christian unity is the result of individuals sharing things in common. When difficult situations arise in the church, they usually can be quickly solved through the leadership of the church. When we behave as a church there will be harmony, joy, and peace.

Notice what Paul said, "Because I have you in my heart, inasmuch as both in my chains and in the defense and confirmation of the gospel, you all are partakers with me of grace. For God is my witness, how greatly I long for you all with the affection of Jesus Christ" (Phil. 1:7b-8 NKJV). Paul was hurting and longing to be with them, and since they were fellow partakers, they had sent word back to Paul saying, "Paul when you hurt, we hurt. When you are in prison, we are in prison. We are in this thing together." You want to know what real fellowship is? Find somebody that hurts and hurt with them. When you suffer with somebody, when you know the meaning of compassion, when you share somebody's hurt and problem; two people who suffer together are never quite the same thereafter. There is a bond of love, there is fellowship, and that is the kind of fellowship we should have if we are going to behave as a church.

Therefore, notice how Jesus explained this. He said, "Every branch in Me that does not bear fruit He takes away, and every branch that bears fruit He prunes, that it may bear more fruit" (John 15:2 NKJV). The idea here in this verse is that of cleansing the vine, or cleansing, purging the church. When the True Gardener sees a branch that is producing fruit, He removes things from the branch that weakens its vitality and strength. Things like sucker branches, useless buds, misdirected shoots, bad spots, discolored leaves, etc. Anything that consumes life but produces no fruit must go! That is what takes place in the life of a believer and in the family of God, the church. There are so many things in us and around us that can slow down our walk with Jesus. When we begin to be fruitful, we can rest assured that He will cleanse us through the pruning process so that we might do even more for His glory. When we allow things into our lives that hinder our walk with the Lord, then we are in danger of a pruning. However, Jesus lets us know that this ministry of pruning is performed on every branch. No on is excluded from the touch of the heavenly Vine Dresser's hand and He challenges us and cleanses us to be fruitful for Him. There is no doubt that when He is purging and cleansing our lives it is going to be painful. Just remember, that even though we are going through this painful pruning Jesus is right there with us having fellowship. His touch, no matter how it may hurt for the moment, is proof that you are His and He cares for you (1 Pet. 5:7). Furthermore, our fellow brothers and sisters in Christ are being pruned as well, maybe at different time than us, nevertheless we are to have fellowship of suffering together.

There is a downside to the ministry of pruning. "If anyone does not abide in Me, he is cast out as a branch and is withered; and they gather them and throw them into the fire, and they are burned" (John 15:6 NKJV). Jesus is letting us know that not every branch responds properly to the challenging and cleansing ministry of the Gardener. When this happens, there is a loss of fellowship and rewards that takes place. Let me point out, there are many people who read this verse and interpret and conclude that it is possible for a branch to be forever cut out of the Vine. That is not exactly what Jesus is talking about. First, Jesus is talking about a loss of fellowship. The phrases "cast out" and "not abiding" is not talking about losing one's salvation. Those phrases are talking about fellowship. Notice the phrase "as a branch", there is no change it still is a branch, it still belongs to the Vine. You cannot lose your relationship. The withered branch still possesses the same nature as the Vine, but it is no longer attached in the sense of drawing life from the Vine in fellowship. Second, Jesus is talking about a loss of vitality. The word withered implies that the branch possesses no life. In other words, the testimony of that branch is just dead and dried up, which describes many Christians today. The testimony and life for the withered branch did not use to be this way. At one time there was life, joy, harmony, unity, fellowship, and a testimony with great power that flowed through the branch from the Vine, but now that it is no longer attached there is deadness. There is weakness where there used to be power. There is emptiness where there used to be fullness. My prayer and advice if you are the withered branch, come back to the Vine and renew that lost fellowship. Once you start to draw that life giving juice from the Vine, then you can begin to produce fruit for Him. Then lastly, Jesus is talking about loss of reward. When this life is over, there will be many children of God, branches, that were unfruitful. They will experience the loss of every reward (1 Cor. 3:13-15). Many think they will be content to just get to heaven, however, they should have had a desire to have rewards so they could place those rewards at the feet of Jesus. Will you hear "Well done?" Only if you are a fruitful branch. Jesus is the True Vine. He exists to bring glory to His Father, the Vine Dresser, by saving sinners, living though them as branches, and causing the branches to bear fruit. Because He formed the church, and brings fellowship to the branches, I am so glad I am a part of the family of God. Behave as a church that abides in Christ.

CHAPTER TEN

People the Chruch could do Without

Likewise also these dreamers defile the flesh,
reject authority, and speak evil of dignitaries.
(Jude 8 NKJV).

IN RECENT YEARS, CERTAIN MEDIA SYNDICATES HAVE BEEN LABELED "fake news"; meaning the news they report has been twisted and altered to fit or push a certain agenda. This kind of goes along with what Peter talks about in 2 Peter, and what Jude writes about in his letter. However, did you know that one of the most successful rackets in the world today is that of selling "fake art"? Even some of the finest galleries and private collections have been invaded by paintings that are clever counterfeits of the great masters. Publishers have also had their share of hoaxes in purchasing genuine manuscripts that were not so genuine after all. If you do not look hard enough, then you could get ripped off, or tricked into buying some that is fake. For example, there is fake leather, fake purses that are supposed to be name brands, fake clothes sold to people as if they were made by the latest fashion designer, and there is even a thing called funny money where counterfeiters are trying to pass off fake money as the real thing.

But counterfeits are nothing new. Satan is the "great imitator" (2 Cor. 11:13-15), and he has been hard at work ever since he deceived Eve in the Garden. Satan also has false Christians (Matt. 13:38; John

8:44), a false gospel (Gal. 1:6-9), and even a false righteousness (Rom. 9:30-10:4). One day, he will present to the world a false Christ (2 Thess. 2). Speaking of snakes, did you know that poisonous snakes have different colors? In North America there are four venomous snakes that are not difficult to recognize. These are the copperheads, cottonmouths, the coral snakes, and rattlesnakes. The eastern coral snake is found from North Carolina to Texas, while the western coral snake can be found in Arizona. The coral snake's coloring gives a good clue that it is poisonous. Any shiny snake patterned with rings of red, yellow, and black is suspicious, however, if the red rings are bordered with yellow then it is poisonous. There is a little poem to remember: "Red and yellow, kills a fellow; red and black, friend of Jack."

When it comes to rattlesnakes, there are fifteen kinds of various size and colors in the United States and Canada. All of them have rattles at the tips of their tails, which is made up of dry, horny rings of skin that lock loosely onto one another. When the rattlesnake shakes its tail, especially when it has been spooked, excited, or defensive; the horned pieces of skin rub against one another resulting in a rasping or buzzing sound. This sound serves as a warning to other animals or humans that might be getting too close.

The copperheads and cottonmouths do not have rattles but can be distinguished by the shape of their heads and color of their skin. The copperheads are brown with hourglass-shaped rings. The cottonmouth also has a similar pattern, but the markings may become dim as the snake ages. Therefore, to make sure it is a cottonmouth, you will have to pick it up and look closely at the rings to tell; but are you willing to do that? Cottonmouths are found in the southeastern United States, as far north as Virginia and as far west as Texas. Copperheads are also found in the southeastern United States. I share this information about how to tell these venomous snakes apart just in case your hobby is collecting snakes' tails. By the way, the best way to collect a snake's tail it to cut the tail off right behind the ears. On a serious note, it is important that you can identify venomous snakes, especially if you live in a house that has a beautiful garden, children at home, or small pets. You need to know what poisonous snakes are in the garden and teach your children how to recognize them as well.

To behave as a church, you need to be able to identify those people the church could do without. Please understand, I am not saying that there are people that we should keep from coming to church because this would go against the Great Commission (Matt. 28:18-20) and we should behave as a church that invites the "whosoever will" may come in. Neither are we to pick and choose what kind of people we want in our church, for God loves the whole world (John 3:16). What I am saying is that there are people who have bad behaviors that the church could do without. In this chapter we are going to discuss those people who exhibit these bad behaviors.

The False Teachers

Peter writes, "But there were also false prophets among the people, even as there will be false teachers among you" (2 Pet. 2:1 NKJV). The people Peter is referring to is the nation of Israel. They were constantly having false prophets come in and lead them astray. Therefore, false teachers in churches are not anything new, as a matter of fact, false religion goes all the way back to the days of Eden. There was Elijah fought against the prophets of Baal, who were promoting a pagan religion. Along with the prophets of Baal, the Jewish false prophets did damage, because they claimed to speak for Jehovah God. Later, Jeremiah and Ezekiel had to expose the counterfeit Jewish prophets and their ministry, but the people followed the pseudo-prophets just the same. Why? Because the religion of the false prophets was easy, comfortable, and popular (Jer. 6:14). Because every man wanted to do what was right in their own eyes (Judg. 21:25). Because the false prophets preaching made them feel good and it was just what they wanted to hear.

When you get into the New Testament, the apostles and the prophets laid the foundation for the church and then passed from the scene (Eph. 2:20). Paul warned the young Timothy that false teachers would come again, he writes, "For the time will come when they will not endure sound doctrines, but according to their own desires, because they have itching ears, they will heap up for themselves teacher" (2 Tim. 4:3 NKJV). This is why Peter wrote about false teachers in the church because false teachers had infiltrated the church. So, to warn us to be alert, Peter presents three aspects about false teachers who we do not need in the church.

Peter writes, "But there were also false prophets among the people, even as there will be false teachers among you, who will secretly bring in destructive heresies, even denying the Lord who brought them, and bring on themselves swift destruction" (2 Pet. 2:1 NKJV). Notice that phrase, "among you", Peter is referring to the church, the bride of Christ, at his time and even in our day and age. There are false teacher in churches today, as a matter of fact, you can believe almost anything you want to believe, no matter how strange and bizarre, or you can live how you want to live, or do what is right in your own eyes; go online, look around your city, and you can find a church where you can be perfectly at home. It is amazing what people will believe. Over in 2 Corinthians 11:13 Paul talks about false teacher who will occupy pulpits, and they do not know the Lord Jesus Christ and yet they stand as false apostles, and angels of light. When you look for the devil, never fail to look in the pulpit. Do not let false teachers take you by surprise, because the Word of God gives plenty of warning and clarity.

Peter calls what the false teacher taught as "destructive heresies" (2 Pet. 2:1 NKJV). The word "heresy" means "a sect, a party, to divide" (Concise Oxford English Dictionary Eleventh Edition, 2004) Paul tells the Galatians that promoting a party spirit in a church is one of the works of the flesh (Gal. 5:20). When heresy comes into a church it causes the people to have to make a choice because, if somebody brings in false doctrine; then the pastor, the teacher, the leadership of the church will have to say, "You cannot do that." The false teacher will say, "Oh yes, we can." There is a division whenever a church member says to another, "Are you on my side or the pastor's side?" He is guilty of promoting a party spirit and causing division in the church. A false teacher is the one who is making a division in the church not the pastor, because they will make you choose between his doctrines and the doctrines of the true Christian faith. But why does Christianity have so many cults, division, and errors in it? Because the Bible says, if there now false cults, the Bible would not be true, but because the Bible says there will be false cults. Peter was right when he said there were false prophets in the past and now there are false teachers among you (2 Pet. 2:1).

THEIR MESSAGE

How do you spot a counterfeit teacher? Let me give you some ways you can spot a false teacher. You can take any preacher or teacher and hold him up with five test questions and you can tell whether he is real or counterfeit. The first test is the source test, "What is the basis of his teaching?" False teachers are better known for what they deny than what they affirm. They deny the inspiration of the Bible, the sinfulness of man, the sacrificial death of Jesus Christ on the cross, salvation by faith alone, salvation is for anyone, and even the reality of eternal judgment. They especially deny the deity of Jesus Christ, for they know that if they can do away with His deity, they can destroy the entire body of Christian truth. Christianity is built upon and has at its core belief the Chief Cornerstone, Jesus Christ. If He is not what He claims to be, then there is no Christian faith. If he has these denials, then does he have revelation other than the Bible? For example, someone might come to your door, and say, "Oh, we accept the Bible as the Word of God, but we also accept Joseph Smith as a prophet" or they may accept William Branham as a prophet. Now they want to lay some source down alongside the Word of God. But the Bible says we are not to add to it, and we are not to take away from it, nor are we to amend it or adjust it.

The next test is the Savior test. Do they believe that Jesus Christ is the Messiah, the virgin-born Son of God, co-equal and co-eternal with God the Father? If they do, then ask if they worship Jesus Christ? They will say, "We believe that Jesus Christ is the Son of God." Good to hear but the question is, "Do you worship Jesus Christ?" They will then say, "We give Him praise and honor." Awesome, however, the question is, "Do you worship Jesus Christ?" They may fidget a little and say, "We reverence Him." Okay one more time, "Do you worship Jesus Christ?" If they get honest, the false teacher will have to say, "No!" You see, the Bible is full of the worship of Jesus Christ. Throughout the Bible, it tells us how to worship Him. If the false teacher is not worshipping Jesus Christ, then they must be worshipping some other god. "And Jesus answered and said to him, "Get behind Me, Satan! For it is written, 'You shall worship the Lord your God, and Him only you shall serve'" (Luke 4:8 NKJV).

The next test is the subject test. Is the primary source of their teaching the gospel of Jesus Christ? Paul said, "For I determined not to know anything among you except Jesus Christ and Him crucified" (2 Cor. 2:2 NKJV). The good news of the gospel is about Jesus Christ. The Old Testament told us that somebody is coming; the New Testament tells us that somebody has come; and the Book of the Revelation says somebody is coming again and that person is the Lord Jesus Christ. He is the hero of the Bible, while theme of the Bible is salvation. What is the subject of the false teacher? What is the motivation behind his message? Do they want to talk to you about what they call kingdom truth or something else? Are they preaching Jesus and salvation by grace through faith? Paul says, "As we have said before, so now I say again, if anyone preaches any other gospel to you than what you have received, let him be accursed" (Gal. 1:9 NKJV). The literal translation is "let him be condemned." You may think that is harsh, but it is not harsh at all especially if he is leading people to hell. If he is not teaching that Jesus died for the church (Eph. 5:25), that He died for the sins of the World (1 John 2:2), that He was buried and on the third day arose for the grave; then the false teacher is teaching something else other than the gospel of Jesus Christ and is leading others to hell along with himself.

Another test is the salvation test. Do they teach salvation by grace, or do they try to mix works, baptism, or something else into it? When someone says that there is something else other than putting your faith in Jesus Christ to be save, you are taking the whosoever out of the Bible. For example, someone might say you must be baptized in order to be saved, do you realize what they have done? Do you know how many people they have eliminated? What about the soldiers that have fought for our country over in the Middle East? They get shot or gassed, and the chaplain comes and says, "Son, are you saved?" He says, "No." "Son, do you want to be saved?" "Yes, I do" says the soldier. The chaplain then says, "Well, son I'm sorry, but I cannot baptize you. Out here there's nothing but sand." Jude accused the false teacher of turning "the grace of our God into lewdness and deny the only Lord God and our Lord Jesus Christ" (Jude 4 NKJV). Please understand why they deny the truth of the Christian faith, it is because they want to satisfy their itching ears and their own lust under the pretense of religion. In Jeremiah's day the false prophets were doing the same thing (Jer. 23:14). This is the reason why many are willing to follow the false instead of the truth. False teachers seem to have successful ministries because of this lewdness; however, statistics is not proof of genuineness. The broad way is the way that leads to destruction (Matt. 7:13-14) and many will claim to be true servants of Christ, but in actuality they are lost and will be rejected (Matt. 7:21-23).

The final test is the sanctification test. Do you teach, and are you endeavoring to live, a holy life? If they are not living a holy life, if they do not teach holiness or a personal holiness and separation from sin, then there is something rotten in their teaching. Let's be honest, most false teachers are interested in one thing, making money. False teachers will manipulate people and use their religion as a disguise (1 Thess. 2:5). Jesus was a poor man and did not even have a place to lay His head. The same could be said for the Apostles and yet they gave themselves to minister to others. False teachers, like snakes, are cleaver rich men who get people to cater to them. Micah had this to say about the false prophets in his day, "Her heads judge for a bribe, her priests teach for pay, and her prophets divine for money. Yet they lean on the Lord, and say, "Is not the Lord among us?"" (Mic. 3:11 NKJV). Yes, you need to pay an employee the worth of the hire (Luke 10:7), however, money should not be his only motive. False teachers are guilty of immorality, love of money and pride. The first step in identifying a false teacher is by their message.

THEIR METHOD

Peter says, "And many will follow their destructive way, because of who the way of truth will be blasphemed. By covetousness they will exploit you with deceptive words; for a long time, their judgment has not been idle, and their destruction does not slumber" (2 Pet. 2:2-3 NKJV). Give the devil credit for being clever. What false teachers secretly do is (vs. 1), lay their false teaching alongside good teaching to confuse others. Paul told Timothy, "Not the Spirit expressly says that in later times some will depart from the faith, giving heed to deceiving spirits and doctrines of demons" (1 Tim. 4:1 NKJV). Instead of openly declaring what they believe, they weave themselves into a church disguised as a sheep and give the impression they are true to the Christian faith. According to Peter they secretly bring alongside the true Christian faith their false teachings making it appear they believe the fundamentals of the faith. Then, before long they remove the true doctrine and leave their false doctrine in its place. In other words, they do a "bait and switch", they use the Bible, not to enlighten, but to deceive. This is the same method Satan used when he deceived Eve.

Take beer ads for example, what are the most beautiful ads on television? What do they tend to associate beer with? Busch beer's tagline is "Head for the mountains" and they will have beautiful scenery in the background. Miller beer's tagline is "It's Miller time" and they will show everybody having a good time. They do not show some drunk in a gutter, covered with flies and vomit. They do not show some drunk man coming home, hitting on his baby girl, hitting her in the face with his fist. They do not show a man slamming his wife up against the wall. They do not show somebody coming into an emergency room, with his face all sliced up, because he just went through the windshield. They do not show any of this. Long ago there was the Marlboro Man who was this dude with a suntan and a big hat. But what does riding a horse and dying of cancer have to do with one another? Yes, today they have taken a lot of those ads off television, but the examples seen here are the same association that the devil does to push his false doctrine through false teachers. There in verse 3 Peter uses the phrase "with deceptive words", that word "deceptive" comes from the Greek word that means plastic (Strong's Concordance, 1984) False teachers are plastic preachers who use plastic words. What is plastic? It is something that is pliable, easy to mold, and simple to imitate, false teachers are good at using deceptive words.

THEIR BEHAVIOR

Peter tells us that false teachers have destructive ways or unbridled lust. You can tell if a person is a false teacher because they do not love the Lord; and they cannot love the Lord because they do not know the Lord. The sum, center, and substance of their behavior is themselves. This means that they have the behavior of apostasy and immorality interwoven in their lives. There are people who want to talk about grace and live in sin. They say, "Well, Calvary covers it all." Listen, that is heresy. Paul said, "What shall we say then? Shall we continue in sin that grace may abound? Certainly not! How shall we who died to sin live any longer in it?" (Rom. 6:1-2 NKJV). Jeremiah agrees, "Also I have seen a horrible thing in the prophets of Jerusalem: they commit adultery and walk in lies; they also strengthen the hands of evildoers, so that no one turns back from his wickedness. All of them are like Sodom to Me, and her inhabitants like Gomorrah" (Jer. 23:14 NKJV). In Jeremiah's day, the so-called prophets were calling themselves prophet and yet they lived in sin. Their destructive ways causing many of the people of God to follow them. They loved to have a preacher who will drink with them, who will tell filthy jokes with them, and who will be crude with them. Why? Because it makes the people fill better. Therefore, their success in ministry, what people call success, did not come from God's work. Statistics are no proof that something is of God because many will follow their own destructive ways. Some people will love the sensual rather than the spiritual. That is why Jesus said, "Not everyone who says to Me, 'Lord, Lord,' shall enter the kingdom of heaven, but he who does the will of My Father in heaven" (Matt. 7:21 NKJV). Many are living double lives and are false prophets, and this is the type of behavior the church could do without.

The Character of the Apostate

Another group of people the church could do without is those who behave with the character of the apostate. An apostate is a person who has received the truth, rejected the truth, and now ridicules and renounces the truth (Concise Oxford English Dictionary Eleventh Edition, 2004) Jude tells us the cause of their rebellion, he says, "Likewise also these dreamers defile the flesh, reject authority, and speak evil of dignitaries" (Jude 8 NKJV). In other words, these people live in a dreamworld of fantasy and delusion. They believe Satan's lie, the same lie that was told to Eve in the Garden of Eden, "you will be like God" (Gen. 3:5 NKJV). Therefore, apostates turn away from God's truth, they feed their minds on false doctrines that inflates their egos and encourages their rebellion. According to Jude, the apostates are inexperienced people who do not know what they are talking about (Jude 10). Jude echoed Peter's description of the apostate as brute beasts (2 Peter 1:12, 22).

Notice also that Jude says that they "defile the flesh" (Jude 8 NKJV). What that means is they generally go into deep sexual sin or some kind of fleshy indulgence and immorality. An unbeliever may not believe the gospel, but he will normally be a moral person. The unbeliever can be nice, happily married, never running around on their spouse, and pay their bills. But that is not an apostate. The apostate participates or practices sexual sin or some kind of immorality, which causes them to defile the flesh. This phrase to describe the apostate comes just after Jude was talking about Sodom and Gomorrah. "As Sodom and Gomorrah, and the cities around them in a similar manner to these, having given themselves over to sexual immorality and gone after strange flesh, are set forth as an example, suffering the vengeance of eternal fire" (Jude 7 NKJV). Then Jude says, "Likewise" (Jude 8 NKJV) referring to verse 7. "Likewise… these filthy dreamers" (Jude 8 NKJV).

Why would an apostate be more prone to sexual immorality or some sort of sensuous sin than an ordinary unbeliever? Because animals live by natural instinct, and so do the apostate. The apostate has willingly and deliberately sinned; he has basically committed soul suicide, and he has kicked his conscience to death. When men rebel against God, they sink to the level of beast. As a result of their rebellion and pride, they defile the flesh, living to satisfy their animal lusts. "But it has happened to them according to the true proverb: "A doge returns to his own vomit," and "a sow, having washed, to her wallowing in the mire"" (2 Pet. 2:22 NKJV). Therefore, the apostate is worse than the unbeliever (2 Pet. 2:20). Peter said it would have been good if he never knew the truth (vs. 21).

During Mardi Gras down in New Orleans, they will put up banners of ancient gods such as Bacchus and Isis. Bacchus is a pagan god of wine, while Isis is the Egyptian deity of darkness. While they celebrate Mardi Gras, they celebrate their human half and the darker half of nature. The streets will reek of fermented sob and trashcans will be filled with oyster shucks. Those who are filled with alcohol shout in the face of the Christian street preacher, "Be gone!" because they do not want to hear him preach. Their guilt, pain, and conscience it suspended in favor of the more pleasant pursuits of drink and sex. Woman put on garter belts and expose their breast. Men parade in masks of leather and masks of demons, their feral tongues extended. They celebrate Mardi Gras (Fat Tuesday) for the return of spring, a return to fertility, after a winter's pause. However, it is also the beginning of Lent (Ash Wednesday), which is the celebration of death and resurrection of Christ. Therefore, these two celebrations are put side-by-side which makes for an interesting bed fellow. They are a contradiction in terms, Ash Wednesday is a time to get ready for the holy season of Easter. People say, "Well, if we are going to spend all that time getting ready for Easter, don't you think we ought to have a big time before we do it? Don't you think we ought to have a Fat Tuesday before we have Ash Wednesday? Don't you think we ought to have a carnival?" The word "carnival" is the word "flesh" (Strong's Concordance, 1984) When we a valedictory, we are saying goodbye. When you put these two words together you get "farewell to the flesh." So, for a certain number of days, they are going to have to say goodbye to the old flesh. They are going to eat, drink, fornicate, booze it up, dance, take drugs, all in the name Christianity. That is what the apostate does. They get away from the Word of God, and let their imaginations and dreams go wild and then wants to bring those filthy dreams into the church.

Let me warn you about something; arrogant speech is a dangerous thing, and so is despising the authority of that God has established. Even the Archangel Michael (Dan. 10:13) did not dare rebuke Satan, but respected the authority given to him by God. The point is that Michael did not rebuke Satan directly but left that to the Lord. It is a dangerous thing for God's people to confront directly and to argue with him, because he is much stronger than we are. If an archangel is careful about the way he deals with the devil, how much more cautious ought we to be! While it is true that we share in the victory of Christ, it is also true that we must not be arrogant. Satan is a dangerous enemy, and when we resist him, we must be sober and vigilant (1 Pet. 5:8-9).

The Character of Cain

Jude says, "Woe to them! For they have gone in the way of Cain..." (Jude 11 NKJV). Cain represents a person who perverts the gospel. In Genesis 4:1-5 is the story of two brothers. It is the story of two offerings, two religions, and two destinies. Adam and Eve had two sons: Cain and Abel. Abel came to make an offering to the Lord from the flock. Abel was a shepherd, a keeper of the flock and took a little lamb, one without spot or blemish and offered it to the Lord as a blood sacrifice. God accepted that offering. How did Cain feel about this kind of salvation? How did he feel about the blood of the lamb? He was not impressed with it, because he made an offering also (Gen. 4:3). Cain was a farmer; therefore, he takes the most succulent fruit, the ripest grain, the sweet-smelling herbs, and the most beautiful flowers and offers them to the Lord. God was not impressed and did not respect nor received Cain's offering. Why? Because Cain was offering the work of his hands, out of something he grew out of the ground and remember the ground is cursed (Gen. 3:17-19). Cain's offering represents his sweat, his toil and he is bringing to God that which God says has a curse upon it. God does not accept a work salvation kind of religion.

Now notice how this represents the perverted message of the gospel. A person who perverts the gospel message is one who does not preach the cross of Christ nor the shed blood of Christ. In other words, he has gone the way of Cain. Did you know there are only two religions in the world; not three, not four, but two and they are the true and the false. Now we like to divide religion up into Confucianism, Muhammadism, Rheumatism, Christianity, etc. We also like to break them down into different kinds of categories. We even break Christianity down into different denominations: Baptists, Methodists, Presbyterians, Episcopalians, Catholics, and so forth.

But the bottom line is there are only two religions: the true religion and false religion. In the lives of Cain and Abel, we can see the two religions represented. Abel represents the true religion because the true religion is salvation by the blood. While Cain represents the false religion because false religion is man trying to get to heaven by his own good works, and all by his own efforts. There are only two religions the way of Cain and the way of the Cross. The way of Cain leads to hell, and the way of the cross leads to heaven. The church does not need the way of Cain taught within her membership.

The Character of Balaam

Jude warns us of another man, "Have run greedily in the error of Balaam for profit..." (Jude 11 NKJV). This is a person who not only pervert the gospel, but also uses the gospel for financial gain and these are represented by Balaam. Who was Balaam? Balaam was an apostate prophet, and his story is told in Numbers 22-25. The way of Balaam is shown in the lifestyle of Balaam who was a soothsayer and a false prophet. His motive was to make money and he used his opportunities not to serve God and His people, but to satisfy his cravings for wealth. He used his religion to make money and entice the people to sin.

Balaam was well known around the region for his prophecies coming to pass and there was King Balak who was intimidating the Jews. As the king was coming out of Egypt one day, he got to thinking about Balaam. He sent word to Balaam that he wanted to hire Balaam to put a curse upon the children of Israel. When the two met in person, the king told Balaam that he would give him a fee for the curse. This made Balaam excited and anxious to get to work, however, Balaam knew that God did not want him to go with the delegation and serve King Balak. Therefore, he told the king that he could not curse Israel. This causes the king to think, "Every man has his price." So, the king upped the ante, and throws in some fringe benefits, and a bigger salary; and he comes back to Balaam. Balaam wants that money so bad that his palms itched so much, and he becomes so greedy, that he tells the king the truth. He says, "As is said before, we cannot put a curse on them.

But I can tell you how you can get them to curse themselves. Do you not have some good-looking Moabite girls? What you need to do is turn them into harlots and you bring the Israelites over here for a sensual feast. You let them fellowship together for a while and before long you will have those Jewish boys committing fornication with those girls. Then I will not have to curse them, they will curse themselves and God will curse them." Somehow Balaam maneuvered around God's declared will and went to Moab with the king. King Balak got those girls and they set up the sensual feast, and they got the Israelites to fornicate, and God slew twenty-four thousand of the Israelites as the curse of God came upon His people. Let me just say, there is not enough demon in Satan's army that can stop the church from behaving as a church by attacking the church from the outside. But the devil knows that we can curse ourselves if we take our eyes off our Lord and Savior, that is when we let the devil infiltrate us. The devil cannot curse the church nor its members, but we can curse ourselves.

So, God decides to use a donkey to rebuke Balaam and tried to get him on the right track, but Balaam's heart never changed. The sight of the angel of the Lord may have frightened him, but it did not bring him to surrender and faith. King Balak had promised him great wealth and he was going to get it one way or another. When can the church or church member walk in the way of Balaam? When deliberately rebelling against God's revealed will and try to change it. When we have selfish motives and ask, "What will I get out of it?" When we cause other people to sin so we can profit from it, either by gaining their position, getting our way, or money. Religion is big business today and it's easy for preachers, musicians, executives, writers, and other in Christian service to become more concern with money, prestige, reputation rather than the spiritual value and Christian behavior of the church.

The Character of Korah

The last person the church does not need in the church is those who behave like Korah (Jude 11). These are people who protest and would prohibit the gospel. In Numbers 16:1-4, we can find the story of Korah. Who is Korah? Korah was an important man, for he was the cousin of Moses, which would make him a prince in Israel. Korah had great influence upon the people. As a matter fact, he was able to raise up two hundred and fifty men to do protest rally against Moses and Aaron. "They gathered together against Moses and Aaron, and said to them, "You take too much upon yourselves, for all the congregation is holy, every one of them, and the Lord among them. Why do you exalt yourselves above the assembly of the Lord?"" (Num. 16:3 NKJV). In other words, what Korah said is, "Moses, who do you think you are? Aaron, who do you think you are? Why are you lifting yourselves up above the rest of us? Do you not know that you are no better than we are? Do you not know that everybody is holy around here?" Basically, with those words this man was rebelling against God's prophetic message; and he was rebelling against God's priestly ministry. Why? Because every apostate is a rebel at heart.

Now Moses knew what was about to happen, he knew how the wrath of God would burn against Korah. "And Moses said: "By this you shall know that the Lord has sent me to do all these works, for I have not done them of my own will. If these men die naturally like all men, or if they are visited by the common fate of all men, then the Lord has not sent me. But if the Lord creates a new thing, and the earth opens its mouth and swallows them up with all that belongs to them, and they go down alive into the pit, then you will understand that these men have rejected the Lord" (Num. 16:28-30 NKJV). The next verse tells us exactly how God feels about Korah. "Now it came to pass, as he finished speaking all these words, that the ground spilt apart under them, and the earth opened its mouth and swallowed them up, with their households and all the men with Korah, with all their goods So they and all those with them went down alive into the pit; the earth closed over them, and they perished from among the assembly" (vs. 31-33 NKJV). Korah had brought his blasphemous accusation, and Moses went to God about these apostates. God told Moses to separate himself from these men, for He was about to send judgment upon them and their households. So, while Korah is in his house, there is a great jagged chasm that opens in the earth; and down goes Korah. Down goes his family; down goes his possessions. The earth closes back up and swallows them up. While the two hundred and fifty men are standing their gaping at what just happened, God sends fire down from heaven to destroy the followers of Korah.

Listen, it does not do the church any good to have members who behave like these apostates. God does not always deal with them like He did with Korah. However, what God did was set an example, just like He did in the early church when Ananias and Sapphira lie to the Holy Spirit (Acts 5:1-11). In that first church, God struck them dead. Again, God does not do that every time somebody tells a lie, however God was setting an example. What I am trying to say is that God, in the most violent and vivid way that could be shown, is showing how He feels about apostasy in the church. The church needs to be warned not to behave as a church who follows the ways of these apostates. The church needs to be aware of the behavior of these apostates: Cain represents those who would pervert the gospel and promote a bloodless religion, Balaam represents the hustlers who prostitute the gospel for money, and Korah represents those who protest the gospel and shake their fist in the face of God. By the way, those who behave like Korah are those who try to tell the pastor what to preach on and what not to preach on. They also turn against other brothers and sisters who resist their ideas. How important is it that we know Christ in these days? How important is it that we behave as a church without the behavior of these apostates? Jude wanted to write about the gospel, but he said, "Beloved, while I was very diligent to write to you concerning our common salvation, I found it necessary to write to you exhorting you to contend earnestly for the faith which was once for all delivered to the saints" (Jude 3 NKJV).

CHAPTER ELEVEN

Church Members the Church cannot do Without

Then He said to another, "Follow Me." But he said,
"Lord, let me first go and bury my father."
(Luke 9:59 NKJV)

THERE WAS METHODIST PREACHER OVER IN GEORGIA AND EVEN thought his style was unusual, meaning he engaged the congregation in dialogue during his sermons, the people loved him. One Sunday morning he said to the congregation, "Let's pretend that the church is a locomotive. What part of the locomotive would you like to be?" One man held up his hand and said, "I'd like to be a wheel that rolls the train down the track." Someone else said, "I would like to be the whistle on that locomotive that sounds God's praises throughout the land." Another person said, "Pastor, I would like to be the coal, and just burn myself up for Jesus." At that point the pastor broke out in a huge smile and said, "Now you are talking. Brothers and sisters, we have got too many whistles and wheels in the church now; what we need is more coal." What that Methodist pastor is talking about is commitment, the willingness to be used for Christ's sake at any cost.

In the ninth chapter of Luke, Jesus sees the cross looming in front of him, and he knew he has some fair-weather followers around him who are more than a quart low on commitment, so he tries to teach some hard facts of life. There are many social observers who

156

believe that we are in a day and age where it seems like there is not any commitment at all. The evidence is clear and proves this to be true in any area of society even in church. People borrow money, but they do not pay it back in a timely and agreed period. Bankruptcy is at an all-time high because people spend more than they earn. The financial experts are pointing to the fact that there is no commitment on the part of the consumer. Employers are even saying that the biggest problem they deal with is the lack of commitment from their employees to the jobs. Even after signing contracts that include bonuses, some employees fail to give fair labor for the wages. The concept of diligence and carefulness in doing our work suffers from a basic lack of commitment to anything.

Take marriage for instance; in the Bible belt of America, (the south), we have seen the loss of commitment in marriage. Divorce is no longer perceived as being out of the ordinary. As matter of fact, it has become as easy as deciding where or not to take a vacation to an exotic place. In fact, the going rate for a divorce, done by a divorce attorney is around fifty dollars. What used to be a rare and not heard of issue, has now emerged a trend with marriage and family counseling offices opening every day. Most young adults would rather just live together out of wedlock than make it official and marry one another. Young people are not being taught about family values and the importance of wedding vows. Therefore, thousands of Christians go through some counselor's door every year because they have not been equipped at home, because of lack of example; or they have been taught at church, because of lack of teaching and discipleship. Young couples are not equipped to deal with any of the adversity in life, marriage, parenting, finances, health, you name it! I am not against or opposed to Christian counseling, praise God for godly counselors and ministers. However, what does bother me is the believer who by-passes God's word, principles, concepts, and precepts, by turning to man or woman who they think can solve all their problems. There has been only one man who has ever been able to solve mankind's problems, and He is usually the last person anybody turns to. Today, it seems as though there is not anything holy about marriage. Young women, who are three to four months pregnant, decide to wear white wedding gowns. Men and women get married three or four times, standing in sacred altars with white dress as if they are the Virgin Mary and no one seems to care! Yes, it is true that Jesus forgives our sins, but what is trending in society should not infiltrate the church. We must do better at sharing the gospel and teaching and making disciples.

Obviously, there is a shortage of commitment towards the church and worship by many Christian church members today seems scarce. It seems odd, that most pastors get excited when twenty percent of their congregation they pastor is the ones pastors can count on any given Sunday. Take for instance Paul's letter to the Philippian church. Paul organized many churches and his interest in them never ceased. This was only natural for Paul. He had put much blood, sweat and tears into building those churches. Some of those churches pleased him, some of them disappointed him, and some he had great joy. The church at Philippi was his favorite. He felt that the church at Philippi represented the crowning work of his life, and of course, it brought him his greatest joy. We can find people like the Christians at Philippi in every church. These are the people the church could not do without.

The Absence of Commitment

Before we get into looking at those the church could not do without let's discuss this subject of commitment a little further. Over in Matthew 5, Jesus is preaching His sermon on the mount sermon, and He begins to talk about adultery in Matthew 5:27-30. Here is what He said, "You have heard that it was said to those of old, 'You shall not commit adultery.' But I say to you that whoever looks at a woman to lust for her has already committed adultery with her in his heart. If your right eye causes you to sin, pluck it out and cast it from you; for it is more profitable for you that one of your members perish, than for your whole body to be cast into hell. And if your right-hand causes you to sin, cut it off and cast it from you; for it is more profitable for you that one of your members perish, than for your whole body be cast into hell" (Matt. 5:27-30 NKJV). While the overall subject of His point is adultery, the underlying point is that of commitment. Today, we are suffering from a loss of commitment at many levels of modern living, but what scares most pastors to death is: our failure to follow through on our promises and commitments, and this is destroying the church. Jesus tells us two things: first we are to throw out anything in our life that keeps us from being totally committed. Notice those phrases, "Pluck it out" and "cut it off." Jesus is trying to shock us into realizing that some things get in the way of allowing us to keep His commandments. Many times, they are the little things that keep us from being faithful and committed to Him. The common drive toward succeeding financially has made many fathers a stranger in their own homes. The compulsion to be the top in any field of work has turned parents into workaholics, making them strangers to their children. The second thing Jesus tells us is that we need to put our focus and motivation into our relationship with our family. Your job is not for the sake of making a living, your job, that gives you an income, allows you to live with those to whom you gave your primary commitment, which includes your spouse and children. They must come before anything else and second to your relationship with Jesus.

The High Price of Commitment

Discipleship is not for the soft or pampered; it involves great sacrifice and self-denial, and many believers are not willing to pay that price. Jesus said, "Foxes have holes and birds of the air have nests, but the Son of Man has nowhere to lay His head" (Luke 9:58 NKJV). This unwillingness to pay the price is prevalent in the church today here in America. Do not believe me, look around at church: most members have not missed a meal. Most churches have cushioned seats, air conditioning, classrooms, musicians, televisions, a roof, security teams, no fear of persecution, and on I could go with the list. I am ashamed to talk sacrifice, especially when I am aware of what many Christians are facing in other parts of the world today.

I once read about Matta Boush who was arrested in March 1986 in his home village of Tabanya, South of Kordofan, Sudan and was charged with: harboring four Sudan people's liberation army guerillas in his home. Matta was sent to a military prison not far from his hometown and during the first few weeks he was tortured and interrogated. Understandably, Matta became depressed, because he did not know why he had been arrested and his judicial appeals were rejected. His wife and daughters did not visit him, and at one point he was told they were in guerrilla-controlled territory and could not visit him. Occasionally, he saw people being executed around him, but he had thirty years to look forward to if he had that long. One day an Irish Catholic sister came and visited, which changed his outlook on his situation. She told him that there were many others in prison whose cases were far worse than his. She encouraged him not to ask why he was in prison, but instead to ask what purpose he was here for. From that point on, Matta began to minister to his fellow prisoners and for the first prayer meeting there was a total of six people. At the next meeting, there was a total of seventy, and in the next there was one hundred and sixty. Seeing the growth, the authorities insisted that Matta not allow Muslims to join in the meetings, but he was not deterred, and hundreds of Muslims converted to Christianity! In most Islamic countries today, you can receive the death penalty if you convert someone to Christianity. Talk about sacrifice.

In China, Xie Moshan spent twenty-six years in prison for illegal preaching in an underground church. While his wife spent her time confined to a sixty-five square foot room for supporting the underground church. If Jesus is truly our Lord and Savior, there ought to be some sacrifice and self-denial in our lives, but where is that kind of sacrifice in the modern church. Yes, I see it here and there, but why does God's people have to be begged to serve the Lord? Why do many churches have to pay people to play an instrument for church worship, why do they have to be begged to serve in the nursery, or teach Sunday School and Bible school? Many churches pay outside college students or seminary students to staff key positions in the church because God's people lack commitment.

The Urgency of Commitment

"Then He said to another, "Follow Me." But he said, "Lord, let me first god and bury my father." Jesus said to him, "Let the dead bury their own dead, but you go and preach the kingdom of God."" (Luke

9: 59-60 NKJV). I know that sounds harsh and insensitive, but there are no suggestions here that the elderly father was seriously ill, or even directly dependent on the son. The would-be follower just wanted to stay where he was a few more years until the father died. Jesus told him that he should not allow a future death to delay him from serving now, because time is of the essence and there is a sense of urgency now!

I remember watching the final minutes of a college football game several years back, between the Georgia Bulldogs and the Alabama Crimson Tide. The game was a thrilling squeaker which was won by Alabama. The key play of the game was when the Alabama quarterback threw a high and hard pass to a receiver, and the pass bounced off his outstretched hands into the air, and then landing in the hands of a Georgia linebacker. Now, linebackers are not accustomed to catching passes, and he tried to hold on, but it slipped right through his fingers. In disgust he fell to his knees and pounded the turf. Our God given opportunities come that way, they come quickly, often without warning, and you either rise to the challenge or it passes through our fingers never to return.

I remember going on a youth mission trip to Colorado with Third Baptist Church Murfreesboro, TN. While we were there, we had some down time, and we went snow skiing. After spending the morning out on the slopes, we took a break for lunch. We had finished eating and resting in the public mountain restaurant/lodge, while people came in and out. Some were gathering outside at the picnic tables of the restaurant. There was this young man standing outside the window of where our group was sitting. The young man was probably the same age I was at the time, seventeen, maybe a little older. However, I took notice of this young man, because he had a tall mohawk that was dyed blue. I have never seen someone in person with this kind of hairstyle, therefore I proceeded to ask the associate pastor and youth pastor if they would let someone like him into the church youth group? The associate pastor spoke up, "Yes, Chris, I would, and I would love on him as Christ commands, and I would share the gospel of Christ." His answer hit me like a ton of bricks. I was called to be a preacher at the age of fifteen and knew what the moving of the Holy Spirit felt like in my life. After what the associate pastor said what he said, the Holy Spirit was so strong and telling me to move outside and talk with that young man about Jesus.

But I did nothing. I sat there in my chair surrounded by my fellow youth group members and youth workers and did nothing about sharing Jesus. Call it resisting the Holy Spirit if you want, but Jesus landed an opportunity in my hands, and I let it slip through my fingers, never to return. I live not knowing whether that young man ever accepted Jesus Christ and I left beating the ground because of that lost opportunity. Today, I stand forgiven by God for that lost opportunity and through many prayers God has shown me the lessons of that experience. I am committed to sharing the gospel, especially when presented with an opportunity from the Holy Spirit. My prayer is that I may never miss an opportunity again.

Life rolls along, alternating between normal hours of boredom and awesome moments of eternal significance. For example, a wife craves some sign that she is more important than her husband's job. The husband, wanting to make his wife happy, works hard and long hours at his job to do so. They never communicate their feelings to one another until it is too late, and they are in court. Here is another example, someone with low self-esteem longs to hear someone tell them, "You are really special!" until it is too late, and they are burying them. While at the funeral everyone who knew her asking the question, "Did you know she was depressed?" Another example, a child hears a parent say, "Let's report your watch as stolen so the insurance will cover it." While the parents put the watch in a safe place waiting for the insurance company to respond. The child never hears anyone say, "but that would be wrong," and then it is too late; the child is in custody for burglary! One last example, there is a young father who for years regarded Sunday as his day for hunting and fishing. His eight-year-old son watches every Sunday as his father leaves to go on his expedition. Then it is too late, the son grows up with no respect for the things of God. Jesus taught us that time is of the essence, for we shall not pass this way again (Luke 9:60-62). King Solomon put it this way, "To everything there is a season, a time for every purpose under heaven" (Eccl. 3:1 NKJV). Do you live with a sense of urgency? Are you carpe diem (Latin for seize the day)? Are you taking advantage of the opportunity God has given you? When is the last time you have worked at fulfilling your commitment to God?

The Faithfulness of Commitment

Paul had his hands in organizing a lot of churches during his day, and from his letters we can gather that he never lost interest in what was going on in those churches. In the book of Philippians, we get the idea this church at Philippi was his favorite church. This church to Paul was the crown of his life's work, and they brought him his greatest joy. He writes, "I thank God upon every remembrance of you, always in every prayer of mine making request for you all with joy, for you fellowship in the gospel from the first day until now, being confident of this very thing, that He who has begun a good work in you will complete it until the day of Jesus Christ; just as it is right for me to think this of you all, because I have you in my heart, inasmuch as both in my chains and in the defense and confirmation of the gospel, you all are partakers with me in grace" (Phil. 1:3-7 NKJV). Later He writes, "Therefore, my beloved and longed for brethren, my joy and crown, so stand fast in the Lord, beloved" (Phil. 4:1 NKJV) and then he says, "Now you Philippians know also that in the beginning of the gospel, when I departed from Macedonia, no church shared with me concerning giving and receiving but you only" (vs. 15 NKJV). The church members of the Philippian church were faithful and that brought Paul great joy. There are some members in churches today who have the same behavior as the members of this church in churches today. But who are they? They are the "faithful people". People who are willing, visionaries, optimistic, giving, and promoters of members of the church. But what exactly do faithful people do?

THE FAITHFUL DRAW NEAR

To answer the question, let us look at the book of Hebrews. The book of Hebrews was written to Jewish converts. New church members who have been saved from an ancient system of bondage to a law they could not keep. However, the rituals and demands of the law were all they knew, and some of the converts were considering returning to Judaism. They were having a difficult time leaving the rituals and ceremonies of their old life. They were clinging to their old religion and their old methods of worship. Some of the converts had already walked away from their commitment to Jesus, from the church, and they had gone back to their old way of life which was Judaism. This prompted the writer of Hebrews to write, "Therefore, brethren, having boldness to enter the Holiest by the blood of Jesus, by a new and living way which He consecrated for us, through the veil, that is, His flesh, and having a High Priest over the house of God, let us draw near with a true heart in full assurance of faith, having our hearts sprinkled from an evil conscience and our bodies washed with pure water" (Heb. 10:19-22 NKJV).

The first challenge is for us to enter in and draw near. These verses tell us how it is possible to enter the presence of God, and for us to draw near to Him. The writer makes a statement in verse 19 that must have sounded strange to his Jewish readers. He tells them to "enter into the Holiest" with "boldness" (vs. 19 NKJV). He also tells them that there is a "new and living way" (vs. 20 NKJV) into the presence of God. The old Jewish system was a closed system, as were most religious systems in the ancient world. Under the Jewish system, no one could approach God but the High priest, and he could only enter the Holies of Holy on the Day of Atonement with the blood of an innocent sacrifice to atone for his own sins. Man was barred from the presence of Jehovah God. When Jesus came and died on the cross, He made a new way, for all to receive Him, to enter the presence of God. When the veil of Christ's flesh was broken, the way was opened to God for all whosoever will enter. When Jesus died the veil that separated the Holy Place and the Holies of Holy in the temple was torn from top to bottom. "And Jesus cried out again with a loud voice and yielded up His spirit. Then, behold, the veil of the temple was torn in two from top to bottom; and the earth quaked, and the rocks were split, and the graves were opened; and many bodies of the saints who had fallen asleep were raised; and coming out of the graves after His resurrection, they went into the holy city and appeared to many" (Matt. 27:50-54 NKJV). When Jesus, Who is our High Priest, entered the Holy of Holies, with His blood, He left the way open for us to follow Him (John 10:9). His shed blood is our invitation to enter the presence of God (Heb. 9:22).

The word "having" is used three times in Hebrews 10:19-22. It speaks of a "present possession" (Concise Oxford English Dictionary Eleventh Edition, 2004) We have some precious possessions of what Jesus did for us on the cross. We have boldness to enter salvation (Heb 10:19). The way has been opened and we are invited to come (Isa. 1:18, Rev. 22:17). If you have not come to Jesus, you should do it today! Next, we have a High Priest (Heb. 10:21). We have a Man on the inside, praying for us and guaranteeing us that we will be accepted when we come (Heb. 7:25; Rom. 8:34; John 6:37). Then, we have clean hearts and new lives (Heb. 10:22). The Jewish worshiper was never truly clean. Even the high priest had to cleans himself every time he entered the tabernacle or temple. Because of Jesus's death, burial, and resurrection things are different for us today! Based on what Jesus did for us and what we He has provided for us; people are challenged to "draw near". Faithful church members draw near to Jesus daily. Daily Bible reading, prayer time, going to worship services, group Bible study, giving of tithes an offering, singing praise, etc. is all part of drawing near to Him. Jesus calls us to come to Him. We must come to Him with a sincere heart, and not come to Him lightly. We are not to come into His presence and treat it like a game. We can come into His presence with full assurance of faith. The means we can come to God with the full assurance that He will receive us. Make good use of this privilege, seek Him, seek His face, and call upon Him often. Find yourself frequently in the throne room, praying to the King, calling on Him to demonstrate His approval of your life, the church, by manifesting His power through you and the church. Call on Him to do the incredible for the lost.

THE FAITHFUL HOLD FAST

The writer of Hebrews goes on to say, "Let us hold fast the confession of our hope without wavering, for He who promised is faithful" (Heb. 10:23 NKJV). Faithful people claim to have a blessed hope in Jesus, and they are looking forward to the day when they arrive in heaven someday, therefore, they live out that hope by being faithful to Jesus. The reason why the writer is writing this is because some of the Jewish converts were having a hard time making a complete break from the ritual of their old religion. They were trying to hold onto their Jewish heritage and Jesus too. The writer tells them to beware lest they turn away from Christ and go back to their old lives. There is a danger in that for the church body today. Most of the church body was not saved out of a religion, but out of the darkness of our old life of sin. Therefore, there is always the danger that we might turn back to the ways of the world. The writer of Hebrews is challenging us to be faithful to the Lord Who saved our souls by His grace. We have all known people who were in church for a while and then they departed back into the world. We must be on guard that the same does not happen to us. There is nothing this world has to offer but pain, suffering, heartache, and death. Listen to what John says about this, "They went out from us, but they were not of us; for if they had been of us, they would have continued with us; but they went out that they might be made manifest, that none of them were of us" (1 John 2:19 NKJV).

Faithful people can endure and overcome with the sure knowledge that Jesus will come back for us because He always keeps His promises. When He saved us and called us out of a life sin; He promised us a new life (John 10:10). He promised us a home in heaven (John 14:1-3). He is not going to fail to deliver everything He has promised His children. We may fall short in fulfilling our commitment to Him, but He will never fail us (Heb. 6:18; 13:5)! Every promise He has ever made to us is an ironclad promise and He is fully capable of fulfilling His promises. The knowledge that God will always be faithful to us should serve to make us desire to be faithful to Him in return! So be a faithful person and hold tight.

THE FAITHFUL LOOK AFTER ONE ANOTHER

Faithful people are ones who think about others. "And let us consider one another in order to stir up love and good works, not forsaking the assembling ourselves together, as is the manner of some, but exhorting one another, and so much the more as you see the Day approaching" (Heb. 10:24-25 NKJV). The word "consider" means "to set the mind on" (Dictionary, 1828) We are to set our minds on our fellow believers to provoke them, stir them up. We are to stir the pot, rock the boat, which should cause them to do good work. This is not a negative motivation like trying to incite a crowd to riot, but it is a positive motivation. Faithful people think about others, which causes faithful people to do something for others and then in turn others will do good work. This is called "exhorting one another" (vs. 25 NKJV). The word "exhort" means "to encourage" (Dictionary, 1828) Taken together these words are a challenge for the saints to look out for one another and to encourage one another in our walk with the Lord. But just a thought, if we would behave as a church full of faithful people, who are looking after one another, then we would not be so self-centered. There are ways we can be thinking about one another.

First, we should behave as a church that loves each other. Love should be the calling card of the church. Jesus put it this way, "By this all will know that you are My disciples, if you have love for one another" (John 13:35 NKJV). God should be the central and foremost love in our lives and the second object of our love should be the love we have for one another. After all, is that not the first and second greatest commandments? "Jesus said to him, "You shall love the Lord your God with all your heart, with all your soul, and with all your mind. This is the first and greatest commandment. And the second is like it: 'You shall love your neighbor as yourself.' On these two commandments hang all the Law and the Prophets" (Matt. 22:37-40 NKJV). Genuine, godly love for one another is one of the sure marks of real salvation (1 John 3:14). The absence of this love reveals the absence of true salvation (1 John 4:7-8, 20-21). We are to behave as a church where people feel loved! It is sad when people receive a warmer greeting at a retail store or restaurant than they do at the house of God! We are to love! Do not wait to be loved, start loving others and love will come your way!

Next, we should behave as a church that works together. We are to help and serve our brothers and sisters in their work for the Lord. We are to encourage them in the work they do. Stirring them up, motivating them to keep up the good fight. Instead of finding fault with everyone and everything they do, we should take the time to notice the positive things people are doing and encourage them. We are in this thing together and we are to be in the building up business, not the tearing down business. Paul writes, "Therefore let us pursue the things which make for peace and the things by which one may edify another" (Rom. 14:19 NKJV). He told the Ephesians something similar, "Let no corrupt word proceed out of your mouth, but what is good for necessary edification, that it may impart grace to the hearers" (Eph. 4:29 NKJV). We should be encouraging one another to continue faithfulness to the Lord and His work.

Also, we should behave as a church that worships together. Some of the Jewish converts had abandoned the public gatherings of the believers. We are not to forsake the assembling of the body of Christ, but we are to seek out the fellowship of the saints and not find ways to avoid them. Church attendance is far more vital than people realize. You are not a number to be counted for attendance, you are a part of a family. Just as a hot coal becomes cold when it is separated from the fire, the believer will become cold when the believer is separated form the fellowship of the presence of God and other believers. We need the excitement, the teaching, the preaching, the worship, the challenges, the encouragement, the fellowship, and the sense of family that is available when we go to church. Many of the saints need to reexamine their commitment to the public worship of the Savior. Nothing will help you stay close to the Lord than regular, faithful attendance to the service at the house of God!

Let me share a humorous story. "We have football in the fall, basketball in the winter, and baseball in the spring and summer, and as a pastor I have been an avid sports fan all my life. But I have had it! I quit this sports business once and for all. You cannot get me near one of those places again. Want to know why? Well, every time I go to a sporting event, they ask me for money. The people with whom I end up sitting with are very unfriendly. The seats are always too hard, and they are not at all comfortable. I went to many of the games, but the coach never called on me when there was not a game. The referee made a decision with which I disagreed with, now I avoid that referee.

I suspected that I was sitting with some hypocrites, who only like our home team because they came to see their friends and to see what others were wearing rather than watch the game. Some of the games went into overtime, and I was late getting home. The band played some songs that I had never heard before. It seems that the games are scheduled when I want to do other things. I was taken to too many games by my parents when I was growing up. I do not want to take my daughter to any games, because I want her to choose for herself what sport she likes best." Now that is a humorous story, is it not? Yet, those are the same kind of excuses people use for not coming to church. Church is far more important than any ball game has ever been. We need to stow our excuses, and just admit that our hearts are not where they need to be with the Lord. We need to repent of our sin of not attending His worship service at His house and get back to where we need to be.

Finally, we need to behave as a church that waits together. As we see the coming of the Lord draw closer each day, we are to encourage one another to faithfulness and holy living. The idea here is this: as we live in these perilous times and each day gets worse than the previous day, and coming of Christ gets closer and closer; it is going to get harder and harder for the church body to remain holy and separated from this world. We are going to need the fellowship of the church more than we ever have before. We have a duty to one another to encourage, challenge, help, and serve one another along the way of this life. Jesus is coming soon, and we need each other. We need the fellowship and strength that we draw from one another if we are going to overcome. We need what the church has to offer while we wait for Jesus.

"But Jesus said to him, "No one, having put his hand to the plow, and looking back, is fit for the kingdom of God" (Luke 9:62 NKJV). Jesus was not a farmer, but he knew that plowing requires that the farmer's eyes be fixed immediately upon what lies ahead in case of rocks or obstructions. He keeps his eyes upon a fixed target somewhere in the distant so that he could keep the row straight. There are church members who behave as though they must forever be glancing over their shoulders worried about something that took place in the past, some mistake, some sin, and because they behave this way, they have missed a God divine appointment or opportunity that lay right in front of them. There are some church members who behave as though they need to look back at some false god, who they never totally renounced. Therefore, they simply can never focus on their commitment to God until they let go of the past. God wants us to focus all our attention on Him and the opportunities He places in front of us.

The writer of Hebrews says, "Therefore we also, since we are surrounded by so great a cloud of witnesses, let us lay aside every weight, and the sin which so easily ensnares us, and let us run with endurance the race that is set before us, looking unto Jesus, the author and finisher of our faith, who for the joy that was set before Him endured the cross, despising the shame, and has sat down at the right hand of the throne of God" (Heb. 12:1-2 NKJV). If we are alert, we will notice the troubled person who needs a good listener. If we stay focused on Jesus, then we will be able to see when a colleague, friend, or family member needs to be introduced to the Savior. We will be able to see the principle that needs to be defended and the underdog who needs someone to stand by them, as we keep our eyes upon the Author and Finisher. Every day is a new kingdom task that we must complete, so we must be alert enough to see them and faithful enough to complete them as we behave as a church member.

In 1904 William Borden, heir to the Borden Dairy estate, graduated from a Chicago high school as a millionaire. His parents gave him a trip around the world. He traveled through Asia and the Middle East. While there he was given God inspired burden for the world's suffering people. Writing home, he told his parents how he was going to give his life to preparing for the mission field. When he made that decision, he wrote in the back of his Bible two words: "No reserves." After graduating from Yale University, he turned down numerous high-paying jobs and headed to seminary, where he wrote two more words in his Bible: "No retreats." After completing his studies at Princeton Seminary, Borden sailed for China and on the way, he stopped in Egypt for some additional training. However, while he was there, he was stricken with meningitis and died within a month. Perhaps you are thinking like I did, "What a waste!" William Borden did not think so. Shortly before he died, he entered two more words into his Bible and now the statement in the back of Williams Borden's Bible reads: "No reserves, no retreats, no regrets." (Flyod, 2018) Success for a Christian is to be able to say at the end of life, "I have fought the good fight, I have finished the race, I have kept the faith. Finally, there is laid up for me the crown of righteousness, which the Lord, the righteous Judge, will give to me on that Day, and not to me only but also to all who have loved His appearing" (2 Tim. 4:7-8 NKJV). We will never be able to say that until we are totally committed to Jesus! The church needs church members who have "No reserves, no retreats, no regrets." There are some people the church cannot do without! Are you faithful? Are you willing? Do you have a vision for your church? Are you a promoter? Are you a giver? Are you willing to behave as a church member?

CHAPTER TWELVE

The Most Important Person in the Church

For no other foundation can anyone lay than that which is laid, which is Jesus Christ.
(1 Corinthians 3:11 NKJV)

IF THERE WERE EVER A PERSON THAT IS SO VITAL AND IMPORTANT to the behavior of the church that person would be the Lord Jesus Christ. He is central to all the church does, after all He is the Master builder of the church. To behave as a church, we are to come together with our hearts, minds, and soul and focus upon the presence of Jesus. When we worship, hear the Word of God preached, tithe, serve, and pray, we are coming into the audience of one. The church should behave as though He is the sole purpose for coming to church in the first place. In Matthew 16:16 it says, "Simon Peter answered and said, "You are the Christ, the Son of the living God" (NKJV). Jesus then responds by saying, "And I also say to you that you are Peter, and this rock I will build My church, and the gates of Hades shall not prevail against it" (vs. 18 NKJV). What is the "rock" which Jesus said He would build His church? What is the foundation of the church that Jesus built His church? The Roman Catholic Church would have you to believe that the "rock" that Jesus was referring to is Peter. Which led the Catholics to believe that Peter was the first pope. Jesus did not promise to build His church upon Peter, but upon Peter's confession.

The church that Jesus built has no human foundation. Jesus is the foundation of the church and when He makes His statement in Matthew 16:18, He is using a play on words. Let us look at the Greek words that Jesus uses to make His point. "You are *petros* and upon this *petra* I will build My church." So, what is the difference between *petros* and *petra*? *Petros* means "a stone" like a boulder; and *petra* means "a large rock formation" like a mountain (Strong's Concordance, 1984) We could read verse 18 this way, "You are Peter, you are a piece of stone, and upon this rock, this foundational stone, this massive stone, or mountain I will build my church." By the way, the Aramaic form of the name Cephas also means "a stone" (Strong's Concordance, 1984) Everyone who put their faith in Jesus, believes upon Him, and confesses Him as the Son, God, and Savior, becomes a "living stones" (2 Pet. 2:5 NKJV).

What is the foundation stone which the church is built on? It is built upon the confession that Peter just made, "You are the Christ, the Son of the living God" (vs. 16 NKJV). Jesus Christ is the foundation rock on which the church is built. Therefore, He is to be the center of the church. He is the most important person the church cannot do without. Someone once said, "There are three things for a person to be happy and to have fulfillment in their life. First, they need something to believe. Next, they need someone to love. Finally, they need something worthwhile to do." I agree with this and believe it to be true, plus I think the Bible would confirm that for us to find fulfillment and happiness and meaning in life we must have something to believe in. Then we must have someone to love and love us. We must have something worthwhile to do rather than just merely drawing our breath, a salary, and fighting to live while we live to fight. There must be more to life.

The Cornerstone of the Church

It possible that the conversation about Jesus building His church is still on the mind of Peter as he wrote his first letter. In 1 Peter 2:4-9, Peter is talking about the church, and how it is built, and how it functions. Peter writes, "Coming to Him as a living stone, rejected indeed by men, but chosen by God and precious" (1 Pet. 2:4 NKJV). Then he says, "Therefore it is also contained in the Scripture, "Behold, I lay in Zion a chief cornerstone, elect, precious, and he who believes on Him will by no means be put to shame" (vs. 6 NKJV). Here we see that Peter is talking about the cornerstone of the church. The cornerstone of the church is Jesus. Our church is built, (my church, your church, or any Christian church), is built upon the Lord Jesus Christ.

Jesus is a supernatural stone meaning that Peter called Him a "living stone" (vs. 4 NKJV). Stones do not have life in them, they are dead. If you want to say something is dead you would use the phrase, "Stone dead" or "Dead as a rock." Even your pet rock is dead, and yet Jesus is called a living stone. What Peter is saying is that Jesus gives supernatural life. Jesus said, "The thief does not come except to steal, and to kill, and to destroy. I have come that they may have life, and that they may have it more abundantly" (John 10:10 NKJV). In other parts of the New Testament, He is called: Living Water and Living Bread. When we behave as a church with Jesus being at the center of what we proclaim and do, we have an abundant life. There are a lot of people who do not have life. There are a lot of people who want to go to heaven, but they do not have life. They exist, but there is no life in them. Jesus Christ came not to give you existence but life. You will always have existence, because when God made you, He breathed into your nostrils the breath of life and you became a living soul. Therefore, you will go on endless, timeless, dateless, measureless. Your soul will be in existence somewhere when the sun, the moon, and the stars have grown cold. But only in Jesus do you have life. He is the most important person in the church, and He is a supernatural stone.

He is also a select stone. Peter said that Jesus was chosen of God (1 Pet. 2:4). There is no one like Jesus our living select stone. He is precious to the Father. Jesus is the beloved Son, in whom God is well pleased (Matt. 3:17; 17:5; 2 Pet. 1:17). Jesus is the object of the Heavenly Father's love. Jesus is vital to the church, because there is no way you can know the Heavenly Father without knowing God the Son. You cannot ignore God the Son without ignoring God the Father. You cannot worship the Father except through the Son. "Jesus said to him, "I am the way, the truth, and the life. No one comes to the Father except through Me" (John 14:6 NKJV). Jesus is a precious stone.

Jesus is a slighted stone. Peter said that Jesus was "rejected indeed by men" (1 Pet. 2:4 NKJV). Then He says, "Therefore, to you who believe, He is precious; but to those who are disobedient, "The stone which the builders rejected has become the chief cornerstone" (vs. 7 NKJV). In other words, not everybody is going to love Jesus. There are some who have rejected Jesus as the Messiah of the world. Think about this, if everyone the world believed on Jesus, then that would prove that Jesus is not the Christ, the Son of God, because Jesus prophesied and said that not everyone is going to believe on Him. "Because narrow is the gate and difficult is the way which leads to life, and there are few who find it" (Matt. 7:14 NKJV). This is a clear prophecy that there are going to be those who will reject the living stone. So, when Peter writes, "rejected indeed by men" (1 Pet. 2:4 NKJV) it implies that men have examined the stone, and after examining the stone they say, "We do not want the stone." What is God going to do with people who sit in an air-conditioned, upholstered church, and hear a preacher preach his heart out about the Lord Jesus Christ, and they examine Jesus, and they say, "I don't want Him?" What is going to happen to those people? Jesus said, "And that servant who knew his master's will, and did not prepare himself or do according to his will, shall be beaten with many stripes. But he who did not know, yet committed things deserving of stripes, shall be beaten with few. For everyone to whom much is given, from him much will be required; and to whom much has been committed, of him they will ask the more" (Luke 12:47-48 NKJV). Jesus also said, "And you, Capernaum, who are exalted to heaven, will be brought down to Hades; for if the mighty works which are done in you had been done in Sodom, it would have remained until this day. But I say to you that it shall be more tolerable for the land of Sodom in the day of judgment than for you" (Matt. 11:23-24 NKJV). Those who have heard the gospel and those of us who have known Jesus and yet reject Him will have a more sever judgment than the vile people of the city of Sodom who lived in open sodomy and rebellion against God.

175

Peter also calls Jesus a stumbling stone. "And 'a stone of stumbling and a rock of offense.' They stumble, being disobedient to the word, to which they also were appointed" (1 Pet. 2:8 NKJV). People stumble on the Chief Cornerstone and in one way or another every human being ever born will encounter Jesus Christ. Therefore, Jesus will be for you either a steppingstone into heaven or a stumbling stone into hell. You can be saved by Him, or you can be judged by Him. If Jesus is not your Chief Cornerstone, then He is your stumbling stone. Furthermore, Jesus becomes a strategic stone placed in your path for you and you alone to decide what to do with Jesus. Notice how Peter puts it, "Therefore it is also contained in the Scripture, "Behold, I lay in Zion a chief cornerstone, elect, precious, and he who believes on Him will by no means be put to shame" (vs. 6 NKJV). During Peter's day, in the architecture world, when a building was built, in the foundation there would be a chief cornerstone. This was the stone that set the angles of the walls. This was the stone that gave symmetry and strength and significance to the building. This was the stone upon which the building rested. It locked the corners together. It was generally a massive stone, not like a little cornerstone we set in a building today to commemorate the building. This stone was such an integral part of the building that if you were to take it out, the building would not be stable, nor would there be any significance. Everything was locked on it and built around it. Jesus is that strategic stone that gives the believer significance, direction, strength, and substance in the believer's life. "And He is before all things, and in Him all things consist" (Col. 1:17 NKJV). Jesus can be strategic in your life and in the church, however, there are so many individuals and churches who have been trying to build without Him. Therefore, it seems as though you cannot get the job done.

After Jesus shared the parable of the wicked vinedresser (Matt. 21:33-39), He asks the people a question concerning the owner who comes back (vs. 40). The people gave the answer (vs. 41), but it seems they missed the mark for Jesus said, "Have you never read in Scriptures: "The stone which the builders rejected has become the chief cornerstone. This was the Lord's doing, and it is marvelous in our eyes?"" (Matt. 21:42 NKJV). The answer the people is unique, they were so intrigued by the parable that they did not know that they just passed judgment on themselves. In verse 42, Jesus is quoting from Psalm 118:22-23 and He used these verses to explain to the people that He is the Son in the parable and the religious leaders are the evil vinedresser. Understand this, in the Old Testament, God is referred to as a rock or a stone (Deut. 32:4, 18, 30-31; Ps. 18:2, 31, 46). The stone is also messianic, therefore to Israel, Jesus was their stumbling stone (Isa.8:14-15; Rom. 9:32-33; 1 Cor. 1:23). However, when they rejected the Chief Cornerstone, through His death and resurrection Jesus created the church. Therefore, to the church, Jesus is our foundational stone, our head and Chief Cornerstone (Eph. 2:20-22; 1 Pet. 2:4-5). Of course, the Jewish religious leaders knew the importance of the messianic stone that Jesus was referring as He quoted Psalm 118:22-23. They were the builders rejecting the stone (Acts 4:11). Because of their unbelief, they stumbled over Him, therefore, they were judged, and the kingdom was taken away from Israel and given to another: the church (1 Pet. 2:9). Those who put their trust in Jesus find Him to be their foundation stone. However, Jesus was also referring to Daniel 2:34-35, 44-45, where the Messiah is pictured as a "smiting stone that crushes all that gets in the way. Those who would attack the stone would be destroyed; those who reject Jesus will be judged, crushed in His wrath in an eternity in hell.

What is odd the Jewish religious leaders knew their traditions, especially the tradition surrounding the building of Solomon's temple. Jewish tradition that tells us about the time when Solomon's Temple was being built, the enormous stones for the walls and the foundation were prepared at the quarry, after that they were shipped and brought to the Temple Mount. The reason they prepared them at the quarry is because they did not want the sound of a hammer and chisel, nor want the workmen to use an instrument on them. All they wanted is for the workmen to lay them into place. As they were laying the foundation, there was one stone of unusual size and peculiar shape that had been brought; but the workmen could not find a place for it at the time. Therefore, this stone was placed in the middle of the construction yard, and the workers kept stumbling on it; they kept falling over it. It was an annoyance, as it lay there in their way. It was in a way the rejected stone because they could not find a place for it. After a while, the construction foreman said, "What is that stone for? Where does it go?" No one could figure it out. So, the foreman had them get rid of it.

The workers take their bars and begin to pry that stone and move that stone, until they were able to tumble it off the Temple Mount, and down between the Temple Mount and the Mount of Olives, into the brook of Kidron, into the valley there, and then they continued their work. Then it came time to lay the cornerstone, and the builders searched for a long time to find a stone of sufficient size and strength, with the proper shape to fit into that corner and bear the great weight which would rest upon it. The foreman sent word to the quarry to send the cornerstone. The quarry sends back that it has already been shipped to them. Must the crew make an unwise choice for this important place which the safety of the entire building would be endangered? What they need is a stone that can withstand the weather elements. They looked at several different stones but there was not one that could stand the immense weight of the building for they would crumble to pieces. Finally, they remembered the stone that for so long was rejected and thrown off the Temple Mount. The rejected stone had been exposed to the air, the sun, and the storms, without the slightest crack. The builders examined the stone and ran every test but one. If it could bear the test of severe pressure, then they would accept it for their cornerstone. The trial was made, and the stone was accepted, brought to its assigned position, and fit exactly like it was supposed to.

The Bible confirms to us that this Cornerstone is Jesus, and it is only upon Him that any spiritual building can safely be places. Jesus says, "And I also say to you that you are Peter, and on this rock, I will build My church, and the gates of Hades shall not prevail against it" (Matt. 16:18 NKJV). Jesus used this illustration of Himself because this world is trying to build without Jesus. As a church we need to behave as a church that is built upon the Chief Cornerstone. The world says, "We are tired of Him. We stumble over Him. He is in our way. Get rid of Him, and we will go on and build our lives." Listen, you cannot build without Jesus Christ. "For no other foundation can anyone lay that which is laid, which is Jesus Christ" (1 Cor. 3:11 NKJV). If you are not building upon Jesus, then you are stumbling over the Chief Cornerstone because He is a strategic stone.

The Standard for the Church

Once you place Jesus in your heart and He is your foundation stone, then you should seek to know Him more by studying His word and worshipping Him in His house. Because Jesus is the most important person to a body of believers, therefore we must never leave Him out. As you study His word and get to know Jesus, your going to discover that Jesus was no ordinary teacher. He did not belong to the order of the scribes or pharisees, and He was not among the religious elite of the day. Jesus did not have a doctorate degree of the Law of Moses. Yet, He talked about the Law in a more penetrating fashion than anyone had ever done before, not hesitating to be critical of the so-called experts. Perhaps more than His words, people were also baffled by His behavior. He did not observe the Sabbath by keeping the oral traditions. He did not enforce their time-honored rules about fasting. To the religious leaders of His day, the most disconcerting behavior of them all was the fact that He associated with sinners; people who would render Him ceremonially unclean.

Because of His behavior some of the religious leaders took this to mean that He was teaching that there were no rules at all. What is ironic about this is the fact that this confusion remains today, maintained by those who suggest that Jesus abolished the Law and introduced an era of grace. Yet Jesus said standing before His disciples, "Do not think that I came to destroy the Law or the Prophets. I did not come to destroy but to fulfill" (Matt. 5:17 NKJV). From the sound of it, He was endorsing the backbreaking law-abiding of the religious hard-liners, advocating a lifestyle of sterile legalism. No, Jesus was no ordinary teacher. If Jesus is our standard, then how can anyone behave as a follower of Christ, or behave as a church member? How can we have this righteousness? Where does it come from?

Jesus went on to say, "For assuredly, I say to you, till heaven and earth pass away, one jot or one tittle will by no means pass from the law till all is fulfilled. Whoever therefore breaks one of the least of these commandments, and teaches men so, shall be called the least in the kingdom of heaven; but whoever does and teaches them, he shall be called great in the kingdom of heaven" (Matt. 5:18-19 NKJV). In the Law of Moses, God certainly revealed His standards for holy living. The pharisees were attempting to keep every letter of the Law but were breaking the spirit of the Law. They not only fell short of the Mosaic Law but fell short of the glory of God. Jesus called for righteousness that would exceed the righteousness of the scribes and pharisees. Jesus was to fulfill the law Himself, therefore His disciples also would share in the fulfillment of the Law of righteousness. Jesus was born under the Law (Gal. 4:4), fulfilled the law in His life and teaching, and He bore the curse of the law by His death on the cross (Gal. 3:13). To this day, He is still fulfilling the law's requirement through believers as He enables us to walk by the Spirit (Rom. 8:3-4).

The ones who were guilty of destroying the Law were the teachers of the law themselves. Because they were always trying to find loopholes that would enable them to obey the letter of the law, while at the same time ignoring the spirit and true intent of the Law. In which the Law revealed the need for a savior. So, the religious leaders were destroying the Law through their rejection of God's Messiah. However, Jesus understood that the purpose of God's Law was to promote holy living among God's people, or they were to behave as a church. Thus, Jesus became our standard by fulfilling the Law. Jesus fulfilled the Law several ways. First, He simplified it by rescuing the Law from all the traditions of man. Which was being added onto throughout the years as a way of control and manipulation. Another way He fulfilled the Law was He intensified it by moving the Law from mere outward conformity to the inner soul of man. This would give believers a righteousness that would exceed that of even the pharisees. Another way He fulfilled the Law was He internalized it by writing the Law upon our hearts and giving us the Holy Spirit. Therefore, He enables us to obey God's Law joyfully. Yes, it is true that there are many parts of the ceremonial law which were fulfilled in Christ which are no longer binding on God's people. But if we want to be the greatest in the kingdom of heaven (Matt. 5:19), we must have a desire to learn, love, and obey the Law of God by following Jesus who is our standard.

The Righteousness of the Church

In His sermon, Jesus took six important Old Testament laws and applied them in terms of daily living, making clear that the Father was not concerned about technicalities but about transformed hearts. He was focusing on prevention rather than punishment. These six applications are more than just ethical lessons, they were examples to show us that all our behaviors and attitudes have one motivating factor. That motivation can be in what Jesus said, "That you may be sons of your Father in heaven; for He makes His sun rise on the evil and on the good and sends rain on the just and the unjust" (Matt. 5:45 NKJV). When we behave as a church, our obedience gives evidence of our relationship with Jesus. We do not obey because we must, but because we want to obey.

WE WANT TO LOVE AND RESPECT OTHERS

Jesus begins with murder, He says, "You have heard that it was said to those of old, 'You shall not murder, and whoever murders will be in danger of the judgment'" (Matt. 5:21 NKJV). Most of us feel comfortable with the command not to murder. But Jesus shattered our self-righteousness by asserting that being angry with another person is just as bad (Matt. 5:21-22). There is a holy anger against sin, but Jesus talked about an unholy anger against people (vs. 23-26). He was talking about a settled anger, or malice that is nursed inwardly, this kind of anger is an irrational thing. It makes destroyers instead of builders. It robs us of freedom and makes us prisoners. To hate someone is to commit murder in our hearts. Jesus insisted that Kingdom people must be deal with their anger quickly and privately, not through public potshots but through private prayer and meditation time seeking restoration with the one we angry with. How can we come to the place of worship while we are stubbornly harboring a grudge with our brother? Unsettled anger imprisons us in bitterness, blocks the joy of our worship, and disrupts our church family fellowship.

WE WANT TO KEEP OURSELVES SEXUALLY PURE

Jesus said, "You have heard that it was said to those of old, 'You shall not commit adultery.'" (Matt. 5:27 NKJV). The very first command that we find in the Bible is found in Genesis 1:28 which says, "Then God blessed them, and God said to them, "Be fruitful and multiply; fill the earth and subdue it; have dominion over the fish of the sea, over the birds of the air, and over every living thing that moves on the earth" (NKJV). Jesus is reaffirming this command and then He explains that the intent of this command was to reveal the sanctity of sex and the sinfulness of the human heart. God created sex, and God protected sex, therefore, God has the authority to regulate it and to punish those who rebel against with immoral lifestyles even those who commit adultery. His purpose in regulating sex is not rob us of its pleasure but to protect its blessings in our lives. This is why Jesus urged His followers to maintain their sexual purity at the very point where it begins, with a lustful look (vs. 28-30). Now, He did not say, not to look, He said do not leer. Listen, I am not trying to create a grey area here, but we need to get a grip on this. Because it is not the glance that entraps a man but the focused stare, the deliberate decision to feed the sensual appetite. So how do we get victory from this? By purifying the desires of our heart and disciplining the actions of our body.

WE WANT TO KEEP OUR MARRIAGE VOWS

Divorce in biblical times was often an independent action on the man's part to rid himself of an unwanted wife. The rabbis of Jesus's day liked to debate the legal scenarios for divorce (Matt. 19:1-9), and some used Moses's instructions about the delivery of the certificate of divorce (Deut. 24:1-4) as convenient permission for ending an undesirable marriage. Jesus said, "furthermore it has been said, 'Whoever divorces his wife, let him give her a certificate of divorce.' But I say to you that whoever divorces his wife for any reason except sexual immorality causes her to commit adultery; and whoever marries a woman who is divorced commits adultery" (Matt. 5:31-32 NKJV). Jesus undercut this self-righteous rationale by reminding them that Moses made this certificate exception as a compromise based on the hardness of your hearts (Deut. 19:8), which hardly made it an honorable precedent to build one's case around. Jesus focused instead on God's original plan of marriage: one man and one woman bound together for a lifetime (Deut. 19:4-7). The divorce statistics in our country continue to mount, and tragically there is little difference when we compare the numbers in the church with those of society. God hates sin, and this sin of divorce creates untold suffering for His children and their children, who have been created as a new creation. "Therefore, if anyone is in Christ, he is a new creation; old things have passed away; behold all things have become new" (2 Cor. 5:17 NKJV). Behave as a church. The church should continue to affirm the importance of the marriage vows that are permanent, while at the same time offering full merc and forgiveness to those who have suffered from failed relationships.

WE WANT TO BE PEOPLE OF INTEGRITY

The rabbis of Jesus's day loved to have hair-splitting discussions about the relative value of different oaths or vows. "Again, you have heard that it was said to those of old, 'You shall not swear falsely, but shall perform your oaths to the Lord.'" (Matt. 5:33 NKJV). The Pharisees, who were unmatched in their ability to weave lavish reason for sidestepping the truth, would scrupulously avoid swearing by the name of the Lord. However, they would substitute something like heaven, the throne of God, earth, Jerusalem, or even inside the Law (vs. 34-36). Jesus cut right to the chase and said, "But let your 'Yes' be 'Yes,' and your 'No,' 'No.' For what ever is more than these is from the evil one" (vs. 37 NKJV). The use of oaths could never compensate the lace of integrity. The need for an oath was an admission of failure in some area of truthfulness. Jesus taught that our conversations should be honest, and our behavior so true, that we do not need extra help from oaths to get people to believe us. Because Jesus is our righteousness.

WE WANT A SPIRIT OF HUMILITY

The Mosaic Law stipulated an "eye for an eye" and a tooth for a tooth" to keep people from forcing an offender to pay a much higher price than his offense merited (Ex. 21:24; Lev. 24:20; Deut. 19:21; Matt. 5:38). Jesus moved beyond this law by calling His followers to a spirit of humility, instructing the offended party not to resort to retaliation. Jesus said, "But I tell you not to resist an evil person. But whoever slaps you on your right cheek, turn the other to him also. If anyone wants to sue you and take away your tunic, let him have your cloak also. And whoever compels you to go one mile, go with him two. Give to him who asks you, and from him who wants to borrow from you do not turn away" (Matt. 5:39-42 NKJV). This encouragement to turn the other cheek and to walk the second mile does not mean that we should never resist evil, nor does it mean that we should submit to injustice in our society. But what Jesus is getting at is that we should check our hearts to see if our first response was to return evil or aggression towards evil or aggression act against us. The behavior of the follower of Christ is designed to stop the escalation of violence. We should behave as a church willing to suffer loss rather than cause another to suffer. We should not only know but actively live out the promise that vengeance belongs to a holy God who is perfect in His retribution (Rom. 12:19-20). Plus, we should be willing to forego legitimate rights if it is helpful in the spread of the gospel. Behave as church members who are peacemakers not backbiters.

WE WANT TO BE PERFECT IN LOVE

Jesus states, "You have heard that it was said, 'You shall love your neighbor and hate your enemy' (Matt. 5:43 NKJV). This is interesting, because you will not find any encouragement in the Old Testament Law for a person to hate his enemy, and yet the rabbis were quoting and practicing this. The Old Testament does make a clear distinction between a person's attitude towards both his fellow Israelite and the non-Israelite. But it appears that this distinction may have been twisted by some to condone a hatred of the Gentiles. But Jesus demanded a love that does not discriminates. He said, "But I say to you, love your enemies, bless those who curse you, do good to those who hate you, and pray for those who spitefully use you and persecute you, that you may be sons of your Father in heaven; for He makes His sun rise on the evil and on the good, and sends rain on the just and the unjust" (vs. 44-45 NKJV). This does not mean we have to like the things some people do; or even like the people themselves, as far as having feelings of affection towards them. But love demands that we be concerned for the welfare of our enemies and pray for them. When we love our enemies, we are behaving like Jesus (Rom. 5:10). If we only love those who love us back, how will people see the need for the gospel of Jesus in their lives? Listen to how Jesus put it, "For if you love those who love you, what reward have you? Do even the tax collectors do the same? And if you greet your brethren only, what do you do more than others? Do not even the tax collectors do so? Therefore, you shall be perfect, just as your Father in heaven is perfect" (Matt. 5:46-48 NKJV). Behave as a church for Jesus is our righteousness. Because of everything Jesus does for us and through us, Jesus should be the most important person in the church and should never be left out. The church should revolve around Jesus, not Jesus revolving around the church or individual Christians. Jesus should be at the center of every ministry, worship service, and fellowship of the bride of Christ. Behave as a church.

CHAPTER THIRTEEN

What Everyone Should Bring to Church

Serve the Lord with Gladness; come
before His presence with singing.
(Psalm 100:2 NKJV)

DID YOU KNOW THAT PEOPLE BRING ALL KINDS OF STUFF TO CHURCH when they come. People bring their emotional baggage, their hurts, their sin, their suffering, their burdens, and we should bring those things for Peter writes, "casting all your care upon Him, for He cares for you" (1 Pet. 5:7 NKJV). Then there are some people who bring snacks, candy, even toys to entertain the kids. I have seen a few people read other books while the sermon is being preached. There are some who think that it is a good time to balance their checkbooks. While other make out a grocery list or plan their activities for after church. There are those who pull out their nail clippers and trim their fingernails or they pull out their fingernail paint and paint their nails. Some play on an iPad or smartphone during the service. There was one lady that came to church with her little Yorkie dog and sat him in the pew with her. He was not even a service help dog, just her pet. These are not necessarily bad things, but they can be a distraction and there are some things that should be left at the house! But of course, there are those who bring their Bible when they come, if they have a Bible. There are some things every churchgoer, especially church members, should bring to church.

For example, we are encouraged in Ephesians 5:18 to be filled with the Spirit of God, and the evidence of this fullness is that we are joyful (vs. 19), thankful (vs. 20), and submissive (vs. 21). Over in Colossians 3:16-25, we are instructed to be filled with the Word of God, and when we are we will be joyful (vs. 16), thankful (vs. 17), and submissive (vs. 20). There are three behaviors of the believer that are controlled by the Holy Spirit and God's Word. These are presented in Psalm 100, which is a psalm of thanksgiving. It is also a psalm of the future millennial kingdom as it describes what worship will be like in the day when the Lord Jesus Christ reigns in glory and power upon the earth. We are not in that glorious day right now, but we are in the family of God, and we are commanded to gather ourselves together and worship Him as we see that day approaching (Heb. 10:25).

I am afraid the bride of Christ today is taking the privilege of going to the church building and assemble as a family is a privilege that we are taking for granted. For instance, how much preparation do you put into going to church? How much time do you spend getting your heart ready for corporate worship? Do you pray for the services? Do you seek the Lord's face and ask Him to move in power when we come together? Most of us just come to church without giving a second thought to what we come together as a church family for. The Bible has more to say about how we are to go to church. Paul wrote, "These things I write to you, though I hope to come to you shortly; but if I am delayed, I write so that you may know how you ought to conduct yourself in the house of God, which is the church of the living God, the pillar and ground of the truth" (1 Tim. 3:14-15 NKJV). King Solomon writes, "Walk prudently when you go to the house of God; and draw near to hear rather than to give the sacrifice of fools, for they do not know that they do evil" (Eccl. 5:1 NKJV). Keeping those things in mind, what should everyone bring to church?

Bring the Right Spirit

The psalmist writes, "Make a joyful shout to the Lord, all you lands! Serve the Lord with gladness; come before His presence with singing" (Ps. 100:1-2 NKJV). There are at least three kinds of spirits you should bring to church. The first is, a shouting spirit. For some church members this is not a problem, however, in the Southern Baptist church there are some that will think a person is weird or that they are over emotional if they shout. I, personally, love to shout and sing in the Southern Baptist church that I attend. There is nothing wrong with shouting God's praise in His house. After all, those who do not want to shout at church, will go down to the stadium for their favorite professional sports team and when their team wins, they go crazy. Shouting things like, "We won!" Think about this, those players on the team do not even know you. The jersey of your favorite player that you wear does not even know you. If you are a true child of God, you are clothed in His robe of righteousness, and He made you a starter on His team when you were not even worthy to be drafted! Therefore, you should have a desire to "make a joyful shout to the Lord" (vs. 1 NKJV). Let me break this command from the Lord. The word "make" implies that we are to make music (Strong's Concordance, 1984) It is used to refer to singing and to the psalms. The Jewish people in those days would sing the psalms and hymns unto the Lord. The next word is "joyful," it means "to give a public confession of attributes and works of God" (Strong's Concordance, 1984) The last word we want to look at is the word "shout." It refers to a "ringing cry" ((Strong's Concordance, 1984) This shout should be a shout that pierces the eardrum. When all these words are put together, we can see that the psalmist is calling on the people of the Lord to raise an anthem of praise from their hearts to the Lord.

The next spirit you should bring to church is a serving spirit. The word "serve" means "to be a slave, to be in bondage to" (Concise Oxford English Dictionary Eleventh Edition, 2004) It refers to doing whatever the master tells you to do. In other words, as a child of God you are to be at His beckoning. When we got saved, we became the Lord's property (1 Cor. 6:20). Therefore, we are to do what He tells us to do without question or hesitation. There are some church members who do not like that idea. There are Christians who do not want anyone telling them what to do. Listen, if you did not like what you just read, then you will not like what I got to say next. We are to serve the Lord with gladness. That little word "gladness" means "with mirth, merriment, joy unspeakable, laughter" (Wood, Marshall, & Millard, 1996) Psalm 100:2 is telling us that we are to serve the Lord, be at His beckoning, with laughter! We are to be so filled with love for Him that regardless of what He has asked us to do, we are tickled pink to do it! This is the behavior that filled David's heart, he said, "I was glad when they said to me, "Let us go into the house of the Lord."" (Ps. 122:1 NKJV). He was filled with mirth when it was time to go worship the Lord!

The last spirit I want to tell you about is, you should have a singing spirit. In verse 2 we are told to approach the Lord our God with singing. This little word refers, as previously stated, a ringing cry, the shout of joy. Our hearts should be so filled with the wonder of Who He is and what He has done for us that we allow His praise to burst forth from our inner beings. The first two verses of Psalm 100 tell us that when God is in your life, you will not be able to hide Him! You will not keep Him a secret for very long! You cannot have someone the size of God in your heart without Him getting out now and then! Sometimes He will run out your eyes, sometimes He will show up in your raised hands; and sometimes He will run up your throat and over your vocal cords and make you shout! The fact is you will not be able to contain Him.

TWO KINDS OF PEOPLE

Over in Luke 18:9-14, Jesus gives us a glimpse into the Temple as some people gathered to worship. Jesus said, "Two men went up to the temple to pray, one a Pharisee and the other a tax collector" (vs. 10 NKJV). As you look at these two men, see which one has the right kind of spirit. The first man that Jesus tells us about is a Pharisee. He was a spiritual leader among the people. He was known and respected as a man of God who knew the scriptures and had many of them committed to memory. When he came to the temple to pray that day, he wore the leather box on his right wrist and forehead that contained certain special portions of the Law (Matt. 23:5). Being a Pharisee, he would have prayed at least three times a day, because the Pharisees made a big deal over prayer. As a matter of fact, Pharisees loved to pray out loud with long prayers and in public so others could see them (Matt. 6:5-8). Adding to this public prayer time, is the fact that Pharisees loved to fast twice a week which would happen to be on Monday and Thursday. This so happens to be at the same time they would go into the markets to buy and sell their wares. This means the Pharisees were letting everyone see that they were fasting (Matt. 6:16-18). The way the people in the marketplace knew that Pharisees were fasting is because they would not comb their hair or wash their face, and they wore the most wrinkled and rumpled clothing they could find. They would even put ashes on their faces to make themselves look as though they were pale from fasting. As the Pharisee would make his way into the temple, he would make his way to the offering box, in front of everyone, and make a big deal over his offering that he was giving to temple (Matt. 6:1-4). He would tithe on everything he possessed, even the herbs that grew in his garden (Matt. 23:23), often giving between twenty and thirty percent.

What we have here is a very religious man, considered to be holy by everyone who saw him, and yet he had the wrong kind of spirit. His spirit was one that loved the adoration that came his way from the common people around him (Matt. 23:5-7). His kind of spirit reminds me that there are many in churches today. There are those in church who think they are pure, holy, and righteous and has everyone around them convinced of these things. If everyone around them does not line up with himself, he is convinced that they are wrong.

The other man who came to pray that day was a publican, a tax collector. This man was a social and spiritual outcast. Yes, he was welcome to come to the temple to pray in the court of the Jews, he was not allowed to attend the meetings at the synagogue. The other Jews hated him and looked down on him because he was a tax collector that worked for Rome; a government that was oppressing Israel at the time. Here is the reason a tax collector was hated in those days. The chief tax collector would pay Rome for a certain area or district, which would give him the authority to collect taxes there. He would then sub-lease that district to tax collectors. The chief tax collector could set his own rates and the men who worked for him could set their own rates. As a result, Rome received its taxes, the chief tax collector would receive his taxes, and the tax collectors would receive his taxes, and all were getting wealthy from extorting large sums of money from the common people. As a tax collector, the man who came to pray at the temple that day would have been know for his greed and his dishonesty. He would have been viewed as a traitor to Israel and not even worthy of any compassion or concern from the Jews around him. This man is a picture of those who do not act like we think they should, or dress like we think they should, or say things like we think they should. But just like the publican, there are folks in our churches that others look down on who think they are more spiritual. Yet, this publican as we will see had the right spirit.

TWO KINDS OF PRAYER

"The Pharisee stood and prayed thus with himself, 'God, I thank You that I am not like other men; extortioners, unjust, adulterers, or even as this tax collector. I fast twice a week; I give tithes of all that I possess.' And the tax collector, standing afar off, would not so much as raise his eyes to heaven, but beat his breast, saying, 'God, be merciful to me a sinner!'" (Luke 18:11-13 NKJV). Both men, the self-righteous pharisee and the wicked publican, are praying in the temple. When they open their mouths and begin to speak that is when the true character of their hearts is put on display. Here we see that you really cannot judge a book by its cover. The man everyone thought was righteous was really a hypocrite, while the Lord accepted the man everyone looked down on. As you look at the two prayers of these men, their words and their behavior have something to teach us about bringing the right spirit when we come to church.

When the pharisee begins his prayer, it was an arrogant prayer, because he was quick to tell the Lord how things really are in his life. Remember he is bragging about being righteous and comparing himself to other men. Because he is praying with eyes open, he can see the publican praying near by and tells God how much more he is than the publican. If you really examine the pharisees prayer you will begin to think that the pharisee did not really go to the temple to pray, he just went to inform God how good he was. Again, think about what he says in his prayer. He brags about being righteous and doing religious works. He brags about his giving and tells the Lord how great and wealthy he is. As he compares himself to others, he feels that he has arrived in the eyes of the Lord. Let me point out, that it was common for pharisees to stand when they prayed, spreading their arms out, lifting their voices as loud as they could launching into long complicated self-serving prayer. His prayer only got as far as the roof of his mouth. May God help us not to behave as a church full of people who pray like this pharisee!

The publican does not offer any swelling words of self-glorification, instead he prays a humble prayer. He knows he has nothing at all to offer the Lord. He knows that he is a wicked sinner, and he prays with no pride, no pretense, no hint of self-righteousness, and there are no attempts to justify himself or his lifestyle in the eyes of the Lord. He just tells the truth and humbles himself before God and asks for mercy. He will not even lift his eyes toward heaven. He beats himself on the chest, knowing that his real problem is a problem of the heart. The pharisee, on the other hand, is blissfully unaware that anything is wrong in his heart. The publican's prayer is short, simple, and to the point.

Let me mention a few thoughts about the prayers of these two men that teach us about having the right kind of spirit to bring to church. Prayer is not to become a ritual in church. The Jews prayed, but often their prayers were scripted, and the form was already set. They either quoted a prayer from memory or read them. Thus, a Jew could pray and not even think about what he was saying. Predetermined prayers were formulated for every aspect of life. Every conceivable turn of life had a prayer that had been developed to deal with the issue. This also led to prayer being something that could be recited from the head and not out of the right spirit. Many prayers were comprised of meaningless repetition and the Jews were notorious for repeating phrases and adding adjectives to the name of God thinking they would be heard by God. This was a pagan practice which sadly found its way into some Christian circles today.

The desire to be seen and heard by others is probably one of the worst offenses of all. Prayer had ceased to be about communion with God and degenerated into an attempt to impress others. Therefore, the Jews held long prayers in high regard. The Jews believed that the longer and more elaborate the prayer, the more likely it was to be heard by God. Jesus warned against this practice (Matt. 12:30). There is nothing wrong with long prayer times, just as long as the Spirit is moving in that time. However, when a person is praying a long time to impress others, which is what the Jews were doing, now they have crossed the line into preaching. Prayer is not a time to preach. When the pharisee prayed, he was not talking to the Lord, he was talking to himself and for the benefit of those around him (Luke 18:11-12). If you want to preach, ask God to call you to preach and do your preaching from the pulpit, but do not use your prayer as an opportunity to correct other people. Prayers should be specific and to the point, rather than general and rambling. We should go before God to honor Him and seek His face. It is not a time to brag, it should be a time that is spent with the Lord focused on Him and His glory. We should be seeking His face to ask Him to bless us, to ask Him to move among us, to pray for those around you, to humble yourself in His presence, to acknowledge your need of Him in your daily life, to praise and glorify Him, to seek His power in your life, and to thank Him for His blessings. How is your prayer life spent? What kind of spirit are you bringing to church?

Both these men went to the house of prayer and stood where God promised He would hear His people when they prayed (2 Chron. 7:15). Both men prayed, but the outcome was different for both men. One man went to church and left with nothing. He went through the rituals, judged others by his standards, prayed a self-serving prayer, and worshipped himself. This man went home feeling good about himself but received nothing from God for his efforts. The other man went to church and left with everything. He did not make a spiritual show, he prayed a simple prayer, and offered God honesty, confession, and worship. He left church right with the Lord. What was the difference between the two? The difference was in the attitude and condition of their hearts. One was full of himself and thought he needed nothing more. The other knew he was nothing and possessed nothing. He humbled himself before God and he was blessed. We should behave as a church by having the right spirit when we come to church.

Bring the Right Submission

When we come to church, we are to come bringing the right submission. The psalmist writes, "Know that the Lord, He is God; it is He who has made us, and not we ourselves; we are His people and the sheep of His pasture" (Ps. 100:3 NKJV). We are told to "know" that Lord is God. This word means "to make a distinction" (Dictionary, 1828) We are to know by a distinct determination in our hearts and minds that He and He alone is God! Therefore, we are to submit to the person of God for who He is. So, who is your God? Is your God the God of the Bible? But how can we know who or what is our God and is it even possible? Well, answer this question: What do you give most of your time, attention, and money to? Whoever or whatever you answered that question with is your God. Have you made the right distinction? Have you acknowledged that God Almighty, El Shaddai, Jehovah as the God of your life? Listen, if you ever get it nailed down in your soul that He is the God and that He is superior to every other person, thing, or activity in your life; then you will have no problem behaving as a church and serving Him as you should. The reason why some people have trouble tithing, going to church, or just serving God as they should is that they have a different god than the God of the Bible.

The psalmist goes on to remind us that we are what we are because He has "made" us. This word simply means "to take some material and fashion something new out of it" (Wood, Marshall, & Millard, 1996) God took the clay, which was us, and formed a new creature out of it by His power. Regardless of what we are, we are what are by the power of God (1 Cor. 15:10). When a person gets saved, accepts Jesus in their heart, God takes that first creation and makes something even newer and better out of it (2 Cor. 5:17). Therefore, because we are saved, He saved us for a purpose, and we are to submit to the purpose of God. He did not redeem us to keep us out of hell nor did he redeem us so that we could feel good from time to time. He did not save us so we could look down our long religious noses at lost people and feel superior. He saved us so we might serve Him. "For we are His workmanship, created in Christ Jesus for good works, which God prepared beforehand that we should walk in them" (Eph. 2:10 NKJV).

Because He is God, and He has made us, we should submit to the promises of God. After all, we are the sheep of His pasture. That statement should remind us that we belong to Him and He is the Shepherd. Just as a shepherd looks after the welfare of his flock, the Lord God will look after us with intimate care. David had this nailed down in his own life and expressed in his psalm (Ps. 23). You and I should get this nailed down in our own lives as well. If we could ever grasp the truth the "The Lord is my Shepherd" (Ps. 23:1 NKJV) then it would transform our lives and we could bring the right submission to church. We would realize that we never have to worry about our needs being met. We would never have to fear anything that comes up against us. We have His promises and His guarantee that everything is in His control. Here are some of His precious promises. "Now He who searches the hearts knows what the mind of the Spirit is, because He makes intercession for the saints according to the will of God. And we know that all things work together for the good of those who love God, to those who are called according to His purpose" (Rom. 8:27-28 NKJV). "Be anxious for nothing, but in everything by prayer and supplication, with thanksgiving, let your requests be made know to God; and the peace of God, which surpasses all understanding, will guard your hearts and minds through Christ Jesus" (Phil. 4:6-7 NKJV). "Let your conduct be without covetousness; be content with such things as you have. For He Himself has said, "I will never leave you nor forsake you"" (Heb. 13:5 NKJV, see also Matt. 6:25-34). If you are saved, you belong to the Chief Shepherd and He will take care of the needs that arise in your life. The problem we have is that we do not bring the right submission into His presence, and we must learn to trust Him as we should.

Bring the Right Sacrifice

The psalmist tells us, "Enter into His gates with thanksgiving, and into His courts with praise. Be thankful to Him and bless His name. For the Lord is good; His mercy is everlasting, and His truth endures to all generation" (Ps. 100:4-5 NKJV). In the Tabernacle and Temple days, the priests had better not enter the presence of the Lord without the right sacrifice because to do so would have meant their death. "But into the second part the high priest went alone once a year, not without blood, which he covered for himself and for the people's sins committed in ignorance" (Heb. 9:7 NJKV). Praise the Lord, we do not have to offer a blood sacrifice at church, because Jesus Christ has already taken care of that sacrifice forever (Heb. 10:10-14). When you read those verses, you must pay special attention to the words "one" and "once". However, even though Jesus made the ultimate sacrifice, there is still a sacrifice that we need to behave as a church member and as a church. The sacrifice is not your money, although you should be bringing tithes to the church where you have your membership, or you are committed to supporting. The sacrifice is not your attendance, although you should be at church at every possible opportunity. There is just one sacrifice the Lord expects every saint to bring to church when they come, and it is revealed in the last two verses of Psalm 100. We are told to bring the sacrifice of "praise."

We are to offer a sacrifice of praise. Someone might say, "But I thought only priests could be the ones who offer sacrifices?" Peter writes, "You also, as living stones, are being built up a spiritual house, a holy priesthood, to offer up spiritual sacrifices acceptable to God through Jesus Christ" (1 Pet. 2:5 NKJV). Notice that phrase, "a holy priesthood." Not only are our bodies temples of God, but we are also priests who minister in the temple; we ourselves are a priesthood. Now I know, someone might be thinking, "The Roman Catholics have priest, the Episcopalians have priest, and the Greek Orthodox have priest, but the Southern Baptist do not have priests." Southern Baptist have priests, and if you want to see them go to a Southern Baptist church and look around at the people in the pews, in the choir, look at the pastor; you are looking at priests. We are all priest of God; the great truth is children of God have been born again and through Jesus we have direct access to the Father. I can go directly to God for myself.

OUR PRIVILEGE AS PRIESTS

"Therefore, brethren, having boldness to enter the Holiest by the blood of Jesus, by a new and living way which He consecrated for us, through the veil, that is, His flesh" (Heb. 10:19-20 NKJV). In the Old Testament, the temple had three parts: the outer court, the inner court, and the innermost court. That innermost court was called the Holy of Holies, and only the priest could go in there once a year to make atonement for the people. He had to lift the corner of the veil and he would slip under. Then he would go in there and sprinkle blood upon the Mercy Seat, which was on top of the Ark of the Covenant. If anyone else went in, or anybody went in without blood sacrifice; it would mean immediate and sudden death. The people had to stay outside while the priest went in on their behalf. Now remember, when Jesus died on the cross, the Bible tells us that the veil of the temple was torn in two from the top to the bottom. Not from the bottom to the top, but from the top to the bottom as though God was the one who tore the veil. The fact that God did this is highly significant. Because by His death on the cross, Jesus is telling us that there is no more need of animal sacrifice. Which means that through His death the Old Testament economy is done, and now every one child of God has become priest and we have a special privilege that we can come boldly into the Holy of Holies into His presence with the sacrifice of praise.

OUR PRACTICE AS PRIESTS

What is our duty as priests? Peter says we are to offer up spiritual sacrifices (1 Pet. 2:5). What are spiritual sacrifices that I am to offer? Romans 12:1 tells me that I am to present my body as a living sacrifice. In other words, we surrender our lives to Him, making ourselves available to Him. In the Old Testament, the priest would burn incense, so, what do I do? The psalmist says, we are to offer up sacrifice of praise (Ps. 100:5). Hebrews 13:15 tells us that we are to offer to Him the sacrifice of praise continually. Our praise and our prayers are just as if the incense would be going up and out of that temple, out of my heart, out of my life, day by day, moment by moment, there is to be praise to my wonderful Lord and Savior. What should I praise Him for?

First, we can praise Him for His goodness. We are told, "The Lord is good" (Ps. 100:5 NKJV). This seems like a limited description for God, but the word "good" means, "good, pleasant, beautiful, delightful, glad, joyful, precious, expensive, correct, and righteous" (Strong's Concordance, 1984) Everything God does is an expression of His goodness! We can praise our Lord because He is good! Regardless of what happens in life, God is good! No matter how things turn out, God is still good! Therefore, praise Him for His goodness!

Second, we can praise Him for His grace. The psalmist tells us that God's "mercy is everlasting" (vs. 5 NKJV). We can praise God because He is constantly extending His mercy to us as we go through life. Mercy is defined as not getting what you deserve. We live in a day and age when everyone wants what is coming to them. Not me, if I got what I deserved from God I would be in a place called hell. If I got what I deserved, I would experience the undiluted wrath and fierceness of the Lord. Instead of getting what I deserved, God showed me mercy. When I accept His gift of grace, through Jesus's shed blood at Calvary, He is holding back His wrath from off my life. Why? Because Jesus took my place on an old, cruel, Roman cross. While He was dying there, all my sins were transferred to Him and He died in my place. As He was dying, God looked at Jesus and saw my sins. He saw me hanging there that day and He poured out His wrath into the Person of His own darling Son. God extinguished His wrath towards me that day, and now I enjoy His mercy, His grace. His Mercy will never be exhausted, and we will never use it up (Lam. 3:22-23).

Lastly, we can praise His guarantee. The psalmist tells us that God's "truth endures to all generations" (Ps. 100:5 NKJV). Simply stated, while the years pile up on our lives, not a single promise of God's word will fail! We know that God cannot lie (Heb. 6:18), and therefore, what He has promised in one year will still be as good in ten thousand years, even as it was the instant, He promised it. When He tells you He loves you, then you can count on it being the truth. When He tells you He will save you if you come to Him, you can count on it being the truth. If He tells you He will take care of you, you can count on it. If He tells you that He is coming back, mark it down you can count on it! If He tells you that He will keep you saved, you can count on it. Suffice it to say that if the Lord tells you anything at all, you can count on it. But FYI, if God tells you anything at all, even from His Holy Word, then there is nothing you can do to change it, stop it, or divert it. It will come to pass just as He said it will. Therefore, all of this would be a good reason to praise the Lord.

OUR PROFESSION AS PRIESTS

Peter writes, "But you are a chosen generation, a royal priesthood, a holy nation, His own special people, that you may proclaim the praises of Him who called you out of darkness into His marvelous light" (1 Pet. 2:9 NKJV). Do you know what I am to be doing as a priest? I am to make God known to man and to bring man to God. I do this by "going" and "telling" people. I am to behave like a follower of Christ representing Christ in front of a lost world, and I am to behave as a church member loving my fellow brothers and sisters in Christ. As a family of God, we are to behave as a church reaching the lost by behaving as fishers of men bringing a lost world to Christ. When I do all this, I am showing forth His praise.

Do you know about the garments the high priest would wear when he would go into the Holy of Holies? In Exodus 28 we find the description of what the high priest had to wear. We know that he had to wear the ephod, robe, and breastplate, but there are other priestly garments he also had to wear. "And upon it hem you shall make pomegranates of blue, purple, and scarlet, all around its hem, and bell of gold between them all around: a golden bell and a pomegranate, a golden bell, and a pomegranate, upon the hem of the robe all around. And it shall be upon Aaron when he ministers, and its sound will be heard when he goes into the holy place before the Lord and when he comes out, that he may not die" (Ex. 28:33-35 NKJV). So, the high priest had to wear on the hem of his robe pomegranates and bells. When the priest would go into minister, the people would be listening for the bells. If they did not hear any bells, they would think that God killed him. They were listening to see if he went in with blood, if he did everything just right, because the Bible says, if those bells do not ring the high priest has died.

Think on this, if I do not confess Christ as my personal Savior and Lord, I have no spiritual light, therefore, I die spiritually if I do not confess Him. The bells speak of profession and the pomegranates speak of possession of the Holy Spirit in my heart. Now, as a believer-priest, you are to ring those bells. If your belles are not ringing, you are dead! Dead! You are not saved. Jesus said, "For whoever is ashamed of Me and My words in this adulterous and sinful generation, of him the Son of Man also will be ashamed when He comes in the glory of His Father with the holy angels" (Mark 8:38 NKJV). Peter says we are to show forth His praise (1 Pet. 2:9). We are to behave as a church because you have a bell to ring. But not only are we to ring the bells, we are to wear the fruit. If a man is always confessing Christ, but there is no fruit in his life, then he is not saved. You are not saved by bearing fruit, you are saved to bear fruit. So, there is something beautiful about a bell and a pomegranate, a bell and a pomegranate, a bell and a pomegranate. There is that profession (telling with your mouth) and the possession (living what you say by your behavior). How beautiful is that? On the hem of my garments today, I want those golden bells and that luscious fruit. I want the fruit of the Spirit of the Lord Jesus to show in my life because He has made me a holy priesthood, and you he has made a holy priesthood, and we have the privilege of going into the throne room every day. Are you bringing the right things to church? Are we behaving as a church?

CHAPTER FOURTEEN

What Does God Think of You?

For I know the thoughts that I think towards
you, says the Lord, thoughts of peace and not
evil, to give you a future and a hope.
(Jeremiah 29:11 NKJV)

POPULATION SCIENTISTS TELL US THAT THERE ARE OVER EIGHT billion people on the face of the earth. This is a number that is almost beyond comprehension. To try and get an idea of how many people this is, try to imagine that you took every person in the world and lined them up shoulder to shoulder in rows of one hundred. The line of people that would be formed would reach almost around the world at the equator. That is an amazing mass of humanity. You may feel that among a number that size, you are an insignificant person. You may feel that the Lord does not have time for someone like yourself. Perhaps you believe the Lord is too busy looking after the universe and maintaining this thing to have time to be concerned about you. Yet, the Bible teaches us that God knows everything there is to know about each of the eight billion humans upon the face of the earth today.

Take the prophet Jeremiah for example. He is the inspired writer of two books of the Bible: Jeremiah and Lamentations. He is known as the weeping prophet and the book of Lamentation is a good example of his behavior. The book of Lamentations is a series of hymns, or songs of mourning, which were written against the backdrop of the

Babylonian invasion and destruction of Jerusalem. In this book, we see the awful sufferings endured by the people of Israel in that city at the hands of their enemies. Yet during all the pain and turmoil, God knew a man, thought about this man, and used this man to bring honor the name of the Lord. Jeremiah did not ask to be a prophet, God already had Jeremiah in mind to call him as a minister (Jer. 1:5-6). When God issued His call to Jeremiah, He told him that he would be preaching nothing but judgment to the people (vs. 9-10). God even told him that he was not to be married, so that he could have a more fulfilling ministry of proclaiming the impending judgment of God (Jer. 16:1-3). Therefore, Jeremiah knew what it means to be alone and think that God is not concerned. Jeremiah was a man of deep sadness, and he wept openly about the sins of the people (Jer. 9:1). He endured depression as the result of his message going ignored for so long. He even came to the point where he tried to get out of the ministry (Jer. 20:9). His pain is understandable, because in the ministry of Jeremiah that had span over fifty years, there is no record of one convert. That is the commitment we must behave as a church with. Jeremiah suffered imprisonment by King Zedekiah, because the king did not approve of Jeremiah's preaching (Jer. 32:5). Even while the Babylonians were invading the city of Jerusalem as a fulfillment of his prophecy, Jeremiah was sitting in the dungeon (vs. 2). After Jerusalem falls and many have been killed or taken captive, the prophet does not gloat nor take an "I told you so" mentality. Instead, he becomes broken with the remnant and enters suffering with them. Thus, the book of Lamentations is written.

After enduring a life like this; after being rejected, hated, mocked, imprisoned, ignored; after seeing his beloved Jerusalem ransacked, desecrated, and destroyed; after experiencing the horror of war, the brutality of the enemy and the pangs of hunger, Jeremiah was still able to stand for amid the rubble of the city and the bodies of the dead and lift his voice in praise to God for His great, unfailing faithfulness to His people. Jeremiah praises the Lord because the Lord said, "For I know the thoughts that I think towards you', says the Lord, 'thoughts of peace and not of evil, to give you a future and a hope'" (Jer. 29:11 NKJV). The truth is this verse teaches us that the

Lord God does think about you and me. Of course, this is a word which was spoke to the people of Israel concerning their Babylonian captivity and the promise of their safe return to their homeland. However, there is an application here for the church. You may feel that God does not think about you at all, but I would like to tell you that He does!

Despite his trials and his troubles, Jeremiah had gotten a good grasp on the reality of just Who God is! Jeremiah knew that whether things went well, or whether everything fell apart, God would still be God and He would be eternally faithful to His people. Jeremiah was still able to find hope in a hopeless situation because he believes in the faithfulness of God and that God knew who Jeremiah was.

How well does God really know you?

God knows the thoughts that He has towards you. Yes, God was saying these words to the nation of Israel because they were in captivity in Babylon. He was reminding them that despite their pain and suffering they were on His mind. He was letting them know He is working out His perfect will in their lives (Rom. 8:27-28). When He is finished, He will change them. When Israel went into Babylon as prisoners, they were guilty of idolatry. When they came out of captivity, they never resorted to that sin again. God used a time when they thought they were forgotten and forsaken, to make them stronger and better for His glory.

This statement is also a reminder that of all the people in the world, God has His mind on you. He sees you not as just another member of the vast human race, but as an individual. He has specific thoughts about you, cares about you, and as an individual you are on His mind. People often wonder just what God knows about them. The fact is, God knows everything there is to know about you and me! The Bible is clear when it talks about the scope of God's knowledge our lives (Jer. 1:5). If you let the truths of the Bible sink into your soul, you may find them a bit overwhelming, but in truth, the knowledge that God has about you can be comforting and should cause us to behave as a church.

First, the knowledge that God has about you is intimate. Jesus said, "Are not two sparrows sold for a copper coin? And not one of them falls to the ground apart from your Father's will. But the very hairs of your hair are all numbered. Do not fear therefore, you are of more value than many sparrows" (Matt. 10:29-31 NKJV). Jesus tells us the value that God places on His creation, all lives matter! Even the little sparrow that falls to the ground does not escape the attention of Jehovah God. The reality for us is that the Father is so concerned about our lives that He knows the very number of hairs which are upon our heads. If He is concerned about something as insignificant as that, then we can rest assured that He will take care to watch over the weightier issues of life. Since His knowledge of our lives is so detailed, then we can be sure that He knows every possible thing there is to know about us in an intimate way. The Lord knows our deepest and darkest secrets; He knows our thoughts, our motives, our plans, and our dreams.

Next, God knowledge about us is infinite. In Psalm 139, David tells us that the Lord is everywhere, beholding everything. Even before we came into this world, God was looking upon us and had already determined exactly how we would turn out. David writes, "Your eyes saw my substance, being yet unformed. And in Your book, they all were written, the days fashioned for me, when as yet there were none of them" (Ps. 139:16 NKJV). While it is plain to see that God knows the most intimate details of our lives, we must never forget that He knows every detail of our lives. David praises that fact, "How precious also are Your thoughts to me, O God! How great is the sum of them!" (vs. 17 NKJV). God misses nothing that we do. He sees it all and regardless of where we go, God is still watching our lives. Remember Jonah? Jonah tried to flee from the presence of God, but he ran right into the Lord. He is everywhere and He sees and knows it all!

Furthermore, the knowledge that God has about us is instant. Job said, "I know that you can do everything, and that no purpose of Yours can be withheld from You" (Job 42:2 NKJV). David writes, "For there is not a word on my tongue, but behold, O Lord, You know it altogether" (Ps. 139:4 NKJV). The knowledge of the Lord regarding our lives is always before the Lord. He knows them the instant things are spoken, and the instant things happen. Solomon writes, "Every way of a man is right in his own eyes, but the Lord weighs the heart" (Prov. 21:2 NKJV). If He knows when the sparrow falls to the ground, then He knows when we stub our toe, make plans, or when we regard iniquity in our hearts. God's eye is constantly upon the affairs of your life and my life. "The eyes of the Lord are in every place, keeping watch on the evil and the good" (Prov. 15:3 NKJV). This should be an encouragement to us because we should know that nothing that happens in our life catches the Lord off guard. He knows about our situation before it happens. "Declaring the end from the beginning, and from ancient times things that are not yet done, saying, 'My counsel shall stand, and I will do all My pleasure'" (Isa. 46:10 NKJV). The situation you find yourself in it had to pass through the filter of grace before it could even make it to you (Rom. 8:27-28). David sums this up like this, "Such knowledge is too wonderful for me; it is high, I cannot attain it" (Ps. 139:6 NKJV). If you are trying to hide something from the Lord, then His knowledge is a terrible thing because you are getting away with nothing! However, when you are striving to serve the Lord, by behaving, His knowledge is a blessing, because the Lord knew everything that came to pass in your life before He ever allowed it to come your way.

What is revealed by God's knowledge of you?

Since we can plainly see from Scriptures that the Lord sees every single detail of our lives, what does all this knowledge about us reveal? There are two areas of life that are constantly before the Lord. The first is, God knows about your sins. God knew all of Israel's sins! There was nothing in their hearts or their lives that He did not know. People can be oblivious when it comes to their sins. They often behave as if God cannot see them or is not aware of what they are doing. However, since the first sin was committed in the Garden of Eden, God has witnessed ever single sin committed (Gen. 3:8-11). God is no less aware today than He was then. "And there is no creature hidden from His sight, but all things are naked and open to the eyes of Him to whom we must give account" (Heb. 4:13 NKJV). Job prayed, "For now You number my steps, but do not watch over my sin." (Job 14:16 NKJV). Moses wrote,

"You have set our iniquities before You, our secret sins in the light of Your countenance" (Ps. 90:8 NKJV). It is easy to see the futility of trying to hide one's sins from the Lord. Solomon gave this counsel, "He who covers his sins will not proper, but whoever confesses and forsakes them will have mercy (Prov. 28:13 NKJV). Every child of God should behave as a church by dealing with the encouragement Solomon gives. Or how about the counsel John gives, "If we say that we have no sin, we deceive ourselves, and the truth is not in us. If we confess our sins, He is faithful and just to forgive us our sins and to cleanse us from all unrighteousness. If we say that we have not sinned, we make Him a liar, and His word is not in us" (1 John 1:8-10 NKJV).

The other area of our lives that is before God is our situations. God knew everything there was to know about the sufferings of Israel. He knew about the wickedness of the Babylonians. He knew about their cruelty. Nothing was hidden from Him! Over in Job 23:10 it says, "But He knows the way I take; when He has tested me, I shall come forth as gold" (NKJV). Here we see that the Lord knew everything was happening in the life of His servant Job. That means God knows all that is happening in your life as well. Nothing that has ever come your way has ever taken the Lord by surprise. In fact, He is the One who allowed it to happen for His own purposes and for your good (Rom. 8:27-29). Often the sufferings and burdens of life are greater than we feel that we can bear, but during them we have some spectacular promises. Sometimes there are storms that darken the way. Sometimes there are burdens that are hard to carry. Other times, there are sorrows and troubles that seem to hide the face of the Lord from us, but do not be deceived into thinking that the Lord does not know or that He does not care. God knows everything that you are going through today, and He will get you through it!

How does God react to His knowledge of you?

Since the Lord has this intimate, detailed, personal knowledge of each of us, what does He do with it? How does God's knowledge of your life and mine cause Him to respond? Allow me to show you three ways that God moves in response to His knowledge of His people. First,

God reacts towards you in your past. God moved in Israel's past by choosing them over all the nations of the earth (Deut. 7:7). He moved by delivering them from Egyptian bondage (Ex. 12-15). He moved by bringing them through the wilderness and into the Promised Land (Josh. 1:1). He had plans for the nation of Israel, not plans of evil, but plans of peace; plans that were designed to bring them to an expected end. God moved like this in the lives of all His children. God took steps in the past to meet the deepest need we have, and that need is a need to be saved. Before God had even made the world, He knew that He would make man in His image and that men would sin against Him. Therefore, before there was ever a man to save, or a sin from which to save him, God had already provided a means of salvation. The plan then, is the same plan God has told us about today. This plan involved the Lord Jesus Christ dying on the cross, shedding His precious blood and paying our sin debt. Three days later, He arose from the dead and later ascended back to His Father to be the mediator between God and man (1 Tim. 2:5). Now, anyone can have their sins taken care of by simply accepting Jesus into their hearts as their Lord and Savior by faith (John 3:16, Rom. 10:13).

Next, God reacts towards you in your present. From Israel's perspective, it looked as though the Lord had abandoned them. They were in captivity in Babylon. They were suffering cruel treatment at the hands of their enemies. It seems their prayers were accomplishing nothing, and that there was no hope for the future. That is merely how things appeared! That is how life appears to us at times too! As we go through life, the Lord stands ready and able to help you along the way. You do not have to face the burdens and trials of life alone! You do have to face them with a heavy burden of fear and worry. God would have you and me to trust Him and to look to Him during the trying times of life (Matt. 6:25-33; Phil. 4:6-7). His promises are as good today as they have ever been! He is there to supply to meet your need (Phil. 4:19). He does this so we can behave as His followers, fishers of men, church members, and as a church. Yet, there is one question that Christians still asks, "Why doesn't God do something about this battle that I am fighting? I have prayed about it, and I trust Him, but nothing ever changes." The logical response is: "God's train does not run on your schedule!" He will move, but not when you think He will. If there is what seems to be a lack of response from the Father, I would ask this question instead: "Is everything in order with my life?" What I mean by that is, you need to ask yourself; "Am I rebelling against the Lord over something He has asked me to do? Do I have a secret sin? Have I been disobedient?" Once you realize you are the one out of line and you confess and repent, then it may have been that the Lord was using this valley to call you back to Him all along. The prodigal son would have never gone home if it had not been for the time he spent in the pigpen (Luke 15:11-24). All I am saying is that the Lord will often use adversity as chastisement for the sin and rebellion that is in our life. Therefore, before you accuse the Lord of being unfaithful, be sure that everything is squared away in your own heart and life.

Lastly, God reacts toward you in His promises. Israel thought the Lord had forgotten about them and about all the promises He had made to their forefathers. Jeremiah wrote this passage in Jeremiah 29 to send to the children of Israel to remind them that God has not forgotten them. According to verses 10-13, God has good thoughts about His people. His desire is to give them an expected end. The same is true concerning His church, every child of God. Not a single promise of the Lord will ever fail. He will keep every promise He has ever made in His Word and the Bible is full of His promises. As a matter of fact, there are 8,810 promises in the Bible (Storms, 1978) There are 7,487 promises from God to man which means that of the 8,810 promises eighty-five percent are from God to man. As God brings us through the valleys and through troublesome times of our lives, we can rest assured that in the end, He is merely working out His will for our lives; and the end will more than justify the means (2 Cor. 4:17; Rom. 8:18). He has a plan for your life, and it would be to our benefit if we would behave as a church.

How faithful is God to you?

Like Jeremiah, we all go through times when life seems to fall apart at the seams. When these times come, we need the blessed assurance that God is faithful! Thankfully the Bible gives overwhelming evidence of the unchanging faithfulness to our great God! The word "faithfulness" found in Lamentation 3:23 means "firmness, fidelity, steadiness, steadfastness" (Wood, Marshall, & Millard, 1996) This word "faithfulness" pictures God as One upon Whom we can depend. We can be sure as we face the storms, trials, and valleys of life, that God will ever prove Himself to be steadfast and faithful to you and me. To put it simply you can count of the Lord.

GOD IS FAITHFUL IN HIS GRACE

In the book of Laminations, Jeremiah writes, "Through the Lord's mercies we are not consumed, because His compassions fail not" (Lam. 3:22 NKJV). The pessimist would call hope, "a pathological belief in the occurrence of the impossible. If you are a child of God, you should not accept that definition. The Christian theologian calls hope, "the divine alchemy that transmutes the base metal of adversity into gold." Peter explains hope like this, "In this you greatly rejoice, though not for a little while, if need be, you have been grieved by various trials, that the genuineness of your faith, being much more precious than gold that perishes, though it is tested by fire, may be found to praise, honor, and glory at the revelation of Christ, whom having not seen you love. Though now you do not see Him, yet believing you rejoice with joy inexpressible and full of glory, receiving the end of your faith; the salvation of your souls" (1 Pet. 1:6-9 NKJV). Jeremiah realizes that God's mercies, compassion, and faithfulness was because God loved mankind. Therefore, because He loves us, He chastens us (Heb. 12:5-11). As Jeremiah contemplates this realization, he remembers that it was the pure grace of God that brought Israel out of slavery in Egypt. It was also grace that had kept them a redeemed people despite their failures and wanderings.

God's amazing grace is the only thing that could have reached us in our lost, doomed condition and saved us (Eph. 2:1-4). We could not get to God on our own merit; therefore, God came to us! He came to this world in the Person of the Lord Jesus Christ to die for our sins (Phil. 2:5-8). He came in the Person of the Holy Spirit to draw us to God so we might be saved (John 16:7-11; John 6:44). God's amazing grace not only seeks us out when we are lost in sin, but His grace keeps us in our saved condition. Since we are prone to failure and spiritual wanderings; and if our salvation rested upon our ability to be faithful to the Lord, then none of us would ever be saved. However, salvation is the Lord's control not ours! We are saved by His grace, and we are kept by that same grace (1 Pet. 1:5, Ps. 37:23-24, 28; John 4:13-14).

GOD IS FAITHFUL IN HIS GIFTS

Because God's loving kindness does not fail, God's mercies "they are new every morning; great is Your faithfulness" (Lam. 3:23 NKJV). God's compassion caused him to be moved from within His heart for the world and caused Him to do something about the lostness of mankind (John 3:16, Rom. 5:8). As we pass through our storms and our valleys, we cannot pass through them alone! God sees our path and His grace gives us all we need for our journey (Phil. 4:19). Let me give you two thoughts about the great gifts of God. First, God's gifts are faithful. God did not promise an easier road, but He promised that His grace would be sufficient for the need (2 Cor. 12:9). That is what He told Paul about his thorn in the flesh. Grace is usually defined as unmerited love and favor of God towards sinners (Dictionary, 1828) It carries that idea, but grace means so much more by referring to the strength of God to face battles and to bear up under times of difficulty. We should remember that regardless of what life sends our way, we can be confident of the fact that the Lord will give us the necessary strength to face the trying times of life, to help us behave.

Second thought, according to Lamentations 3:23, the grace of God is as fresh as the new day itself. We do not have to worry about there not being enough for us to make it through; for God's grace in our lives is as fresh as the morning dew. Jesus encourages us this way, "Therefore do not worry about tomorrow, for tomorrow will worry about its own things. Sufficient for the day is its own trouble" (Matt. 6:34 NKJV). Just as every new day brings with it its won set of burdens and problems, equally if not more, each day witnesses a new, unfailing, all-sufficient, supply of God's marvelous, matchless, wonderful, amazing grace! God's faithfulness is seen in the fact that we woke up today, in our right mind, and in reasonable health. We woke up with air to breath, food to eat, people we love around us; and I could forever make a list of things we should be thankful for all because of God's amazing grace! What a mighty God we serve! Behave as church because of what God thinks of you.

CHAPTER FIFTEEN

How Big is Your Vision?

Call to Me, and I will answer you, and show you
great and mighty things, which you do not know.
(Jeremiah 33:3 NKJV)

NOW THAT WE HAVE BEEN REMINDED OF WHAT GOD THINKS ABOUT us; and if we are going to behave as a church, then we need to ask ourselves this question: "How big is your vision?" Solomon tells us, "Where there is no vision, the people perish: but he that keepeth the law, happy is he" (Prov. 29:18 KJV). Have you ever tasted a nice, cool refreshing Coca-Cola? Congratulations! So have hundreds of millions of other people all around the world. It is all Robert Woodruff's fault... well, not all his fault, but he is largely to blame. You see, Woodruff, while president of Coca-Cola, had the audacity to state during World War II, "We will see that every man in uniform gets a bottle of Coca-Cola for five cents, wherever he is and whatever it costs the company." (Coca-Cola Company, 2012) When the war ended, he went on to say that in his lifetime he wanted everyone in the world to have a taste of Coca-Cola. Talk about a vision! With careful planning and a lot of persistence, Woodruff and his colleagues reached their generation around the globe for Coca-Cola.

How big is your vision? Have you ever thought about what God could do through you to influence your generation? What if God told you He was going to send you to speak to people that would fight against you and not hear what you had to say? The book of Jeremiah was written against the backdrop of supreme evil. The people of God, Israel, had walked away from God and had embraced the gods of the pagan nations around them. Because of their sin, God is bringing His judgment upon the people. It was a time of pain, sorrow, death, and judgment. It was into this atmosphere that Jeremiah was sent to preach the Word of God. Jeremiah was sent to people who would not hear his message (Jer. 1:19). He was sent to people who would turn a deaf ear to all his pleas for repentance. He was sent to a people who were so given over to their sins they had no desire to hear anything God or the man of God had to say. Jeremiah preached in this climate for fifty years and there is not one record that he had even a single convert. I wonder just how big Jeremiah's vision was, if it was a vision given to him by God!

It was a tragic time for the nation of Israel. Jeremiah was sent to them to preach a message of judgment. He was sent to let the people know that they have angered God and were about to be judged. Jeremiah was commanded to tell them that their nation would be invaded. He was sent to tell them that they would be taken captive. He was sent to deliver a message of final judgment to their king. As a result, Jeremiah was not the most popular man in his nation. In fact, he was arrested and thrown into prison by King Zedekiah for preaching the truth (Jer. 32:1-5). Therefore, Jeremiah prays for understanding of what is going on, and for direction of how to achieve the vision God had given. Out of that tragic and difficult time came a ray of hope through a vision from God. While Jeremiah languished in prison, the Lord came to him to give him hope, encouragement, promise, and clarity of the vision.

Every child of God knows we are living in perilous times (2 Tim. 3:1). These times we live in are tough spiritually, economically, on the church, families, and for individuals. Praise the Lord, the same God Who spoke to Jeremiah in that prison cell is the same God Who knows where you are today. He was the God of the impossible then, and He is still the God of the impossible today. He can give you a vision so big that you may feel it is impossible for you to fulfill it. "But Jesus looked at them and said to them, "With men this is impossible but with God all things are possible" (Matt. 19:26 NKJV). From Jeremiah's situation let me show you how God is the God of the impossible.

Jeremiah's Confidence

In Jeremiah 32:16-27, Jeremiah prayed this great prayer of hope. He presents the evidence he has collected about God that shows Him to be the God of the impossible. Jeremiah found hope in a desperate time by considering the nature of God. Since God does not change (Mal. 3:6; Heb. 13:8), we can rest in this same hope Jeremiah had. The first thing that Jeremiah looked at was God's creation. He said, "Ah, Lord God! Behold, You have made the heavens and the earth by Your great power and outstretched arm. There is nothing too hard for you" (Jer. 32:17 NKJV). The heavens above us and the world around us declare the power and the Person of God. His creation declares Him to be the God of the impossible. Genesis 1:1 is perhaps the greatest commentary on God's power, but there are other verses in the Bible that declare the greatness of God in His creation; verses like Psalm 8:1-3, 19:1-4; Isaiah 40:12; and Romans 1:20. Regardless of what lies in your path today remember that if you are His, you belong to God Who made it all. If He can make everything out of nothing, then He can be trusted to take care of you and help you with your big vision.

The next thing Jeremiah looked at was God's character. He says, "You show lovingkindness to thousands, and repay the iniquity of the fathers into the bosom of their children after them; the Great and Mighty God, whose name is the Lord of host. You are great in counsel and mighty work, for Your eyes are open to all the ways of the sons of men, to give everyone according to his ways and according to the fruit of his doings. You have set signs and wonders in the land of Egypt, to this day, and in Israel and among other men; and You have made Yourself a name as it is this day" (Jer. 32:18-20 NKJV). The language Jeremiah uses to describe God in these verses serves to remind us of Who He is. He is the God of grace, love, mercy, and provision. He is the God of miracles and power. He is the God Who moves heaven and earth, and suspends the very law of nature, if necessary to meet the needs of His children. (Examples: Elijah, the three Hebrew children, Daniel in the lion's den, Widow of Zarephath, feed the five thousand, the disciples in the storm, Mary the mother of Jesus, Martha, and Lazarus, the list could go on.) God has not changed! He is the same God not that He was then. He still knows what it takes and possesses what it takes to see you through whatever you may face in this life (Heb. 13:5; Phil. 4:19; Matt. 6:33). Therefore, behave as a church.

The last thing that Jeremiah looked at was God's conversion. He says, "You have brought Your people Israel out the land of Egypt with signs and wonders, with a strong hand and an outstretched arm, and with great terror; You have given them this land, of which You swore to their fathers to give them; a land flowing with milk and honey" (Jer. 32:21-22 NKJV). With so much uncertainty that may be going on in our lives, goals, plans, or ideas of doing something great, where does your strength come from to accomplish or overcome them? Jeremiah, sitting in the prison, finds confidence from the Lord's power as it was displayed in Israel's deliverance from slavery in Egypt. He recounts how the Lord moved to deliver them from Egypt. He remembers how God brought them into the Promised Land. He writes of how the Lord demonstrated His power to save His people. God's power is what gave Jeremiah confidence, and it should do the same for us as well. When I think of God making the world, I am amazed. When I think of the vastness of the universe and how He created the stars, moon, and planets just by speaking them into existence, I am speechless. However, when I think that a holy, eternal, infinite, omnipotent, omniscient, and omnipresent God would condescend to love the likes of a sinner like mankind, I am brought to my knees in worship. When I contemplate His love, I realize that if He can take a hardened heart, wash it in the red blood of His Son, and make it whiter than snow, He can do anything! That gives me confidence! He is the God of the impossible! That should give you confidence today as well; regardless of what we face in this life, if He can save us then nothing is too big from Jehovah God.

Jeremiah's Crisis

The next thing Jeremiah prayed about the situation he was in. He begins with telling God about the problems he faced. "And they came in and took possession of it, but they have not obeyed Your voice or walked in Your law. They have done nothing of all that You commanded them to do; therefore, You have caused all this calamity to come upon them. Look, the siege mounds! They have come to the city to take it; and the city has been given into the hand of the Chaldeans who fight against it, because of the sword and famine and pestilence. What You have spoken has happened; there You see it!" (Jer. 32:23-24 NKJV). While the people of God have been blessed, they have refused to walk in the will of the Lord. As a result, they are experiencing His judgment on their nation. Seeing the wrath of God being poured out firsthand causes Jeremiah some inner disturbance of the soul. He is perplexed by what he sees happening around him. It brings him to a time of crisis in his life, and yet, he knows that this is what the Lord said would happen (vs. 24). So, you have a holy man of God living among an unholy people. They are suffering for their sins, and he is suffering right along with them. I do not care how strong, or how well grounded you are, that would cause anyone emotional problems.

We have somehow gotten this notion that know the Lord somehow guarantees us freedom from the problems in life. Nothing could be farther from the truth. In fact, serving the Lord in a wicked hour like the one in which we live will guarantee us that we will face problems in our day just like Jeremiah had. God is judging the United States of America, and the children of God will suffer right along with it. As our economy suffers, churches, church members, families, and individuals will suffer too. As morality and wickedness grow, it will take its toll upon godly people and affect the Christian home and church. Add to that the fact that Satan will see to it that God's children are hated, attacked, and persecuted (2 Tim. 3:12), and that is all the makings for a spiritual crisis. If we do not behave as a church, there is always the potential that our brothers and sisters in Christ will fall by the wayside when trouble comes their way.

Next Jeremiah tells God about the plan he followed. "And You have said to me, O Lord God, "Buy the field for money, and take witnesses"! Yet the city has been given into the hand of the Chaldeans" (Jer. 32:25 NKJV). After Jeremiah is thrown into prison, he is commanded by the Lord to purchase a piece of property from his uncle (Jer. 32:6-12). This transaction caused Jeremiah some serious moments of doubt. Think about it, he is preaching to the people that judgment is coming, that their nation is about to be destroyed, and all the people are about to be taken away to Babylon as slaves; yet God wants Jeremiah to buy a piece of property? Why do you buy property in the first place? Most people buy property because they have plans for future purposes. Maybe they are going to build a home, start a business, make an investment, or just something to pass along to the next generation in their family. Jeremiah is buying a piece of property he probably will never see, much less use. This transaction brought Jeremiah to a moment of crisis in his life. The fact is, the Lord works in ways we do not understand, it leaves us perplexed as well. "Oh, the depth of the riches both of the wisdom and knowledge of God! How unsearchable are His judgments and His ways past finding out!" (Rom. 11:33 NKJV). I must confess there are many things I do not understand. I do not understand why the Lord calls young teenagers to come home to be with Him. I do not understand why some of our fellow church members are having medical problems. I do not understand why some folks seem to have such a hard time making it through life. There are many things I do not understand, but if I continue to focus on those things, I will have a moment of crisis as well. I must learn to lay those things I cannot fathom at the altar; give it and leave it in the hands of God Who controls all things.

Jeremiah also told God about the predicament that he feared would happen (Jer. 32:25b), the land was given over to the Chaldeans. I think part of Jeremiah's crisis came from the fact that he did not want to look like a fool. Here he was, in prison, buying a piece of land, when the nation was on the brink of destruction. Surely, he thought the people around him would think he had lost his mind. Is that not part of our problem sometimes? We know what the Lord wants us to do by the vision, guidance, and instructions He gives us, and sometimes we do it, but it seems so unnatural and so strange to us, that we worry about what the rest of the world thinks about our actions. Nobody wants to look foolish to other people, but sometimes God's commands just do not make sense. Think about this, Moses was commanded to hold a stick over the Red Sea when the people were under attack (Ex. 14). Moses was commanded to cut down a tree and throw it into a pool of water to make it drinkable (Ex. 15). Moses was commanded to strike a rock so that the people of God could have water to drink (Ex. 17). Then later Moses is commanded to speak to the rock to bring water for the people to drink (Num. 20). The people of Israel were commanded to look at a snake on a pole to be healed of snakebite (Num. 21). Isaiah was commanded to walk around naked as an object lesson to the king of Israel (Isa. 20). None of those things make sense to us, but they were all the will of God. That goes for us too, the Lord's will does not always make sense to our minds, but the secret to contentment in behaving as a church and serving Him is absolute obedience even when we do not understand what He is up to. The fact is, we will never understand the Lord's ways. "For My thoughts are not your thoughts, nor are your ways My ways," says the Lord. For as the heavens are higher than the earth, so are My ways higher than your ways, and My thoughts than your thoughts" (Isa. 55:8-9 NKJV). We are to behave as a church by trusting Him despite what we do not know, or what we cannot see!

Jeremiah's Comfort

After making his petitions know to God, the Lord speaks to Jeremiah to bring him comfort in the hour of his crisis. We can see God's words to Jeremiah in Jeremiah 32:26-44. What God says to Jeremiah brought comfort to his heart and they should bring a comfort to our hearts as well. God tells Jeremiah that He will indeed bring judgment upon the people of Israel because of their sins. Everything He has promised to do, He is able to bring to pass. Therefore, God reminds and comforts Jeremiah by telling him about His power. God says, "Behold, I am the Lord of all flesh. Is there anything too hard for Me?" (vs. 27 NKJV). God will judge Israel, and He will use the lost pagans of Babylon to do it. God declares His power by asking Jeremiah a simple, straightforward question: Is there anything to hard for the Lord? God is simply saying that nothing is impossible with God, nothing is beyond His power, and there is nothing too difficult for Him to do! May that truth sink into our hearts and encourage us! God is still the God Who possesses all power in heaven and in earth (Matt. 28:18). He is still the God "who is able to do exceedingly abundantly above all that we ask or think, according to the power that works in us" (Eph. 3:20 NKJV). He is still the God Who "works all things according to the counsel of His will" (Eph. 1:11b NKJV). Because God's great power He is still the God that should comfort our hearts today.

Jeremiah was also comforted by God's great promises. In Jeremiah 32:36-44, God tells Jeremiah that the people of Israel will fall, and they will go away captive into Babylon. He also tells Jeremiah that He will bring them home again. He will gather them to Himself, and they will serve Him. He will be their God and they will be His people. In other words, the judgment they face will serve to purify them and they will return to Him, and to the place of His blessing. That is the same way it works for us. God will give us the vision He wants us to focus on, and when it does not seem like it is going to work out, He shows us it will. The Lord uses the crisis in our lives to mold us, grow us, and develop us. He uses pain, hardship, suffering, and the trials of life to make us more like Jesus (Rom. 8:28-29). He is the God of the impossible. He can take our situation that may seem impossible and transform it into a time of blessing for you and glory for Him. The very God Who made the world and all that is within it, came to the prophet in his prison and makes one of the greatest prayer promises in the Bible. "Thus says the Lord who made it, the Lord who formed it to establish it (the Lord is His name): 'Call to Me, and I will answer you, and show you great and mighty things, which you do not know'" (Jer. 33:2-3 NKJV). Think about where Jeremiah is when this promise is made. He is in prison, living in the middle of a wicked people. Living in a nation that is experiencing the awful judgment of God, yet the Lord wants Jeremiah to know that God cares about Jeremiah and about what the prophet is facing in his life as he is trying to achieve the vision God had given him.

How big is your vision? When it comes to visions, goals, ideas, or your focus what you want to accomplish in your life for Jesus just how big do you dream or are you just playing around with the notion of "wouldn't that be great to do something like that?" The Lord Jesus Christ was not playing around when He called His disciples to gain a vision of impacting the world for His name. He said, "Most assuredly, I say to you, he who believes in Me, the works that I do he will do also;

and greater works than these he will do, because I go to My Father. And whatever you ask in My name, that I will do, that the Father may be glorified in the Son. If you ask anything in My name, I will do it. If you love Me, keep My commandments" (John 14:12-15 NKJV). Please do not underestimate those words, because as Jesus challenges His disciples, I believe that He also meant them for you and me; to dream great dreams, plan great plans, pray great prayers, obey His lite commands, and behave as a church.

Dream Great Dreams

In the disciples' minds, time was running out fast. For more that three years they had hoped Christ would be the one who would redeem Israel and reign as Messiah. But now He is saying that one of them would betray Him and deliver Him up to the Jewish leaders to be crucified. Imagine what the twelve thought when Christ went on to promise, that if they would put their faith in Him, they would do what He has been doing. Around the upper room table sat Peter, who had almost drowned trying to walk on water. There was Philip, who wave his arms in exclamation, stating the impossibility of buying enough bread to feed the multitude. Plus, there was Andrew, who, with a few of the other disciples, could not heal a boy who was demon-possessed. To every disciple in the upper room that night, Jesus told them that they would continue the work He started. Plus, He made this promise to every child of God. Jesus calls us to dream great dreams of what we can do to impact the world for His glory. Then went on to add to this promise, not only would we continue His work that He started, but we would do greater works than what He did when He was on earth (vs. 12). The works that Jesus is talking about is that of mission work, sharing the gospel and making disciples. He is not talking about performing miracles like feeding the five thousand, walking on water, exorcisms, or raising the dead.

The works that He is talking about can be traced back to what John has already stated in his gospel. "For the Father loves the Son and shows Him all things that He Himself does; and He will show Him greater works than these, that you may marvel" (John 5:20 NKJV).

What Jesus is implying here is, just as God raised the physical dead, Jesus gives spiritual life (vs. 21). The greater work that Jesus is doing is greater than raising the dead. "Most assuredly, I say to you, he who hears My word and believes in Him who sent Me has everlasting life, and shall not come into judgment, but has passed from death into life" (vs. 24 NKJV). In other words what He is talking about is salvation, about hearing the gospel. The greater work that we will be doing is greater than raising the dead, it will be leading a lost soul to Jesus Christ. Of course, it is not the believer himself who does these greater works; it is the Holy Spirit working in and through the believer (Mark 16:20). I would rather have the power to lead souls to Christ than to raise the dead from the grave. Remember, "Jesus said to them, "My food is to do the will of Him who sent Me, and to finish His work" (John 4:34 NKJV). When Jesus came to earth, He had a work to do, a vision to accomplish. He did not come as a miracle worker, walk on water, raise the dead, nor feed the multitudes all though He did all that. Jesus came to do the greater works that God had given Him. Now Jesus is giving His disciples in the upper room the vision of this greater works for them to accomplish and to dream great dreams. Just as God sent Jesus, now Jesus is sending us out into the world to continue to do greater works than He did. That means we are going to bring even more people to Jesus Christ than Jesus Himself, brought to Himself when He was on earth. Therefore, we must behave as a church dreaming great dreams.

More people were converted in day on the day of Pentecost than Jesus ever saw converted. How is this possible? The key to this possibility has two answers. First, because Jesus was going to the Father, He assured the disciples He would send the Comforter, the Holy Spirit to dwell in the hearts of believer (John 14:16-17). On the day of Pentecost, the Holy Spirit came (Acts 2:1-4). Christ would now continue His work through us! Second, Christ qualified His promise with a condition. So, how is Christ going to continue His work through us? If anyone who has placed their faith in Jesus, they will do what Jesus has been doing (John 14:12). The challenges us to have faith; not necessarily more faith, but faith in Him, an ongoing faith. This does not mean we are going to upstage Him, that we know how to do it better that He did. It means that Jesus wants us to dream great dreams and He will accomplish His works through us.

Renew Your Vision

If we are to behave as a church what should be the vision for the body of Christ? There should be at least one vision that every local true body of Christ should have. If that local body does not have one, then they are going to perish (cease being a church). Pastors and leaders should be casting God's vision before the congregation, and individuals should be renewing that vision in their daily lives. Ask yourself, "Have I stopped seeing greater thing happen in my life?" Perhaps you have stopped believing that God can work in a mighty way in our generation. But what limits the work of God here on earth? Is God somehow incapable of turning the hearts of multiple thousands to Himself? Is He incapable of spreading the fires of revival throughout this country and beyond? Of course not! Yet God has chosen to limit His work, at leas in some measure, to those things we trust Him to do through us.

For the most part the reason why, it seems that God is not doing anything, is not that God cannot, it is because we have forgotten the vision and/or have placed so many regulations and stipulations on God that He chooses not to do great things through us. Why is it that so few Christians never accomplish great things for Christ? I believe it is because we have lost the ability to dream great dreams. We have lost the vision; and as we know where there is no vision the people (the church) perish. For God to use us again, we need to confess our unbelief and say: "Lord Jesus, renew my vision of Your power. Renew my confidence in Your abilities. Renew my trust in Your resources." Once we renew our vision then we can begin to dream again. Christ Himself never limited His disciples' vision; even though He restricted His own public ministry to Palestine, He came and lived and died for all mankind. After His resurrection, He commissioned His followers to go and make disciples (Matt. 28:18-20). He sent them first to Jerusalem, then to Judea, then to Samaria, and ultimately to the ends of the earth (Acts 1:8).

Where have your own personal dreams stopped? Have they been lost somewhere between your living room and the house next door? If your dreams are not greater than finishing your education, paying off your bills, building a home, being promoted at your job, raising your children, or succeeding then your vision is not divine. Maybe it is time to consider how God could use you to make a difference in the lives of others. The opportunities are great throughout the globe. But how can we impact our generation for Christ? Is it possible to preach the gospel to all nation? I believe it is possible by taking God at His Word and make plans to accomplish great things by His power working in us and through the church.

Plan Great Plans

The fact that Jesus tells us that if we will believe in Him, that we will do greater things than He did because He goes to the Father is fantastic! It so unconceivable, yet it is a true promise, nonetheless. The promise was made from the very lips of Jesus and has been proven trustworthy many times. Jesus promises we can do greater works than He did! Perhaps it would help us to look at the ministry of Paul to get an idea of what Jesus is saying in John 14:12. Without a doubt, God used Paul tremendously during the crucial formative years of building up the New Testament church. Even His opponents admitted Paul had saturated the entire provinces with the gospel and turned the world upside down. Some scholars have even claimed, that from a human point of view, that Paul influence history more than Jesus Christ Himself.

What was Paul's secret? Simple, he dreamed great dreams, but he was more than a dreamer. He planned great plans and carried them out in the power of the Holy Spirit. These plans included utilizing ministry teams, traveling extensively, taking advantage of opportunities to witness for Christ, and establishing local churches to nurture new believers. Paul was not content to saturate one small area with the gospel at the expense of rest of the world. He had a strategy for reaching the entire Roman empire! He could say, "But now no longer having a place in these parts and having a great desire these many years to come to you, whenever I journey to Spain, I shall come to you" (Rom. 15:23-24 NKJV). Paul goes on in that chapter to explain his itinerary. In his mind, he could visualize every major city where he would stop on his way to Rome. He longed to win the people of that capital city to Christ. But beyond that, his goal was to reach Spain, the western limit of the empire. His strategic planning is what motivated his ministry. He did not consider it carnal or beneath his dignity to plan, instead he used it as a tool to reach the masses more effectively. That is how we should be thinking as we behave as a church.

Obey His Great Commands

Overall, we must recognize God's role in our planning. As Solomon says, "Unless the Lord builds the house, they labor in vain who build it; unless the Lord guards the city, the watchman stays awake in vain" (Ps. 127:1 NKJV). No matter how nice a job the architect did on the blueprints. Our planning is never intended to replace God's sovereign leading in our lives. This is an exciting concept to me; on the one hand, God intends for us to be logical and strategic while planning to fulfill the Great Commission. But on the other hand, God can redirect our plans when necessary. One does not cancel out the need for the other. So, just how big is your vision? What is the vision you have for your life? For your church? Do you have dreams and plans of what God might do through your life? Or are you just too busy with life's routine, ordinary tasks? We might even ask, "how big is your God?"

The Lord Jesus Christ challenges us to abandon our complacency when He says that we can do even greater things that He has done through the Holy Spirit who dwells in us. He does not intend for us to sit idly by and dream of what could happen for His glory. He wants us to plan great plans so that dreams can come true! William Carey upset the status quo of the church in his day when he proposed sending missionaries from Britian to evangelize other parts of the world. Older Christians told him to give up his preposterous ideas. Carey countered their boredom and doubt by writing, "Expect great things from God, attempt great things for God." (Smith, 1887) That statement became the creed of the modern mission's movement as men and women followed Carey's example and went to the ends of the earth with saving message of Christ's gospel. Like Carey, God wants us to attempt great things for Him to reach our generation.

Are you expecting great things for God? Are you attempting to do great things for God? Or are you letting the opportunities pass you by? If the Lord wants the gospel preached worldwide; then we cannot remain passive. Whatever our gifts or abilities or resources, we must behave as a church as faithful stewards of what God has given us. Dream a little. Envision the four million people who have not accepted the gospel in this generation. Many have not even heard it explained to them. What are you going to do about it? Start doing something by making a specific plan of action. Determine how God could use you to share Christ at work, at school, in your neighborhood, on your vacation, and beyond. Are you willing to gain a big vision of God could do through you to win others to Himself?

CHAPTER SIXTEEN

There is Work to be Done

And He opened their understanding, that
they might comprehend the Scriptures.
(Luke 24:45 NKJV)

To behave as a church, we need to be fulfilling the Great Commission. A Great Commission church is a church that goes where the people are and shares the good news that Jesus saves. All the way back to the days of the Garden of Eden in the Bible, God is the one Who takes the initiative to reach out to people. In Christianity, God is the one reaching out to people, but in other religions man must reach out to their gods. Therefore, since man is searching for something to fill their void in their lives there are countless millions around the world who live in fear. Their lives are dominated by worry. They fear the unknown and they do not know Jesus as their Savior. In the state of Arkansas, there are over one hundred thirty identifiable people groups, and seventy of them are considered unreached with the gospel of our Lord and Savior Jesus Christ.

Because most people have never heard the gospel clearly proclaimed, we should behave as a church with a strong conviction that God has ultimately brought them to where they are so they might have an opportunity to follow Jesus. Jesus says, "The thief does not come except to steal, and to kill, and to destroy. I have come that they may have life, and that they may have it more abundantly" (John 10:10 NKJV). That is a message that the world needs to hear, that is what your country needs to hear, your state needs to hear, your county, your hometown needs to hear. If we are going to behave as a church, then we must continue the work of the Great Commission, until He comes back for us (Luke 24:49).

In Luke 24:44-53, Jesus is going over His life, which includes His death and resurrection. Then He turns to His disciples and tells that they are chosen to carry the gospel of God to all the world. After that, Jesus tells the disciples to wait at Jerusalem to be endued, or clothed upon, with power from heaven. Then He ascends into heaven (Acts 1:9-11). Goodbyes are not easy, especially if the one leaving will be gone for a long time. Babe Ruth said goodbye at Yankee Stadium with tears in his eyes, while he was being eaten up with cancer. In the Watergate hearings, Nixon said goodbye to his staff, walked across the lawn, then said goodbye and waved from Marine 1. If you have ever said a final goodbye to a child, a spouse, a sibling, or a parent then you know how bad goodbyes can be. When Jesus ascended into heaven, He left behind the memories of a three- and half-year ministry, intertwined with good times and bad times with His disciples. He had changed their lives and they have never been the same. They spent forty incredible days after His resurrection together; and now it is time to say goodbye. He is leaving and going home; and He tells them to His work until He gets back (Matt. 28:18-20; Mark 16:15; Luke 24:49; Acts 1:8).

A few days after Jesus ascends, the disciples find themselves in the world; scared, hunted, and with a big job that needs to be done. The disciples took Jesus at His word, they went back to Jerusalem and waited for Jesus to fill them. When they received His power, they went into all the world. The impact these guys made was literally turning the world upside down (Acts 17:6). They were able to accomplish great things all because they did what Jesus said. They tarried until Jesus empowered them. Because of the early church and His disciples, today, we are organized, have a nice building, there is music, pews, lights, air conditioning, trained preachers, and complete copies of God's word. When Jesus ascended into heaven, He left some things behind for us to do, and we are to tarry until. We have everything we need to impact this world for Jesus, we even have the power of

God living in each church member. However, it seems today that His power is not working in and through the church. Why? Because many Christians, many churches, are not behaving like a church. They are not carrying out His command in their lives. Many have never allowed the Holy Spirit to work through them, or they do not have a motivation for evangelism. That is why I believe the greatest need for churches is to be filled with God's Holy Spirit and His power.

Motivation from Jesus' Ministry

"And He said to them, "Why did you seek Me? Did you not know that I must be about My Father's business?" (Luke 2:49 NKJV). Very early in His ministry Jesus made it very clear that He was here for a purpose. The Father's business is reaching out to the lost. Right after Adam's sin and fall, God took the initiative to seek him. "Then the Lord God called to Adam and said to him, "Where are you?" (Gen. 3:9 NKJV). Jesus said, "For the Son of Man has come to seek and to save that which was lost" (Luke 19:10 NKJV). God takes the initiative in reaching out to man, and he expects the church to do the same while He gone. As long as there is one person who has not heard the message, the task is not finished. The mission field cries out, "unfinished". The remote areas of every city and town cry out, "unfinished". The whaling of the unsatisfied soul cries out, "unfinished." The voices of your neighbor cry out, "unfinished." You have loved ones who cry out, "unfinished." Perhaps your own soul is crying out, "unfinished." Are you actively participating in carrying out the Great Commission, His unfinished task? If you do not help, much of it will go undone (John 9:4).

Just as the Holy Spirit was a part of the birth of Jesus, the Holy Spirit is a vital part of empowering us to fulfill the command to go win the lost (Eph. 5:18). Jesus promised the disciples that God would send His Spirit, the Comforter, into the world (John 14:26). This promise was literally fulfilled on the Day of Pentecost when the disciples were filled with the Holy Spirit (Acts 2:4). Jesus assures us that we are supernaturally empowered to carry out His work, just as the disciples and the early church were able to carry out the Great Commission (Acts 1:8). As we receive the Lord Jesus as Savior into our hearts, we receive the Holy Spirit (John 14:16). As believers we do not need to wait for a new empowering by the Holy Spirit, we are already empowered. We do not need to wonder whether it is God's will that people be saved, we already know it is! "The Lord is not slack concerning His promise, as some count slackness, but is longsuffering toward us, not willing that any should perish but that all should come to repentance" (2 Pet. 3:9 NKJV). God clearly revealed His will to His people and has empowered His children to go with confidence and share the gospel message! If we are to experience God's presence in our worship, both public and private; and experience His power in our witness, then we need to allow God to doo all He wants to do in and through us.

The Holy Spirit is given to every born-again believer. "But you are not in the flesh but in the Spirit, if indeed the Spirit of God dwells in you. Now if anyone does not have the Spirit of Christ, he is not His" (Rom. 8:9 NKJV). Every child of God possesses the Holy Spirit. By ourselves, we are weak and can do nothing. "For I know that in me (that is, in my flesh) nothing good dwells; for to will is present with me, but how to perform what is good I do not find" (Rom. 7:18 NKJV). If there is any power in any person, it is the direct result of the Holy Spirit indwelling and in-filling! We use Philippians 4:13 to say that with Christ we cand do all things, and it is true! However, I am not strong simply because I know Him, I am strong because I allow Him to work in my life. There is no limit to the power of the almighty God! He has the ability to do whatever needs to be done. God's power can soften the hardest of hearts, move the highest mountains, and lift the greatest burdens. His power is absolutely unlimited! The problem today is not God, but His people. We have a righteous God, but He does not have a people who behaves as a church.

The word "power" comes from the word "dunamis" and means "the ability to perform anything" (Concise Oxford English Dictionary Eleventh Edition, 2004) This is the power that works in every child of God. Basically, what this teaches us is that we are indwelt by His Spirit, God's power resides in us, and when it is needed, it will explode from us and work in the world. We need this power because souls are perishing from lack of power. Churches and church members are drying up due to a lack of power. Sin is running rampant because there is no manifest power and presence of God among His people. If you are saved, the power of God is there, but it never gets manifested because few are paying the price in prayer. Few are totally yielding to the control of the Holy Spirit. The secret to His power is not getting more of God! No! You got all of Him when you were saved! The secret is giving more of yourself to Him!

Let me say that I am tired of reading about what God did 2,000 years ago. I am glad He did, but I want to see it happen now! I am hungry to see Jesus Christ adored and worshipped as He deserves today. I long to see a church that is a New Testament church in every sense of the word. I just want to experience the awesome power of God in these days in which we live! Pray that God would demonstrate His approval of the church by manifesting His power through the church!

Motivation from Jesus' Teaching

Jesus once quoted from the book of Isaiah, he said, "The Spirit of the Lord is upon Me, because He has anointed Me to preach the gospel to the poor, He has sent Me to heal the brokenhearted, to proclaim liberty to the captives and recovery of sight to the blind, to set at liberty those who are oppressed; to proclaim the acceptable year of the Lord" (Luke 4:1-19 NKJV, Isa. 61:1-2). Jesus gave us a very clear description of those who were lost. There was another occasion, where Jesus used a fishing experience with His disciples to teach them the priority of reaching out to the lost. After following His command to let the nets down, those who were there were astonished. As a matter of fact, "and so also were James and John, the sons of Zebedee, who were partners with Simon. And Jeus said to Simon, "Do not be afraid. From now on you will catch men."" (Luke 5:10 NKJV). They were astonished because of the miracle that they had witnessed, but what the did not understand was that Jesus had been empowered by the Holy Spirit. Being empowered by the Holy Spirit is vital for the ministry of reaching the lost. The church, the body of Christ, God's adopted children who have place their faith in Jesus has this same empowerment due to the indwelling of the Holy Spirit. We have received spiritual power for service in fulfilling the great commission. Whereas we are commanded to "go" and "make disciples. These words from the great commission have a promise built into them "I will be with you." Therefore, since we have been commanded to go and make disciples, then it is safe to assume with great confidence that His power and presence will go with us.

Listen to this promise that John tells us about, "Now this is the confidence that we have in Him, that if we ask anything according to His will, He hears us. And if we know that He hears us, whatever we ask, we know that we have the petition that we have asked of Him" (1 John 5:14-15 NKJV). The command of Jesus for all genuine believers is to go and make disciples, and as believers it is our response to obey our Lord and Savior. So, the promise John writes about is that if we pray and obey, God will grant our petitions. We can go in confidence to serve Him in His power. But why is prayer vital to evangelism and discipleship? First, because spiritual warfare is supernatural (Eph. 6:12). This battle for lost souls is not fought against people who do not trust Jesus as their Lord and Savior, no! The enemy, Satan, has blinded them to the gospel, making it necessary that we do the work of reaching the lost with the gospel we need to tap into that internal power; we do so through prayer. Prayer had a priority in the life of Jesus. He prayed before calling the twelve disciples. He prayed during His forty days of temptation. He prayed early in the morning. He prayed on the cross. If prayer was important to Jesus, then payer should be a priority to the believer.

Jesus told the disciples, "Behold, I send the Promised of My Father upon you; but tarry in the city of Jerusalem until you are endued with power from on high" (Luke 24:49 NKJV). The word "tarry" comes from the Greek word "kathizo" simple means to "sit down" (Strong's Concordance, 1984) It reminds me of all the times through out the Bible that God told His people to be still. "And Moses said to the people, "Do not be afraid. Stand still, and see the salvation of the Lord, which He will accomplish for you today. For the Egyptians whom you see today, you shall see again nom more forever" (Ex. 14:13 NKJV). Moses told the Lord, "Fear and dread will fall on them; by the greatness of Your arm, they will be as still as a stone, till Your people pass over, O Lord, till the people Passover whom You have purchased" (Ex. 15:16 NKJV). (Other instances of people being told to be still: 2 Chron. 20:17; Neh. 8:11; Ps. 4:4, 46:10; Isa. 23:2; Jer. 8:14). There in Luke 24:49, Jesus basically tells His disciples to just "sit down" in Jerusalem until they were filled with the Holy Spirit. What did they do? They sat down in Jerusalem in the upper room and waited on Jesus. They spent ten days in the upper room sitting down and praying together (Acts 1:14, 2:1), waiting for God to fill them for service. These guys prayed until something happened. This is one crucial element that could be missing in our day. There are few who are willing to spend extended periods of time in prayer calling on God. We fill our altars with shallow, embarrassed, and hurried prayers. May God help us to learn the value of waiting on God until the answers come. The secret is in tarrying, sitting down before the Lord. The spot where we pray should look worn out if you are truly waiting upon the Lord. There should be tear stains if we are truly waiting on the Lord. When you decide to tarry before the Lord in prayer, other things are going to take a back seat and the things of God will come to light and become a priority. What is more important in your life; those you love so dearly or the power of God?

When the power of God comes into your live there will be a since of urgency in Jesus' words. Take the words Jesus shared with Nicodemus. "Do not marvel that I said to you, 'You must be born again.'" (John 3:7 NKJV). It is dangerous for the lost to put off being born again. Jesus said, "No one can come to Me unless the Father who sent Me draws him; and I will raise him up at the last day" (John 6:44 NKJV). If these statements from Jesus are true regarding the lost, and they are, then we need to behave as a church and respond with a sense of urgency to share the gospel with them. Jesus defined His ministry and gave us the motivation for the ministry by stating, "For the Son of Man has come to seek and to save that which was lost" (Luke 19:10 NKJV). He wants us to have that same purpose and motivation, "So Jesus said to them again, "Peace to you! As the Father has sent Me, I also send you" (John 20:21 NKJV). Our motivation is to share the message of the gospel to every person in the world. Sharing the message of salvation can be challenging, but the message of salvation cannot be challenged. Man cannot challenge the message of salvation, and yet man has attempted to produce numerous methods of salvation without the shedding of blood (Heb. 9:22).

Paul had the same problem with the church in Galatia. "I marvel that you are turning away so soon from Him who called you in the grace of Christ, to a different gospel, which is not another; but there are some who trouble you and want to pervert the gospel of Christ. But even if we, or an angel from heaven, preach any other gospel to you than what we have preached to you, let him be accursed. As we have said before, so now I say again, if anyone preaches any other gospel to you than what you have received, let him be accursed" (Gal. 1:6-9 NKJV). The Galatians were abandoning their freedom in Christ for legalism of religion. They have become infatuated with the religion of the Judaizers, just the way little children follow strangers who offer them candy. The Galatians were not simply changing religions or changing churches, but they were abandoning the very grace of God! To make matters worse, they were deserting the God of grace for man made additions to gospel. We must never forget that to behave as a church, you and your fellow brothers and sisters in Christ are to be living together while holding fast to your relationship with God. You cannot mix grace and work because one excludes the other. Salvation is a gift of God's grace, purchased for us by Jesus Christ on the cross. It you challenge the message of salvation you are forgetting God.

The message of salvation will live on even during the tribulation. "Then I saw another angel flying in the midst of heaven, having the everlasting gospel to preach to those who dwell on the earth; to every nation, tribe, tongue, and people" (Rev. 14:6 NKJV). The message of salvation is a fool proof gospel. "For I am not ashamed of the gospel of Christ, for it is the power of God to salvation for everyone who believes, for the Jew first and also to the Greek" (Rom. 1:16 NKJV). When any man or woman comes and invites you to accept a better way than the gospel; just tell them, that you are born again by the shed blood and the grace of the Lord Jesus Christ. That you are going to live forever in heaven with Him. That will blow their minds because they cannot challenge the message of salvation. However, think about everyone who challenges the gospel message of Jesus Christ. They are the ones that will be in the number mentioned in Revelation 20:14-15. "Then Death and Hades were cast into the lake of fire. This is the second death. And anyone not found written in the Book of Life was cast into the lake of fire. You cannot challenge it and still go to heaven. If you attempt to go to heaven any other way other than through Jesus Christ, you will go to hell. If you challenge the message of salvation with baptismal regeneration, you will go to hell. If you challenge the message of salvation with your good works, you will lose and go to hell.

No one can question the love exhibited by the Son of God. Look at the love Jesus endured for you as pointed out by Luke, "to whom He also presented Himself alive after His suffering by many infallible proofs, being seen by them during forty days and speaking of the things pertaining to the kingdom of God" (Acts 1:3 NKJV). "Many infallible proofs" tells us that He gave His life so you and I could live forever. He gave His body at the whipping post. He who shed His blood for an uncaring world and a generation of perverts. He who left His home in heaven and came to a world of sinners who rejected Him and nailed Him on the a cross. He who in love cried out to the Father, "Then Jesus said, "Father, forgive them, for they do not know what they do." And they divided His garments and cast lots" (Luke 23:34 NKJV). He who bowed His head in shame and suffering, then died for a world that hated Him and wanted nothing to do with Him. That is unquestionable love! No one in the world would do that for a world of people who do not care. But this Jesus whom you crucified only commands that you follow Him. "Then He said to them, "Follow Me, and I will make you fishers of men" (Matt. 4:19 NKJV). As we follow Him, He makes us fishers of men by discipling on His teachings and motivating us to go out and share His great love and sacrifice.

Jesus declared, "I am the true vine, and My Father is the vinedresser. Every branch in Me that does not bear fruit He takes away, and every branch that bears fruit He prunes, that it may bear more fruit. You are already clean because of the word which I have spoken to you. Abide in Me, and I in you. As the branch cannot bear fruit of itself, unless it abides in the vine, neither can you, unless you abide in Me"

BEHAVE AS A CHURCH

(John 15:1-4 NKJV). John later writes, "And now, little children, abide in Him, that when He appears, we may have confidence and not be ashamed before Him at His coming" (1 John 2:28 NKJV). What exactly does it mean to abide in Christ? It means that we as believers are to remain stable, fixed in a position of complete faith and trust in God. It means we are consistently obeying or putting into practice what God has commanded of us in His Word. Jesus made our mission as clear as He could and obeying His command our motivation.

Mandate to Witness

So, if Jesus commanded us to go and make disciples in the great commission found in Matthew 28:18-20; then why do so few Christians take the initiative to share the gospel of Christ? First, those who do not share are misguided because they have a misguided sense of ethics. The current view of ethics tells Christians that they would be imposing their convictions on others. Would God command us to do something that is unethical? Of course not! We are not seeking to impose or force our theology upon them, we are simply informing of the dangers of living with Jesus Christ in their lives. God does not force people to respond to His free gift of gracious salvation, He want them to know that He loves them and for them to make an informed decision to accept that gift or reject that gift.

Next, those who do not share have misjudged the lost. Some how Christians, that do not share the gospel, has gotten the idea that those without Christ do no want to hear the gospel. They believe that people without Christ will be hostile and unresponsive. But "Then He said to His disciples, "The harvest truly is plentiful, but the laborers are few. Therefore, pray the Lord of the harvest to send out laborers into His harvest" (Matt. 9:37-38 NKJV). One of Satan's best lies is to try to convince Christians that lost people do not want to hear the gospel. He will insult by trying to get us believe a twisted version of God's Word. Jesus told us that there are plenty of people who will hear the gospel, Satan says you know that cannot be true. Think about the truth of God's Word, in most cases we will get a polite response from hearing what we have to say. Furthermore, we must remember that

God is our protector and do not need to fear as we go in faith and obedience to share the gospel.

Plus, those who do not share are misinformed. There are those church members who feel that for a witness to share the gospel, the witness must have certain spiritual gifts to witness. Jesus said, "But you shall receive power when the Holy Spirit has come upon you; and you shall be witnesses to Me in Jerusalem, and in all Judea and Samaria, and to the end of the earth" (Acts 1:8 NKJV). Again, would God command us to do something that we could not do? A witness is sworn to tell the truth of what he or she saw or experienced. Sometimes we make mistakes, and we fumble over words while we share the gospel. However, make not mistake about, we are called to be witnesses not a super salesman attempting to persuade the person with special abilities. Besides that, man cannot persuade another man to be saved. Jesus puts it this way, "No man can come to Me unless the Father who sent Me draws him; and I will raise him up at the last day" (John 6:44 NKJV). The only person who can persuade men to be save is the Holy Spirit that lives in the Christian. Christians are only witnesses to that which has happened to them.

Last, Christians who do not share the gospel with others may have their priorities misplaced. Some people get themselves into all types of difficulties by trying to figure out how to prioritize God, self, family, job, church, etc. Why do we seek to make this complicated? Jesus said, "But seek first the kingdom of God and all His righteousness, and all these things shall be added to you" (Matt. 6:33 NKJV). In other words, put God first. As we honestly do this, we will find greater order and freedom in our lives and He will prioritize the rest of our lives. We will then learn to behave as a church. How tragic it is for people to miss out on the abundant life found in Christ. We must go and tell them the good news! We as Christians have a divine mandate to go and witness to the lost; we have biblical motivation for evangelism!

An Unstoppable Force

The angels said, "Men of Galilee, why do you stand gazing up into the heaven? This same Jesus, who was taken up from you into heaven, will so com in like manner as you saw Him go into heaven. Then they returned to Jerusalem from the mount called Olivet, which is near Jerusalem, a Sabbath day's journey" (Acts 1:11-12 NKJV). The disciples went back and tarried just as Jesus commanded them to (Luke 24:49). Luke tells us that on the Day of Pentecost, "They were all filled with Holy Spirit and began to speak with other tongues, as the Spirit gave them utterance" (Acts 2:4 NKJV). The disciples, along with some of the other saints were in the upper room praying when the Holy Spirit came in. Then in Acts 2, we see there were three thousand people who got saved, and later in Acts 4:4 we read about five thousand more people were saved. In Acts 5:14 it says, "And believers were increasingly added to the Lord, multitudes of both men and women" (NKJV). The point is this, the early church was an unstoppable force, because they were doing what they were commanded to do by the power of the Holy Spirit which dwelt inside them. Therefore, the church today can be an unstoppable force as well if we would behave as a church allowing the power of the Holy Spirit to flow through us.

The fear of man did not stop them from doing God's work. In Acts 5 the disciples were brought in before the council for preaching the gospel. They said to them, "Did we not strictly command you not to teach in this name? And look, you have filled Jerusalem with your doctrine, and intend to bring this Man's blood on us!" But Peter and the other apostles answered and said, "We ought to obey God rather than man" (Acts 5:28-29 NKJV). The disciples took their command personally. They were not going to let some two-bit politicians hinder their work, because they had the power of the Holy Spirit in them (Acts 4:31). When the people of God fall in in love with their Lord and Savior Jesus Christ and yield their bodies to the control of the Holy Spirit, you have an unstoppable force. The gates of shall not prevail against them, because "now when they saw the boldness of Peter and John, and perceived that they were uneducated and untrained men, they marveled. And they realized that they had been with Jesus" (Acts 4:13 NKJV). The New Testament church suffers today because those who would oppose us cannot see Jesus in our lives. These disciples had Jesus written all over them. It makes a difference when you are doing the work of God through the power of the Holy Spirit.

As the early church went out to share the gospel then did not let the fear of persecution stop them either. "As for Saul, he made havoc of the church, entering every house, and dragging off men and women, committing them to prison. Therefore, those who were scattered went everywhere preaching the word" (Acts 8:3-4 NKJV). Yes, it is true the early believers did become scattered and literally run for their lives because of the persecution. Who was leading the persecution against them? None other than Saul, who later became Paul, the church planter of several early New Testament churches. The persecution allowed them to take the gospel to the uttermost parts of the earth. The persecution and other fears they may have had, become a great motivation tool in the spread of the gospel. "And this continued for two years, so that all who dwelt in Asia heard the word of the Lord Jesus, both Jews and Greeks" (Acts 19:10 NKJV). The church, today, has not begun to behave as a church who has gotten a hold of this motivation like the first century church did. We seem to huddle up and hunker down trying to protect our little flocks. When will we wake up and realize that we are an unstoppable force that the world must reckon with? When will we be willing to go out on the limb a little farther or get out of the boat and walk on water keeping our eyes on the Author and Finisher of our faith? Until we do, we will never begin to see the fruit like the early church had.

Over two thousand years ago, Jesus stood on a mountain overlooking Jerusalem and said to His disciples, "Let not your heart be troubled; you believe in God, believe also in Me. In My Father's house are many mansions; if it were not so, I would have told you. I go to prepare a place for you. And if I go and prepare a place for you, I will come again and receive you to Myself; that where I am, there you may be also" (John 14:1-3 NKJV). That is an unfailing promise. If it was not so, He would have told us. I believe it! I am holding on to that promise! I am looking for Him to coming back at any time! Until He comes, you are part of what He left behind to do, His work! The disciples were willing to "tarry" before the Lord and as a result. They were rewarded with power. They literally changed their world through the power of God in their lives. We can see God moving in our churches today. We can see many sinners saved, homes salvaged, and lives reclaimed. We can experience the manifest presence of God in our worship services. We can experience God's conviction moving on the hearts and lives of all those who come to church. If we are willing to behave as a church. Have you ever tarried before the face of God until He filled you with His power? Have you wrestled in prayer for your family, your church, your country, or yourself? Are you guilty, as I have often been, of being too busy to pray? We are needy people, but one thing we need the most is the very thing God wants to give His children, His power! Will go before God and call on His name, and expect Him to move mountains and do miracles? Will you "tarry" until? There is much work to be done.

CHAPTER SEVENTEEN

Seeking Christ and Lifting Him Up

When they had finished the days, as they returned, the
Boy Jesus lingered behind in Jerusalem. And Joseph and
His mother did not know it; but supposing Him to have
been in the company, they went a day's journey, and
sought Him among their relatives and acquaintances.
(Luke 2:43-44 NKJV)

IT HAS BEEN MY OBSERVATION THAT PEOPLE SAY THINGS IN SUCH A
way that they really know what they are saying. For example, there
has been some who have said to me, "I found Jesus at the age of such
and such age." Or "I found Jesus when I went with my parents to a
revival many years ago." What they do not understand, by the way
they are making that kind of statement is they are implying that
Jesus is lost. Wayward Christians make similar statements, such as,
"I found Christ again from just going to that old fashion gospel music
concert at church." Again, this implies that they lost or misplaced
Christ. I understand what they are trying to say when they make
those statements, however, we must never forget that the Lord found
us before we ever found Him. You cannot find someone who is not
lost, and the Lord never was lost, but you and I were.

Look at what happened to Joseph and Mary in Luke 2. Jesus, who
at the time was twelve years old, went with His parents to present to

the Passover. While they were at the celebration, with a lot of people, family, and friends; somehow Jesus gets separated from Joseph and Mary. As far as they knew He was within their traveling caravan or with one of the family members. Therefore, they go ahead a pack up to leave and head back home. His parents went a day's journey before they recognized that Jesus was not with them or even in the caravan of people. They had lost Jesus during the celebration of the Passover, which was all about Jesus the Lamb of God. Then after three days of seeking to find Jesus, they found Him in the temple, among the teachers. He was listening to them as well as asking them questions (Luke 2:47). "So, when they saw Him, they were amazed; and His mother said to Him, "Son, why have You done this to us? Look, Your father and I have sought You anxiously" (Luke 2:48 NKJV). Let's make the statement again, you cannot find someone who is not lost. "And He said to them, "Why did you seek Me? Did you not know that I must be about My Father's business?" (vs. 49 NKJV). What His Father's business? Luke tells us, "For the Son of Man has come to seek and to save that which was lost" (Luke 19:10 NKJV). While Jesus is not lost, I cannot help but wonder how many people has had this same thing happen to them?

In What Sense May We Lose Jesus?

As you know, Joseph and Mary were related to Jesus. Joseph is His foster father and Mary is His biological mother. Now, being related to Jesus in what sense did they lose Jesus? They did not lose Jesus in the sense of relationship for they are still His earthly parents. They lost Him in the sense of fellowship. Let's apply this question to us, if we are related to Him, adopted children of God, then in what sense do we lose Jesus? Listen, if you are saved by the grace of God through faith (Eph. 2:8-9), then you can never lose that relationship with Him. Jesus said, "My sheep hear My voice, and I know them, and they follow Me. And I give them eternal life, and they shall never perish; neither shall anyone snatch them out of My hand" (John 10:27-28 NKJV). If you read that verse 28 from the King James Version it reads like this, "And I give unto them eternal life; and they shall never perish,

neither shall any *man* pluck them out of my hand" (John 10:28 KJV).
Notice that the word "man" is in italics. That means it is not in the
original language. Therefore, the publisher of the KJV you have made
it italicized, so you know it is not in the original language. Now what
is being said is this: "Neither shall any pluck them out of my hand."
Any what? Any man, any event, anything. Some people have the idea
that the devil can take you out of the hand of God. That is ridiculous!
If the devil could take you of God's hand, then why has he not done
it? The only reason he has not is because he cannot! You cannot lose
the Lord Jesus Christ in the sense of relationship.

But let's use the whole council of God. We looked at the security
of the believer in the New Testament, let's move to the Old Testament.
A great corresponding verse to the one we just looked at is found in
Psalm 37:23-24 which says, "The steps of a good man are ordered by
the Lord, and He delights in his way. Though he falls, he shall not be
utterly cast down; for the Lord upholds him with His hand" (NKJV).
The word "ordered" means "secured, established" (Dictionary, 1828)
and if a believer was to stumble God would be there to pick the
believer up, dust the believer off, and put the believer back on the
right path again. For God can keep us from stumbling (Jude 24) and
restore us if we do stumble. Why would a righteous Heavenly Father
do such a thing? Because He is a loving Father who delights in and
wants to see His children succeed. For example, if you are trying to
teach your child to walk, when the little toddler gets old enough to
take a few steps, he may fall and get up, and fall again and get up. But
if you are in a particular situation where you do not want him to fall,
what would you do? Suppose you are crossing the street; you do not
just give him your finger like you would if you were just walking. No,
you would put his entire hand in your hand, and now he is not holding
on to you, you are holding on to him. Then you would start across
the street and when his little knees buckle because he can only go so
far, "though he falls, he shall not be utterly cast down, for the Lord
upholds him with His hand" (Ps. 37:24 NKJV).

So, there can be a loss of fellowship, but not a loss of relationship.
In Luke 2, Mary and Joseph said, "Your father and I have sought
You anxiously" (vs. 48 NKJV). Their hearts were filled with torment,

sorrow, pain; they were anxious to find Jesus. There was a time when I was physically lost. My family and I were on a trip to Washington D.C. We had just visited the Washington Monument and were heading back to where we parked, which was near the Jefferson Memorial. I decided to go ahead of the group and make it back to the van before them. As I was walking in such a fast pace, due to my emotions being upset, I missed the turn on the sidewalk I was supposed to take and kept on walking straight. I had walked several blocks before I realized I was lost. When I came to my sense of direction, I was filled with anxiety and nervously headed back towards the turn I was supposed to take. When I got to the turn, I met my dad and my younger brother walking in a fast pace trying to find me. When my dad sees me, he lets out a deep sigh of air, as if to be relieved he found me. He must have been filled with anxiety and me being physically lost must have caused him pain. We then met up with the rest of the group. May I tell you that if you are out of fellowship with the Lord, I am certain that you have no joy in your walk with Christ. You might have happiness; you may have fun, but you are not going to have joy. The most miserable person in the world is not an unsaved person. The most miserable person in the world is a saved person who is out of fellowship with Jesus Christ. Mary and Joseph looked for Jesus, and they were filled with sorrow; they had no joy at that moment in time. Let me ask you, is there joy in your heart right now? Do you have "joy unspeakable and full of glory" (1 Pet. 1:8 KNJV)? You might be thinking, "Well, nobody is supposed to be joyous all the time." I am going to have to disagree. Paul writes, "Rejoice in the Lord always. Again, I will say, rejoice" (Phil. 4:4 NKJV)! Anxiety is a thief that robs you of your joy. The only way you can rejoice is to stop and rejoice in the Lord for He never changes.

Who may lose Jesus?

It may surprise us to read that it was Joseph and Mary were the ones who lost Jesus (Luke 2:43). Might I just add, those who we least expect to lose the Lord Jesus are the ones who do. It could be a deacon of a church. It could be one sitting to the right of the pastor when he is preaching, could be the one who sits on the left of the pastor. It could be the man behind the pulpit who is in danger of losing the Lord Jesus Christ. If you study the Bible, you will find out that God's men got out of fellowship with Him from time to time. Noah, David, Moses, Samson, Peter, all of these, and others in the Bible got out of fellowship with the Lord. Paul puts it this way, "Therefore let him who thinks he stands take heed lest he fall" (1 Cor. 10:12 NKJV). One theologian said, "An unguarded strength is a double weakness." (Unknown, 2015) Do you think you are beyond getting away from the Lord? Mary did. Joseph did. The great saints of the Bible have at one time, or another gotten away from the Lord. Sometimes people tend to think, "You know, if I were just like our pastor and lived in a holy atmosphere, then I would never have any temptations. Our pastor just does not know what I am facing out there in the dirty old world." Listen to me, as a pastor, you do not know that the devil aims his biggest guns at God's servants. Furthermore, it does not matter who you are, you have never come to a place where you are not in danger of slipping away from the Lord.

Where do we lose Jesus?

Notice what was going on when Joseph and Mary lost Jesus. "His parents went to Jerusalem every year at the Feast of the Passover" (Luke 2:41 NKJV). These parents lost Jesus during a religious ceremony, in a spiritual celebration. They did not lose Him in a dance hall. They did not lose Him in a nightclub. They did not lose Him in some den of iniquity. They lost Him during a church service, a religious ceremony! The Passover was all about Jesus, and it was there that they lost Jesus. Do you know what I found out when I was going to seminary? I found out that a great number of seminary students would backslide with a Bible under their arm in seminary. I mean, amid studying about the Lord Jesus Christ, somehow, they lost that fellowship with the Lord Jesus.

As a matter of fact, the Lord Jesus argued with the church of Laodicea in Revelation 3. He said, "Because you say, 'I am rich, have become wealthy, and have need of nothing', and do not know that you are wretched miserable, poor, blind, and naked" (Rev. 3:17 NKJV). Then He ends that letter to Laodicea by saying, "Behold, I stand at the door and knock. If anyone hears My voice and opens the door, I will come into him and dine with him, and he with Me" (Rev. 3:20 NKJV). Where is He knocking? Well, He is not knocking on the door of the sinner's heart. He is knocking on the door of the church, on the door of the hearts of the church members. Yes, it is true, "For where two or three are gathered together in My name, I am there in the midst of them" (Matt. 18:20 NKJV), but sometimes we have so forgotten His name He is out there on the outside knocking trying to get in. This is like what the psalmist pondered on in Psalm 44. In verses 9-22, he states what Israel was going through at the time and was wondering why God would allow them to go through it since they were doing what they were supposed to do. However, he makes a statement that answers his own ponderings, which prove the reason why they were going through it and why Jesus is on the outside knocking on the church members hearts door. He says, "Our heart has not turned back, nor have our steps departed from your way" (Ps. 44:18 NKJV). There are two possible ways of looking at what he says. First, he is saying, "We have been faithful to you Lord and our hearts have not turned back to the things of the world." Second, he is saying, "Our hearts have not turned back to the Lord." In other words, the people of Israel had not truly repented of their sins of worshiping idols. The church of Laodicea had not repented of their sin of pride and had quenched the Holy Spirit (1 Thess. 5:19). We can lose Jesus where we are when we quench the Holy Spirit in our hearts. Will any holiday take you from Jesus? It could, but it does not have to be a holiday, any day we can quench Him and lose Him. Again, not talking about losing your salvation, just want to make that very clear. The very Passover celebration was that which separated Joseph and Mary from Jesus. What a lesson that ought to be to us! What a warning that ought to stand for us today! They lost Jesus during a religious celebration.

How may we lose Jesus?

How did Joseph and Mary lose Jesus? By assumption, they just assumed He was with them, and they did not even check. "But supposing Hime to have been in the company, they went a day's journey" (Luke 2:44

NKJV). They did not lose Him by getting drunk. They did not lose Him by opposing Him or denying Him. They went a day's journey and went one step at a time. Every step they took, they were getting further from Him, supposing the whole time He was with them.

I wonder if that is true about you. I had to ask myself this question. "Chris, are you just supposing that you are right with God? Are you just supposing that Jesus is a reality in your life?" It is easy to just suppose, I mean you can preach, you can sing, you can be a deacon, you can go to church, you can teach a class, you can give your tithes, and you go day to day and say, "Well, I am fine." Well, you might want to think again, for example: look at Samson the strongest man. The Bible says, "And she said, "The Philistines are upon you, Samson!" So, he awoke from his sleep, and said, "I will go out as before, at other times, and shake myself free!" But he did not know that the Lord had departed from him" (Judg. 16:20 NKJV). They went a day's journey, a step at a time, just simply supposing that Jesus was with them.

I wonder are you willing to investigate your own heart and see if the presence of Jesus is a reality or mere assumption? Neglect is often the way to get away from Jesus, and that neglect is often based on assumption. It is often the cause of backsliding. The church members of Laodicea said, "I am rich, have become wealthy, and have need of nothing" (Rev. 3:17 NKJV). Do you know what a danger that is? The danger is that I could be writing this book and supposing that Jesus is real in my heart. May I suggest that from time to time you take a spiritual inventory of your heart instead of taking another step and getting further away from Him and supposing He is with you?

How can we find Jesus Again?

Where did Mary and Josephe find Jesus? Right where they left Him. They found Him by going back to where they first lost Him. If Jesus is not real to you as He once was; if you do not have that conscious awareness of His presence in your life, then go back to where you first left Him. This is the command that Jesus sent to the church at Ephesus. He said, "Nevertheless I have this against you, that you have left your first love. Remember therefore from where you have fallen; repent and do the first works, or else I will come to you quickly and remove your lampstand from its place, unless you repent" (Rev. 2:4-5 NKJV). Jesus told them to remember where they left Him and to repent. Repentance is the turning around from the direction you are going, a turning around to come back to Jesus (Wood, Marshall, & Millard, 1996) You are probably thinking, "Well I do not know where that was." I believe, if you would open your heart, by humbling yourself to the Lord, He will show you where it was. If you will pray this prayer, "Search me, O God, and know my heart; try me and know my anxieties; and see if there is any wicked way in me and lead me in the way everlasting" (Ps. 139: 23-24 NKJV).

If you will let God lead you to search you to deep down, then I believe you will know where you have gotten away (lost) from Jesus. Maybe you have just been neglecting your quiet time, where you read your Bible, pray, and meditate upon the Scripture. Maybe you have loved the newspaper, television, FaceBook, or social media app more than you have loved the Bible. Maybe you have stopped attending the worship services like you used to, and now it is more convenient to catch a service when you can on a social media page. Do not get me wrong those social media apps are tools to get the message of God out, however you miss out on the fellowship you can have with fellow believers. Or maybe you have lost Jesus because you have some bitterness, some grudge in your heart. Or maybe it is carelessness, going on day after day without tuning your heart in and getting to know the Lord Jesus Christ. Where will you find Jesus? Right where you left Him when you repent and confess that sin.

There is a story about a father and son who were living together. The wife to the father and mother to the son had died, and the father and the son had a sweet fellowship living in the little cottage. It was a chilly night, and the father said to his son, "Son, the fire is going out. Will you go get another piece of wood and put it on the fire?" The son said, "Dad, I'm busy. You get the wood." The Father said, "Son, I'm asking you if you'll go get the piece of wood to put on the fire. I'm your father. I'm older than you are. That's not an unthinkable thing that I would ask you to do." The son said, "I'm busy." The father then said, "Son, listen. I'm sorry it must come to this. I'm not asking you now; I'm telling you. 'Go get another piece of wood and put it on the fire!'" The son said, "Well, since you are telling me, I'm going to give you the answer, No, I will not do it." It got cold in the room, not only physically, but there was that clash between the two wills. Then the father said to his son, "Now, son, this serious matter, more serious than a piece of wood. You have defied me. You have refused to do what I have asked you to do and then told you to do. Now, son, this is my house. You are a grown man. You are living under my roof. The least you could do would be to obey your father." The son said, "I am not going to do it." "Well, son, it is come down to this; either you obey me, or you cannot stay here anymore." "Very well," said the son, "I will not stat here anymore." He then jumped up, walked out of the cottage into the night, and slammed the door behind him. He walked away from his father and from the house; the broken-hearted, perplexed father continued to sit there.

The days came and went. The son began to think of himself, "I have been a fool. Why was I so selfish? Why was I so stubborn? How can I treat my own dear father that way? How can I fail to obey him? I have been wicked. I do not deserve to be forgiven, but I want to be, and I am going to humble myself and go back to the father." He went back, like the prodigal son. He said, "Dad, I am so sorry. I do not know what got into me. I am sure it was just sheer wickedness, sheer pride, sheer selfishness. Daddy, you have been a wonderful dad to me. Thank you for taking care of me. Thank you for loving me. Forgive me, dad, for my arrogance, for my selfishness. Dad, I would like to come back and spend my days with you. Can I come in?" The father with tears, reached out his arms and said, "Son, that is an answer to my prayers. I am so glad you have come home. Thank you for doing that. Come on in. But, son, before you sit down, would you put another piece of wood on the fire?" You know where you left Him. You know where you got away from God. How are you going to get back to Him? Just go right back where you left Him. Whatever it was, go back to that spot, go back to that place, go back to that disobedience, and deal with it. Until you do, you cannot have that fellowship with Jesus.

What to do after you find Jesus?

As redundant as it may sound, when you come back to place where you first lost Jesus, this is where you are to start obeying what he first commanded you to do by lifting up Jesus. Jesus said, "And so Moses lifted up the serpent in the wilderness, even so must the Son of Man be lifted up, that whoever believes in Him should not perish but have eternal life. For God so loved the world that He gave His only begotten Son, that whoever believes in Him should not perish but have everlasting life. For God did not send His Son into the world to condemn the world, but that the world through Him might be saved. He who believes in Him is not condemned; but he who does not believe is condemned already, because he has not believed in the name of the only begotten Son of God" (John 3:14-18 NKJV).

A SINFUL REBELLION

To understand what Jesus means, you need to understand the history behind when Moses lifted up the serpent in the wilderness. That history is found in Numbers 21:5-9. Which says, "And the people spoke against God and Moses: "Why have you brought us up out of Egypt to die in the wilderness? For there is no food and no water, and our soul loathes this worthless bread." So, the Lord sent fiery serpents among the people, and they bit the people; and many of the people of Israel died. Therefore, the people came to Moses, and said, "We have sinned, for we have spoken against the Lord and against you; pray to the Lord that He take away the serpents from us." So, Moses prayed for the people. Then the Lord said to Moses, "Make a fiery serpent, and set it on a pole; and it shall be that everyone who is bitten, when he looks at it, shall live." So, Moses made a bronze serpent, and put it on a pole; and so, it was, if a serpent had bitten anyone, when he looked at the bronze serpent, he lived" (Num. 21:5-9 NKJV).

The people had a problem they had lost Jehovah God due to a rebellious state of mind. God was present with them and was working on bringing them from the land of bondage, which was the land of Egypt, through the wilderness to the Promised Land. The Promised Land was a land that was flowing with milk and honey, it was the goal of their journey. However, right in the middle of their journey they started murmuring, then started complaining, where they finally rebelled against God. The lost God when they took their focus off God's promise and put their focus upon what they were going through at the time. They even asked, "Moses, did you bring us out here to die?" In God's promise to them He never said anything about dying in the wilderness. God had promise that He would bring them to a land that flowed with milk and honey, a land of grapes and pomegranates and figs, a land of victory. But they doubted God's promise. This is going to be most of the reasons why we lose Christ in the first place it is because of the sin of doubting God's promises. Unbelief is the major sin, the mother sin, the father sin, the sin out of which all other sins grow, and it is the one sin that will condemn and send a lost person to hell. Men do not go to hell because they lie, steal, cheat. Jesus said, "He who believes in Him is not condemned; but he who does not believe is condemned already, because he has not believed in the name of the only begotten Son of God" (John 3:18 NKJV). That is why the Holy Spirit has come to convince the world of sin, because they believe not (John 16:9). Unbelief is a terrible sin. It is not an intellectual matter; it is always a moral matter. The children of Israel doubted God and when you doubt God you are calling God a liar. "He who believes in the Son of God has the witness in himself; he who does not believe God has made Him a liar, because he has not believed in the testimony that God has given of His Son" (1 John 5:10). Would you point a finger in the face of God and call Him a liar? Basically, that is what you are doing when you doubt Him.

Not only did they doubt God's promise, but they did not like God's provision, bread from heaven which was the manna. They said, "Our souls dislike this light bread." In John 6:30-35, Jesus explained to people, that the bread that fell from heaven represented the Lord Jesus Christ. Just as the bread that God gave to the children of Israel in the wilderness, even so Jesus came down from heaven. The manna was round which speaks of His eternality, meaning Jesus never had an ending nor a beginning. The manna was white which speaks of His purity. The manna had the flavor of oil which speaks of the Holy Spirit that was upon Him. The manna was sweet, just as Jesus is sweet. The manna was found upon the ground to show us the humanity of Jesus. The manna had to be picked up show us the resurrection of Jesus. The manna had to be eaten giving us the why of salvation by putting our trust in the Lord and absorbing the Lord. Manna gave life to the Israelites, just as Jesus gives everlasting life to those who invite Him into their hearts. However, the children of Israel said they did not want it. They hated it, despised it and would rather have the world's garlic than to have the bread of life.

They despised God's prophet as well. In Numbers 21:5, it tells us that the people spoke against God and against Moses. Since they were angry with God, then it is only logical that they were angry with Moses. This is something I have learned in my years as pastor and minister, which is pastor and ministers should not get upsell if nobody like them. There are some people who do not like a certain kind of preaching. The people of Israel did not like how God was taking care of them. Instead of being grateful for their blessings and joyful for the food that the Lord was giving them, they robbed God of His glory by rejecting Him and His messenger. God was patient with Israel throughout her history and sent one servant after another, but they refused to obey. Finally, He sent His only begotten Son, and they killed Him. Pastors and ministers should not get upset because their message is not well received, people did not like the message Jesus had either. If we are going to behave as a church, then we need to stop rebelling against God and His messengers.

A SURE RETRIBUTION

Why did God send serpents to bite the rebellious children of Israel? In the Bible the serpent is always a symbol of sin. Since the first time the serpent crawled his slimy frame into the pages of history in the Garden of Eden, the serpent always represents sin. God want to show them if they were bound to sin, they were bound to suffer, and so everywhere they walked that day there were these reptiles lying in wait. They got into their tents, their beds, their pots, and people were being bitten by these serpents. God did that. Some people do not like the idea that it was God that did it, but it was fitting that God should do it this way.

251

There are even some who think that God has no right to punish sin. If the Supreme Court of America put this issue on trial, they would vote to outlaw hell as cruel and unusual punishment. They would say God has no right to do that. Let me clarify, it is not that God is too good to punish sin; it is that God is too good not to punish sin. It is the goodness of God, the righteousness of God, and the holiness of God that says sin must be punished. If you die without Jesus in your heart, you will go to hell, and it will not be God's fault! It will be your fault!

The serpents bit the people, and many died from those bites. Which means that with every bite of the serpent, those fatal fangs sank into the flesh, and sent an awful excruciating pain like a liquid fire. Their joints would stiffen, and their eyes would become glazed over. God was teaching them that it is a painful thing to rebel against God. God was teaching them, that "the wages of sin is death" (Rom. 6:23 NKJV); "the soul that sins, it shall die" (Ezek. 18:4, 20 NKJV). This is not a physical death but an illustration of the greater spiritual death. James puts it this way, "Then, when desire had conceived, it gives birth to sin; and sin, when it is full-grown, brings forth death" (Jam. 1:15 NKJV).

A SAVING REMEDY

The children of Israel came to Moses and repented (Num. 21:7-8). They said, "We have sinned and come short of the glory of God." They asked Moses to go to God on their behalf of their sins and ask God to forgive them. Now, Israel had complained and rebelled many times, and once had submitted, "We have sinned" (Num. 14:40), but this is the first time their "We have sinned" seems to be sincere. In the past, Moses would fall on his face before God and intercede for the people, but not they are asking him to go to God. Moses prayed for a solution for the people's serpent problem. However, the Lord did not answer Moses's prayer the way the people were expecting Him to. They were expecting him to remove the serpents and heal the people who had been bitten. Instead, He instructed Moses to make a bronze serpent and place it on a pole and lift it up so all the people had to do was simply look upon it and they would be instantly healed. Jesus used the bronze serpent as an illustration, as He talked to Nicodemus, it was a story that he would have been familiar with. Jesus was using it to illustrate His own death on the cross (John 3:14). "Lifted up" was a phrase used in that day to refer to crucifixion (Wood, Marshall, & Millard, 1996) The comparison between the bronze serpent in Moses' day an the cross of Christ gives us a better understand of what God's grace in salvation means. All people have been infected by sin and will one day die and face the judgment of God (Heb. 9:27), but when they look to Jesus by faith, He will save them and give them eternal life. When the children of Israel looked upon the bronze serpent it saved them from physical death, but when lost sinners look to Jesus, He saves them from eternal death. But why should Moses make a model of a serpent, the very creature that was causing the people to die? Because on the cross, Jesus became sin for us; the very thing that condemns people; and bore in His body that which brings spiritual death (2 Cor. 5:21). Jesus was willing to become like that bronze serpent. He became sin for you and me.

But why was the serpent made of brass? Because throughout the Bible brass is symbol of judgment. What God was saying is that sin must be judge before man can be saved. God cannot overlook our sins. Jesus became our sins, and therefore took our curse for us. He was placed on a pole (cross). Paul said it this way, "Christ has redeemed us from the curse of the law, having become a curse for us (for it is written, "Cursed is everyone who hangs on a tree")" (Gal. 3:13 NKJV). Jesus was impaled upon that cross just as the serpent was impaled upon that pole and lifted up. That is why Jesus is using this illustration to teach Nicodemus, He knew He would be crucified.

THE SIMPLE REQUIREMENT

Did you know how simple it was to be healed from the snake bite? "Then the Lord said to Moses, "Make a fiery serpent, and set in on a pole; and it shall be that everyone who is bitten, when he looks at it, shall live"" (Num. 21:8 NKJV). That is so simple, it is almost absurd. You could expect God to have some complex plan for man to have to go through to be saved, but it is not for God made salvation simple as simple can be. All the Israelites had to do and live was look. Salvation is easy, it is not hard to believe. All you must do is "Believe on the Lord Jesus Chris, you will be saved" (Acts 16:31 NKJV). They did not have to work for it; they did not have to pray for it; or pay for it; all the Israelites had to do was look and live. "For by grace are you saved through faith, and that not of yourselves; it is the gift of God, not of works, lest anyone should boast" (Eph. 2:8-9 NKJV). The gospel of the Lord Jesus Christ is easy to understand, so simple that little children can understand it.

Do not think that because salvation is free and because it is simple that it is not important. Because that would be a tragic mistake. But that is how the mind works. We think, "Well if it is simple, then it must not be important. If it so easy, then it must be cheap." Salvation is not cheap it cost God everything, His only begotten Son (John 3:16). Jesus died in agony and shed His blood to pay the sin debt, and there is no other way. God only has one plan. "Nor salvation in any other, for there is no other name under heaven given among men by which we must be saved" (Acts 4:12 NKJV). "Jesus said to him, "I am the way, the truth, and the life. No one comes to the Father except through Me" (John 14:6 NKJV). God does not force anybody to look. Some of the Israelites looked, and some did not. Some were healed, some were not. I preach the gospel, but those who hear the message are the ones who must decide. I cannot make them decide. Jesus did not win everyone that He talked with. The rich young ruler went away sorrowful (Matt. 19:22). God gives you the privilege of saying yes or saying no.

If we are going to behave as a church, we need to be lifting up Jesus and telling them how to be saved and teach them how to behave as a follower of Christ. It is our job, our duty, our responsibility as a church to lift up Jesus.

CHAPTER EIGHTEEN

Great is Thy Faithfulness

Through the Lord's mercies we are not consumed,
because His compassions fail not. They are new
every morning; great is Your faithfulness.
(Lamentations 3:22-23 NKJV)

IF WE ARE GOING TO BEHAVE AS A CHURCH, AND IF WE ARE TO
be lifting up Jesus, then we must focus on the faithfulness of God;
for our benefit and being a lighthouse to the world. However, I
know that struggles are real. We face them on a regular basis, and
therefore it does make life difficult, little lone trying to behave.
The church is no different from that of regular life, for the church
is made up of incomplete Christians. However, to keep from losing
Jesus in the church, we must rally around one another, encourage
one another, love one another, lift up one another, all by focusing
on the author and finisher of our faith (Heb. 12:2). He is the
faithful God (Deut. 7:9) and when we consider the faithfulness of
God, we can be strengthened to conduct the commissioning work
that He commanded us to do. His faithfulness nurtures us, grows
us, holds us up, therefore, we can have the "blessed assurance that
Jesus is mine, O what a foretaste of glory divine" (Crosby, 1873)
If you were to look for someone in the Bible who knew about
struggles of life, then you should take a look at Jeremiah who
wrote Lamentations.

The book of Lamentations is a series of songs of mourning which were written against the backdrop of the Babylonian invasion and destruction of Jerusalem. In Lamentations we can see the awful sufferings endured by the people of Jerusalem at the hands of their enemies. Even amid all the pain and turmoil, God had someone in Jerusalem who would record the events and bring honor to His Holy name. Jeremiah was known as the Weeping Prophet and when you study his life, you see a life that reveals a portrait of unending sadness and deep depression. Let me give you a list of things that Jeremiah went through and was still able to lift up the faithfulness of God. He received an unwanted call to be a minister (Jer. 1:5-6). He was commanded to only preach about the judgment of God (Jer. 1:9-10). He was forbidden to marry, so he could give himself fully to his ministry (16:1-13) and therefore had to deal with loneliness. Jeremiah had bouts of deep depression which caused him to weep openly about the sins of the people (9:1). His depression was caused by the prolonged unconcern of the people who heard his message and paid him no mind. This caused him to want to get out of the ministry (20:9). His pain can be seen in the span of a fifty-year ministry without even one convert. Jeremiah was put into prison by King Zedekiah because the king did not approve of Jeremiah's preaching (32:5). Even while the Babylonians are invading the city in fulfillment of Jeremiah's prophecy, Jeremiah sits in the dungeon (32:2). After Jerusalem falls and many have been killed or taken captive, Jeremiah does not gloat or take the "I told you so!" approach. Instead, he becomes broken with the remnant and suffers with them (Lam. 1-5).

After enduring all of this in his lifetime; being rejected, hated, mocked, imprisoned, ignored, after seeing Jerusalem ransacked, desecrated, and destroyed, after experiencing the horror of war, the brutality of the enemy, the pangs of hunger, Jeremiah was still able to stand forth amid the rubble of the city and the bodies of the dead and lift his voice in praise to God for His great, unfailing faithfulness to His people (Lam. 3:22-23). How did he possibly do it? Despite his trials and his troubles, Jeremiah had gotten a good grasp on the reality of just Who God is, so he would never loss God in his life. Jeremiah knew whether things went well, or whether everything fell apart.

God would still be God and that God would be eternally faithful to people (Lam. 3:21-23). Jeremiah was still able to find hope in a hopeless situation because he believed in the faithfulness of His great God. Again, like Jeremiah, we all go through times when life seems to fall apart at the seams. When these times come, we also need to His blessed assurance He is faithful. Thankfully, the Bible gives overwhelming evidence of the unchanging faithfulness of our Lord and Savior Jesus Christ.

God is Faithful in His Grace

"Through the Lord's mercies we are not consumed, because His compassions fail not" (Lam. 3:22 NKJV). The word mercy which is translated "loving-kindness" (Strong's Concordance, 1984) is used over thirty times in the Old Testament. It is a very expressive word that conveys all the ideas of "love, grace, mercy, faithfulness, goodness, and devotion" (Wood, Marshall, & Millard, 1996) From this word it gives us the picture of God as the Divine lover of His creation mankind. This word finds its New Testament equivalent in the principle that God loves the whole world (John 3:16). Jeremiah seems to have turned from contemplating his misery to remembering that it was the pure grace of God, which brought Israel out of their slavery in Egypt. It was also grace that had kept them a redeemed people despite their failures and wonderings. Here are some things we can remember that God did for us through His grace.

THERE IS GRACE TO SAVE US

It was only by the grace of God that reached down into our lost, doomed condition to save those whosoever who would accept (Eph. 2:1-9). We in our wretched state could never do anything on our own to save ourselves, for we would always fall short (Rom. 3:23). Therefore, it was God Who came to us! He came in the Person of the Lord Jesus Christ to die for our sins (Phil. 2:5-8). He came in the Person of the Holy Spirit to draw us to God so that we might be saved (John 16:7-11; 6:44).

THERE IS GRACE TO SECURE US

God through His grace has the power to keep us saved and forever in His hands (John 10:28). Yes, we are prone to failure, to spiritual wanderings, therefore, if our salvation rested upon our ability to be faithful to the Lord, none of us would ever be saved. Praise God, salvation and eternal life is God's responsibility not ours! We are saved and kept by His grace (1 Pet. 1:5; Ps. 37:23-24, 28; John 4:13-14). Thank you, Lord, for Your unfailing, unchanging, faithful grace!

THERE IS GRACE TO HELP YOU SOAR

Isaiah writes, "Have you not known? Have you not heard? The everlasting God, the Lord, the Creator of the ends of the earth, neither faints nor is weary. His understanding is unsearchable. He gives power to the weak, and to those who have no might He increases strength. Even the youths shall faint and be weary, and the young men shall utterly fall, but those who wait on the Lord shall renew their strength; they shall mount up with wings like eagles, they shall run and not be weary, they shall walk and not faint" (Isa. 40:28-31 NKJV). This passage of Scripture shows us the blessing of God's grace because what He does for His people through His grace. Verse 31 makes it clear that those who wait upon the Lord will renew their strength. The word "wait" has the idea of "looking to or hoping in" (Dictionary, 1828) In other words, those who do not look to their own power, but who rest in His unfailing, unchanging, faithful grace will have their own strength renewed by His abundant unending resources. The word "renew" means "to sprout again like the grass" (Dictionary, 1828).

There are times when it seems there is little energy left in our spiritual sails. There are times when we feel defeated and unable to rise above our circumstances. Regardless of you may feel spiritually, there is God's grace to help you soar. He promises to help you "mount up with wings like eagles" (Isa. 40:31 NKJV). The word "mount up" means "to ascend" (Wood, Marshall, & Millard, 1996) When an eagle flaps it wings and head into the sky, it is a wonderful thing to behold. This great bird, held to the ground by the same gravity that binds us to the earth, stretches out those massive wings and with one great flap, it is airborne. It quickly rises, breaking the grip of gravity, rising higher and higher, until it can soar high above this world with its dangers, its strife, and its problems. Those who learn to wait on the Lord find they have that same kind of liberty in Christ Jesus. He has a way of helping us break free from the things that bind us. He has a way of helping us to get above our problems, other people, sins, valleys, emotions, etc. He has a way of allowing us to soar above the difficulties of life. Have you ever experienced such a time in your life? Has there been a time when it seems like there was no hope and no way out, until waited upon the Lord and He gave the strength to rise above it all? As we wait on the Lord, He enables us to soar when there is a crisis, to run when there are challenges, and to walk faithfully day by day in regular ordinary life. Yes, it is harder to walk in daily pressures of life than it is to soar. However, every day begins with one step at a time. The greatest heroes of faith are not always those who seem to be soaring; often they are just patiently plodding along. Blesses are the plodders, for they will eventually get there.

When an eagle in the sky encounters a storm, it does not have to land. It does not have to fly through the storm. The eagle turns its eyes towards the heavens, and it rises above the approaching storm. While the storm lashes the earth beneath with its wind and rain, the mighty eagle flies above the clouds with its face towards the sun. Did you know that is possible for you as well? The Lord promises to give you the strength you need to be able to surmount your storms and fly above them through His grace. He did that for His disciples. When Jesus died on the cross, the disciples were divided, discourage, and defeated. They were ready to quit. They believed that all their efforts to serve God had been wasted, and their faith in Jesus Christ had been misplaced. Now, fast-forward to after the resurrection to the Day of Pentecost. They become fearless in their proclamation of the Gospel, over three thousand people are saved, five thousand are saved a brief time later, and millions are saved by the end of the first century. Why? It all happened because God gave them the grace to soar by His power!

I think about the life of Paul, he was empowered to soar high for the glory of God. God took Paul and transformed him into a dynamic missionary for Christ. Paul writes, "Brethren, I do not count myself to have apprehended; but one thing I do, forgetting those things which are behind and reaching forward to those things which are ahead, I press toward the goal for the prize of the upward call of God in Christ Jesus" (Phil. 3:13-14 NKJV). Paul penned those words while he was in a Roman prison. However, that was just his physical location. Spiritually, Paul was flying high in Jesus Christ, making a difference in his world. When most others would have given up, Paul was enabled to "mount up with wings as eagles" and touch his generation for God. Paul discovered there is grace to help you soar. It is my prayer you will make the same discovery and you will soar high in Jesus above your storms for His glory.

THERE IS GRACE TO HELP SPRINT

Isaiah says, "They shall run and not be weary" (Isa. 40:31 NKJV). The word "run" means "to dart, to move swiftly" (Dictionary, 1828) This word reminds us that the Christian life is classified as a race. Paul saw his own life as a race, two times he wrote, "Therefore I run thus: not with uncertainty. Thus, I fight not as one who beats the air. But I discipline my body and bring it into subjection, lest, when I have preached to others, I myself should become disqualified" (1 Cor. 9:26-27 NKJV). "I have fought the good fight, I have finished the race, I have kept the faith" (2 Tim. 4:7 NKJV). Where did Paul get this strength? He got it from looking to the Lord. He got it from waiting before the Lord. He got it from the only dependable, reliable, unfailing source. He got it from the Lord. Paul tells us that his strength was renewed day by day. "Therefore, we do not lose heart. Even though our outward man is perishing, yet in the inward man is being renewed day by day" (2 Cor. 4:16 NKJV). Paul was able to tap into this vast resource of spiritual strength because he was a man of prayer, he was a man of the Word, and he was a man of faith. He trusted the Lord to give Him strength for the battles of life and the Lord Jesus Christ did not fail Him. Therefore, if we are going to behave as a church, then we must look to Jesus, asking for His grace to help us sprint.

Jesus will not fail you or me. Remember what the writer of Hebrews said, "Therefore we also, since we are surrounded by so great a cloud of witnesses, let us lay aside every weight, and sin which so easily ensnares us, and let us run with endurance the race that is set before us, looking unto Jesus, the author and finisher of our faith, who for the joy that was set before Him endured the cross, despising the shame, and has sat down at the right hand of the throne of God" (Heb. 12:1-2 NKJV). The secret to successfully running this race of life day by day is found there in verse 2, we are to be looking unto Jesus. When we look to Him in prayer, in His Word, in waiting before Him for guidance and help, He will enable us to run our race without growing weary. I cannot speak for you, but I want to end my race of life well. I do not want to drop out along the way, nor do I want to become weary while in the race. I would like to keep my eyes on Jesus and sprint to the finish for His glory. It is possible, but I must keep my eyes on Him and every now and then, I might have to lean on His everlasting arms.

THERE IS GRACE TO HELP YOU STROLL

This last gear of life describes most of life. Not every day of life is filled with excitement and adventure. Most of the time, our day-to-day life is just spent walking with the Lord. There are days when you are flying high, and it seems like blessings are falling all around you. Then, there are days when you are in a dead run, sprinting from one thing to the next. Those kinds of days are exciting, but they are only a small part of our existence. Most of the days we live will just be spent in a long stroll Jesus. This is what it must have been like for Adam in the Garden of Eden. "And they heard the sound of the Lord God walking in the garden in the cool of the day, and Adam and his wife hid themselves from the presence of the Lord God among the trees of the garden. Then the Lord God called to Adam and said to him, "Where are you?" (Gen. 3:8-9 NKJV). The Lord showed up, probably like He had done before, to commune with Adam and for Adam to walk with God. It seems like God just desired for Adam to have that special relationship as they walked together.

Micah writes, "He has shown you, O man, what is good; and what does the Lord require of you but to do justly, to love mercy,

261

and to walk humbly with your God?" (Mic. 6:9 NKJV). John puts it this way, "He who says he abides in Him ought himself also to walk just as He walked" (1 John 2:6 NKJV). There is something special about consistently walking daily with Jesus. We walk with Him daily when we read His Word, meditate on His Word, and pray through His Word. We are to take His teachings, His promises, His love and consistently show it to a lost and dying world. We are to behave in an attitude of prayer, "Rejoice always, pray without ceasing" (1 Thess. 5:16-17 NKJV). There is something special about the saint of God who is steady (Deut. 6:7; 28:1; Prov. 4:23). There is something special about the believer who is just always walking with the Lord. Paul told the young Timothy, "Be diligent to present yourself approved of God, a worker who does not need to be ashamed, rightly dividing the word of truth" (2 Tim. 2:15 NKJV). The writer of Hebrews talks about this consistent stroll with God as a rest, "Let us therefore be diligent to enter the rest, lest anyone fall according to the same example of disobedience" (Heb. 4:11 NKJV). There are those who are behaving as church members because if you were to meet them on the street today, they are still walking with Jesus yesterday, the day before yesterday, or even from the past year. They will possibly be the ones who are still walking with Him next year. "Therefore, by their fruits you will know them" (Matt. 7:20 NKJV). Their fruits will prove they are walking with Christ. How about you are you behaving as church member that is strolling with Jesus?

Here is some motivation. Jesus gives grace to those who are walking with Him, through mundane events of their daily existence. We think we are only serving the Lord, however, there is something big happening in us and through us. The fact is, there is nothing bigger than a Christian who simply walks with the Lord day by day. There is something to be said for finding yourself in His Word every day. There is something to be said for simply walking with Him every day. There is grace for that stroll! There is grace to get up in the morning. There is grace to bow your head in prayer. There is grace to open the Word of God, read it, and meditate on it (let it speak to you). There is grace to honor the Lord throughout your daily walk. There is grace to consistently be walking with Him on a regular basis. Think about

God said to Paul, "And He said to me, "My grace is sufficient for you, for My strength is made perfect in weakness." Therefore, most gladly I will rather boast in my infirmities, that the power of Christ may rest upon me" (2 Cor. 12:9 NKJV). God was telling Paul that He was going to give him the support that he needed to make it through this day and all the days that laid ahead! We have that same promise! He is with us to help us be faithful day in and day out. Here is the promise from Jesus, "And I will pray the Father, and He will give you another Helper, that He may abide with you forever; the Spirit of truth, whom the world cannot receive, because it neither sees Him nor knows Him; but you know Him, for He dwells with you and will be in you. I will not leave you orphans; I will come to you" (John 14:16-18 NKJV).

As we faithfully walk with God on a regular basis, with His help and His grace, we will be ready when those times of sprinting and soaring come. Our success in those special times always comes from our faithfulness to stroll with the Lord every day. What I am saying is this: keep on praying, even when it appears He is not listening. Keep on going to church, even when it seems like nothing is happening. Keep on preaching the Word of truth pastor, even when it seems God is not moving, and the people are not listening. Keep on witnessing even when no one is getting saved. Keep on giving even when your finances are tight. Keep on living for Jesus, day by day, even when others around you may be falling away; refuse to turn back or waiver from behaving as a church member. In His time, He will bless you and reward you for being faithful during the routine times of life. When He does, you will be ready to soar or sprint, because you have been faithful in your daily stroll!

God is Faithful in His Gifts

Jeremiah continues his thoughts about God's mercies by saying, "... because His compassion fail not. They are new every morning; great is Your faithfulness" (Jer. 3:22b-23 NKJV). The word "compassion" literally means "womb" (Strong's Concordance, 1984) It gives us the idea that we are to be moved in the heart out of a love for another person. This word is beautiful picture of the grace of God which is actively moving in the life of the believer. As we pass through our storms of life, and go through our valleys, we are not do so alone! God is observing our path and knows what lies ahead, therefore His grace gives us all we need (gifts) for our journey.

Jeremiah tells us that God's gifts are consistently coming in every morning. If we would just during our prayer time grab ahold of them in the morning, those faithful gifts will see us through our day. Yes, God did not promise us an easier road, but He did promise that His grace would be sufficient for the needs (2 Cor. 12:9). Grace is usually defined as "the unmerited love and favor of God toward sinners" (Wood, Marshall, & Millard, 1996) It carries the idea; however, this is a word that has come to mean so much more that just an idea. As previously stated, it refers to the strength of God to face battles and to bear up under times of difficulty. What we need to remember is regardless of what life sends our way, we can be confident of the fact that the Lord will give us the necessary strength to face the trying times of life each morning. You will never have to face a situation as a believer which God has not given you the grace to make it through each day.

Here are some of those gifts which are faithful. First there is the gift of His presence. "Let your conduct be without covetousness; be content with such things as you have. For He Himself has said, "I will never leave you nor forsake you" (Heb. 13:5 NKJV). "Teaching them to observe all things that I have commanded you; and lo, I am with you always, even to the end of the age" (Matt. 28:20 NKJV). These verses, along with others reveal the great truth which God is always present with His children. Even when He cannot be seen, He is there. When you cannot trace God in your life, He is there! I challenge you to search your heart and come to the place where you can fully rely on God. Second, there is the gift of His performance. "Now to Him who is able to do exceedingly abundantly above all that we ask or think, according to the power that works in us" (Eph. 3:20 NKJV). Did you catch that word "able"? When you take this verse for what it says, then it becomes clear that our God is greater, by far, than any problem we have or will ever face. There is no big problem He cannot handle, nor is there any small problems that should be taken to Him in which He desires to hear from us. God is an awesome God, and His children need to remember this great truth. God will take care of you!

Third, there is the gift of His provisions. "And my God shall supply all your need according to His riches in glory by Christ Jesus" (Phil. 4:19 NKJV). "But seek first the kingdom of God and His righteousness, and all these things shall be added to you" (Matt. 6:33 NKJV). "I have been young, and now am old; yet I have not seen the righteousness forsaken, nor his descendants begging bread" (Ps. 37:25 NKJV). These verses teach us the great truth that God is interested in meeting the needs of His children. God has promised to take care of His children, and He will! It may be that His idea of taking care is different than yours, but here is where faith in the trustworthiness of God comes in. We must come to the place where we are willing to trust the Lord to take care of us in any way that He sees fit. Fourth, there is the gift of His person. "Jesus Christ is the same yesterday, today, and forever" (Heb. 13:8 NKJV). "For I am the Lord, I do not change; there you are not consumed O sons of Jacob" (Mal. 3:6 NKJV). These verses reveal the truth about God's nature which always makes Him reliable, because He does not change. God is the same God today as He has ever been and will be forever. He was faithful in the beginning from creation and in the Garden of Eden. He was faithful to Jacob and his sons as He brought them to Egypt and out of Egypt. He is the same God that brought the plagues upon Egypt and parted the Red Sea. He is the same God that helped a shepherd boy defeat a giant, that protected three Hebrew boys in a fiery furnace, and delivered Daniel from the lion's den. He is the same God that brought forth a little baby through a virgin just like it had been prophesied. He is the same God that feed the five thousand, calmed the sea, and brought sight to the blind. He is the same God that laid down His life for you and for me and had the power to pick it up and come out of the grave for us. Since He has always been the same God for all this time, then we can count on Him to be the same God today in the life of every believer who will trust Him. God is a steadfast and trustworthy God!

Jeremiah also said that God's mercies and compassion is fresh and new every morning (Lam. 3:23a). The grace of God is as fresh as the new day sun. We do not have to worry about there not being enough for us to make it through the day, because God's grace in our lives is as fresh as newly baked buttermilk biscuits. Fresh hot buttermilk smells so good and is so delicious. I am blessed to have a wife who bakes fresh buttermilk biscuits for me. She makes big catfish head biscuits. I cannot even wait to eat one, because they smell so good. That is the way God's grace should be to us, we cannot wait to grab hold of His blessings and grace early in the morning to give us the nutrients we need for the day. His grace should be a sweet aroma to us, and we are to be a sweet aroma to Him when we do grab hold of those fresh gifts (Phil. 4:18). Jesus said, "Therefore do not worry about tomorrow, for tomorrow will worry about its own things. Sufficient for the day is its own trouble" (Matt. 6:34 NKJV). Just as every new day brings with it, its own set of burdens and problems, each day also witnesses a new, unfailing, all-sufficient, supply of God's marvelous, matchless, wonderful, amazing grace! God's faithfulness is seen in the fact that we woke this morning, in our right minds, with reasonable health. We woke up with air to breath, food to eat, people we love, people who love us, and so on. God is faithful in His gifts He gives.

God is Faithful in His Goodness

Jeremiah said, "The Lord is my portion," says my soul, "Therefore I hope in Him!" The Lord is good to those who wait for Him, to the soul who seeks Him. It is good that one should hope and wait quietly for the salvation of the Lord" (Lam. 3:24-26 NKJV). The word "good" has the idea of "pleasant, agreeable, and excellent" (Strong's Concordance, 1984) It refers to the character of God. It should remind us that God is forever engage in what is best for His children's lives. Jeremiah describes God as his soul's "portion". Meaning his "share or booty" (Strong's Concordance, 1984) Jeremiah is talking about the spoils of war. What he is saying is: "In the battle of life, God is my reward, my share, and my portion." When the Lord is viewed in this perspective, He will be all a person needs to be satisfied in their souls. David writes, "Who satisfies your mouth with good things, so that your youth is renewed like eagle's" (Ps. 103:5 NKJV). "For He satisfies the longing soul and fills the hungry soul with goodness" (Ps.

107:9 NKJV). God may not give us the things we desire in life, but He will always give us the best things we need. He will five us those best things which will satisfy the soul (Rom. 8:28).

God is the sustainer of life. God will never fail those who place their trust in Him (Isa. 49:23; Rom. 10:11). Not a sing Word of any of His precious promises will ever fail to be honored by Him. "Forever, O Lord, Your word is settled in heaven. Your faithfulness endures to all generations; You established the earth, and it abides" (Ps. 119:89-90 NKJV). "The grass withers, the flower fades, but the word of our God stands forever" (Isa. 40:8 NKJV). If you come to Him for salvation, He will not send you away lost. "All that the Father gives Me will come to Me, and the one who comes to Me I will by no means cast out" (John 6:37 NKJV). If you trust Him for salvation, He will never send you away into Hell. "And I give them eternal life, and they shall never perish; neither shall anyone snatch them out of My hand" (John 10:28 NKJV). If you look to Him for the need in your life, you will never be disappointed. "Do not fear, little flock, for it is your Father's good pleasure to give you the kingdom" (Luke 12:32 NKJV). He will sustain you through this life and into eternity.

God is our savior. Jeremiah said, "It is good that one should hope and wait quietly for the salvation of the Lord" (Lam. 3:26 NKJV). What he is saying is; those who wait upon the Lord will see Him bring them out of their troubles and trials. He will not fail His children, but in His time, He will deliver them from all their valleys. We need to remember today that God is able to deliver both the saint and the sinner. God knows where you are today. He knows what you are going through (Job. 23:10). He will not forsake you, but He will faithfully keep you and bring you out, in His time (Ps. 34:15-22).

Great is the faith that can stand amid the wreckage of life and declare the praises of God. Jeremiah was that kind of believer. Are you? During the early years of the missionary movement in China, four members of one family accepted Jesus as their personal Lord and Savior. However, the youngest member of the family did not. Later he came to his dad and said that he wanted to confess and accept Jesus into is heart and let everyone know. The dad was not excited and felt his son was not old enough. He went on to explain to his son that he might fall away from his profession when he got older. The boy said to his well-meaning, concerned father, "Jesus has promised to carry the lambs in His arms. I am only a little boy. It will be easier for Jesus to carry me." This genuine, but simple statement made the dad realize his son knew what he was talking about. Therefore, he allowed his son to let it be made known of his faith in Christ and was baptized.

As soon as we face the battles, burdens, valleys, storms, and trials of life, we must always remember we are His little lambs, and He is well capable of carrying us through. What kind of battles are you fighting? Take them to the Great Shepherd and trust in His unchanging, unfailing faithfulness.

CHAPTER NINETEEN

Parables, the Kingdom of Heaven, and the Church

Then He said to them, "Therefore every scribe instructed concerning the kingdom of Heaven is like a householder who brings out of his treasure things new and old."
(Matthew 13:52 NKJV)

JESUS CHRIST IS ANOTHER INSTANCE OF GOD'S FAITHFULNESS. JESUS Christ, being fully God and fully man, came to seek and to save that which is lost. He did this by revealing God to us through His teachings, not to mention Jesus taught a whole lot more. In Matthew chapter 13, we see a multitude gather around Jesus. There were so many people, Jesus thought it would be a good idea to get into a boat on the water and sat down to teach them. He began to teach them by telling them a parable. "And the disciples came and said to Him, "Why do you speak to them in parables?" He answered and said to them, "Because it has been given to you to know the mysteries of the kingdom of heaven, but them it has not been given" (Matt. 13:10-11 NKJV). The fact we have an inspired Word of God, called the Bible, means we too have been given the knowledge to know the mysteries of the kingdom of God. But what is a mystery? A mystery is a spiritual truth which you could only know by divine revelation, and you cannot understand the mystery without the divine revelation. It is something our human wit, wisdom, ingenuity, and learning would never figure out no matter how intelligent you are. It is something God must reveal to you for you to know it.

Therefore, Jesus speaks in parables to the multitude, and explains the meaning of the parables, at least some of them that we know of, to His disciples. What is a parable? The word "parable" means "to lay alongside of" (Holman Illustrated Bible Dictionary, 2003) A parable is a lesson or a story in the physical, material world, and laid alongside a spiritual truth. A parable is a story, or comparison placed alongside the mystery, spiritual truth, to make the lesson clear. The easy-to-understand version of the definition of a parable is: an earthly story with a heavenly meaning. Jesus is using parables to unlock for us some deep, deep mysteries to help us understand the kingdom of heaven, therefore helping us to behave as a church. Understanding these things is key to the ministry of the church in the world we live in now, because let's face it, the world we live in is confusing and it is all going to become worse the closer we get to the end times.

Here in this chapter, we are going to look at two misunderstood parables of Jesus: The Parable of the Devil's Dirty Birds (Matt. 13:31-32) and The Devil's Bakery (Matt. 13:33). Let me set the stage for these two parables. People ask the question, "What is wrong with the preacher? What is wrong with the Bible? What is wrong with the church? It just does not seem like people want to get saved when they are presented with the gospel message." To be honest, there may not be anything wrong with the preacher. Remember Matthew 13, Matthew records Jesus first parable as the Parable of the Sower (Matt. 13:3-9). In that parable, the seed, which is the Word of God, fell on stony ground, by the wayside, and among the thorns. There was not anything wrong with the preacher who was the sower, who by the way represents Jesus. The seed the sower was sowing was the message, and there was nothing wrong with the seed. However, the problem was with the soil which the seed fell upon. This Jesus explained was the unconverted world. Another question we ask is: "Why are there so many hypocrites in the church?" The next parable Jesus gives is the Parable of the Wheat and Tares (Matt. 13:24-30). In this parable Jesus shows us how the devil sows tares among the wheat. The tares represent the counterfeit Christians, while the wheat represents true genuine Christian. This teaches us that there are fake Christians who grow up among true children of God in the church.

The Devil's Dirty Birds

Since the world we live in is confused and people are believing in anything, therefore Jesus points out another problem called the apostate Christianity. The word "apostate" means "falling away" (Concise Oxford English Dictionary Eleventh Edition, 2004) It is amazing at some of the things people will believe in today. Even those things whom people parade under the banner of Christianity. However, it is still strange how people will not believe the gospel, while there are others who have strange ideas surrounding the gospel. There is a great, wide display of church and denominations who are far removed from the Holy Word of God and people are believing anything they hear if it is on television or on the world wide web. Those so-called churches are not preaching the true Word of God. They are not honoring the name of the Lord Jesus Christ, nor are they under the blood of Christ. They are not filled with the Holy Spirit and yet there are thousands of people who will march Sunday after Sunday to these churches and come away with their heads fuller, their hearts emptier, bound in the chains of a false gospel. Not only are they not helped by it, but they are literally hurt by this kind of teaching from these false churches. Jesus said, "Woe to you, scribes and Pharisees, hypocrites! For you travel land and sea to win one proselyte, and when he is won, you make him twice as much a son of hell as yourselves" (Matt. 23:15 NKJV).

How did all this false, apostate religion begin? Well, first, Jesus said it would happen, we know this because of the parable of the devil's dirty birds, or you may know it as the Parable of the Mustard Seed. This message is the mystery of the mustard seed, which Jesus tells us about the apostasy which will occur in the last days. We are living in the last days because we can see there is apostasy all around us.

271

A STRONG DECLARATION

"Another parable He put forth to them, saying: "The kingdom of heaven is like a mustard see, which a man took and sowed in his field" (Matt. 13:31 NKJV). We know from listening to Jesus tell the other parables the seed represents the Word of God. Again, the man represents Jesus Christ, the Son of man, our Savior. He is the one doing the sowing of the seed. The field is the world, we can deduct from the other parables. Now, in the East, the mustard seed symbolizes something small and insignificant. Why did Jesus say the kingdom of heaven is like a mustard seed? Why something so small and insignificant? Well, it has to do with the strength of the mustard seed. The mustard seed is so strong, it can produce a very large plant, not a tree in the strictest sense. Let make that very clear, the mustard seed produces a plant! If you have ever eaten mustard, there is a kick, a bite, a fiery pungency to it. If you do not know what that is like, try going to a Chinese restaurant, and get one of those egg rolls put on it some of that mustard they have in the packages and take a big bite; then you will know what I am talking about. Back in the olden days of our forefathers, when people thought they had pneumonia, or whatever they had, they would make up some mustard plaster and put it on their chest. I do not know if this home remedy was the cure for pneumonia, but I have heard from my grandparents it will take the hide from your chest. Talk about the power of mustard seeds. When the mustard seeds are ground up the power, the strength which is on display is what Jesus is talking about when He talks about the mustard seed. The gospel message when it is proclaimed in its purity, it bites, it burns, it blisters, it has power, it has pungency. The gospel message in not a bland message which we preach, "For I am not ashamed of the gospel of Christ, for it is the power of God to salvation for everyone who believes, for the Jew first and also for the Greek" (Rom. 1:16 NKJV). I we are going to behave as a church, I believe we need to get back to going, telling, preaching, and proclaiming the Word of God with the understanding it is a zesty gospel we preach. This is an exciting message we have the privilege to share, and the proclamation of the gospel of Jesus has a strong declaration.

But not only is the strength of the seed on display in this parable, you will notice the size of the seed. According to verse 32, Jesus tells us the mustard seed is the least of the seeds. What this is telling us is, the gospel does not have to have a lot of pomp and circumstance, nor does it have to have trappings with all the trimmings man wants to add to it. It may start out tiny, but it grows to be a large plant which is big enough for birds to sit in the branches. Therefore, let's give thought as to where the strength and size comes from because there is a secret, a mystery to the mustard seed. The mystery is this seed has life! So does the gospel of our Lord and Savior Jesus Christ! Jesus put it this way, "It is the Spirit who gives life; the flesh profits nothing. The words I speak to you are spirit, and they are life" (John 6:63 NKJV). Therefore, Peter writes, "Having been born again, not of corruptible seed but incorruptible, through the word of God which lives and abides forever" (1 Pet. 1:23 NKJV). I do not believe in a dead gospel, nor do I preach a dead message. I preach and believe in a risen Savior Who is alive forevermore. The gospel message is life; therefore, I do not depend upon my own ability but on my faithfulness to the Word of God. The Word of God is life, and the kingdom of heaven is like a mustard seed.

A STRANGE TRANSFORMATION

"which indeed is the least of all the seeds; but when it is grown it is greater than the herbs and becomes a tree, so that the birds of the air come and nest in its branches" (Matt. 13:32 NKJV). Did you see the transformation that took place in this parable? What happened? Something went wrong. As I made clear earlier, the mustard seed produces a large plant NOT a tree. There is a huge difference between an herb and a tree. Herbs have no wooded tissue to it. An herb dies back and must be replanted; but a tree and an herb are totally different, especially since God in His creation made them different and distinguishes between the herb and tree. "Then God said, "Let the earth bring forth grass, the herb that yields see, and the fruit tree that yields fruit according to its kind, who seed is in itself, on the earth"; and it was so. And the earth brought forth grass, the herb that yields seed according to its kind, and the tree that yields fruit, whose seed is in itself according to its kind. And God saw that it was good" (Gen. 1:11-12 NKJV). Under ordinary circumstances, herbs do not transform into a tree. God made a difference between an herb and a tree. An herb never produces a tree, and a tree never produces an herb; there is a difference.

But here in this parable, we have a strange and weird development. Suddenly, an herb becomes a tree. Let me again emphasize this; this is not meant to be. Mustard never becomes a tree. If you have ever grown mustard greens in your garden, you should at least know this by now. Mustard is one of the greatest of herbs. As a matter of fact, in the Middle East, a mustard plant will grow almost seven feet tall, but it is still an herb; it never becomes a tree. Jesus tells us the mustard seed which grows, grows to be an herb, and then it becomes a tree. What Jesus is talking about is evil; something which is not meant to be, something which is twisted, something which is perverted. He is talking about the development of abnormal Christianity. The development of the apostate Christianity. The people who were present that day as Jesus taught them from the boat, knew and were familiar with the Law of Moses and the writings of the prophets, the collection which we call the Old Testament. Therefore, when they hear Jesus talk about this tree with birds lodging in its branches it is a good possibility some of His hearers' mind went back to the writings of Daniel. "The tree that you saw, which grew and became strong, whose height reached to the heavens and which could be seen by all the earth, whose leaves were lovely and its fruits abundant, in which was food for all, under which the beasts of the field dwelt, and in whose branches the birds of the heaven had their home; it is you, O king, who have grown and become strong; for your greatness has grown and reaches to the heavens, and your dominion to the end of the earth" (Dan. 4:20-22 NKJV). Daniel had a vision of a great lofty tree, and in that tree the birds were roosting in its branches. Daniel explained that this was a vision of Babylon and in the Bible Babylon is always a symbol of apostate religion. Isaiah writes, "And look, here comes a chariot of men with a pair of horsemen!" Then he answered and said, "Babylon id fallen, is fallen! And the carved images of her gods he has broken to the ground"" (Isa. 21:9 NKJV). John writes,

"And he cried mightily with a loud voice, saying, "Babylon the great is fallen, is fallen, and has become a dwelling place of demons, a prison for every foul spirit, and a cage for every unclean and hated bird" (Rev. 18:2. NKJV).

Let me just say, the devil is not against religion! As a matter of fact, he is in religion up to his ears, however, it is a false religion, apostate religion, something which is abnormal, something not meant to be. The herb is not meant to be a tree. The tree speaks of pride over far-reaching branches, and becoming a habitation for beast and birds, and all kinds of unclean and creeping things, which God never really intended, and this is a strange development. This evil tree, Jesus is telling us about, is the final form of the false super church which will be in the last days. It is the giant corporation of the incorporated sons of old Adam. The fact Jesus is telling us this while He was here upon the earth should encourage us, because what He is saying lets us know this did not take Him by surprise.

A SATANIC HABITATION

Some try to make this parable teach the worldwide success of the Gospel. They say, "Oh, isn't it wonderful? The church starts with just a little seed, and then it becomes an herb, and then it becomes a great big kingdom tree, and then we get all the sweetest birds. We have the little blue jays, the red birds, the little canaries, and the hummingbirds." That is not what Jesus is talking about at all, because that kind of message contradicts what Jesus taught in His first parable of Matthew 13. Jesus intended for the kingdom of heaven to stay the way He designed it. He intended the church to stay a vine (John 15:5). He intended Israel to stay an olive tree (Rom. 11:11-24). Bottom line is plants do not become trees, and trees do not become plants. Think about it, Jesus said, "I am the vine, you are the branches. He who abides in Me, and I in him, bears much fruit; for without Me you can do nothing" (John 15:5 NKJV). When we are saved, we are grafted into the family of God (Rom. 11:24). Therefore, as we are grafted into the true Vine, Jesus, we are to grow looking like Jesus. We cannot stay or look like the natural man; we are to become more like the vine. The mustard seed, the kingdom of heaven, was to grow up to be a plant and as more were grafted into the mustard seed it is to remain a plant.

Yes, I believe in kingdom growth. I think it is wonderful when the church can see multiple people receive Jesus into their hearts and people join the church. It is beautiful to see a church that had such humble beginnings grow into a large church reaching their community for the kingdom. In truth, most people believed nothing would come of Jesus and His ministry. The people could see the tiny seed, but they could not see the great plant it could become. Consider some of the facts: Jesus was born in the tiny town of Bethlehem in abject poverty. He was reared in Galilee, and no one believed a man of God could come from there (John 7:52). He was raised in Nazareth, where the inhabitants of the city were wicked and worldly by the Jews. He had no family connections, no money, no support from the religious leaders of the day. Jesus was thought to be a nobody from nowhere Who would amount to nothing. His ancestry was questioned (John 8:41) by His enemies. His followers were, for the most part, the dregs of society. His Own people rejected Him. He was despised and rejected by men. The Romans eventually nailed Him to a cross and buried Him in a tomb. His followers preached His resurrection, but most people ignored their message and considered them fools for following a dead man. There is no question the kingdom of heaven was like a mustard seed. When the tiny mustard seed is planted in good soil, it germinates and produces a very large shrub-like plant that eventually gets so large it does look like a tree, but it is not a tree. Some mustard plants have been known to grow as high as fifteen feet tall. Something so small, with such humble beginnings, can become something truly amazing to behold.

The growth of the mustard seed is a picture of the growth of the kingdom of heaven. When the seed was planted in ancient Israel, the prospects for success seemed far away. In the beginning there was Jesus and a few followers. His followers consisted of some uneducated fisherman, a few revolutionaries, some women, and a traitor. By the time the Day of Pentecost came around, after the ascension of Jesus, there were one hundred and twenty devoted followers (Acts 1:15). On that day, something amazing took place! Over 3,000 people came to faith in Christ (Acts 2:41). A short time later, another 5,000 were saved (Acts 4:4). Then after that, it is said the Lord began to multiply the church and the church grew at an astounding rate. The church in Jerusalem is said to have 50,000 members. This was just the beginning! As the message was carried around the world, vast multitudes began to come to Jesus. Cities and nations fell on their knees in the face of the message of the gospel of grace. This amazing growth has continued down to this day. The church had continued to grow and the kingdom of heaven on earth has continued to expand. Yet, the intension for the kingdom was it is supposed to be a plant.

There will come a day when the plant becomes a tree just as Jesus said. Remember this tree is evil and those sweet little birds roosting in the branches of the tree are the dirty birds which are the devil's demons, who take pleasure in apostate religion. How do we know this? Well, since Jesus did not explain this parable, we must look at what He did explain in the other parables to find the meaning of the parable of the mustard seed. The birds in the Parable of the Sower represent Satan (Matt. 13:19). Passages like Daniel 4:12 and Ezekiel 17:23 indicate a tree is a symbol of world power. These facts suggest the Parable of the Mustard Seed is teaching about an abnormal growth of the kingdom of heaven, this should make us think it is possible for Satan to work with in the church or kingdom of heaven. What started out in a humble manner, today boasts of material possessions and political influences.

However, let's be honest, the devil has sent more people to hell through religion than any other way. It is not religion people need. It was a religious crowd who crucified Jesus Christ. People today need to turn from religion and turn to Jesus Christ! It is a personal faith in a living Savior, Who can come into your heart and give you a new nature, make you born again, and graft you into the family of God. Do you know how to detect one of the devil's dirty birds? Some people would not know one of the devil's dirty birds if he flew in their window. What we need today is a course in spiritual bird watching. Here are just a few ways to identify these dirty birds. First, these dirty birds know how to use the Bible. Why? Because the devil knows how to quote the Bible. Second, these dirty birds know how-to do-good work (Matt. 7:22-23). They may teach Sunday School, hold church services, do radio programs, host revival meetings, Bible conferences, write an article in a magazine, author a book, give out Christian tracts, serve at church camp, or help in the youth department all in the name of Jesus. However, while they may do these good works, they have an undermining agenda. Third, they can perform miracles (Matt. 24:24). Just because a man is a miracle worker, does not mean the power of God is on him. The Bible speaks of the spirits of demons having power to do miracles (Rev. 16:14). Therefore, we need a course in bird watching, don't we? These dirty birds come and lodge in the branches, building their nest, transforming the makeup, DNA, inner workings of the church, the kingdom of Heaven.

Let me give you a series of tests you can ask any bird who pecks at your door. This will help you find out whether they happen to be one of these in Babylon's branches or whether he is one who is a true servant, a representative of the Lord Jesus Christ. First, is the source test. If you will ask, someone who comes up to you preaching another Jesus, "What is the source of your information? Where did you get your belief? Do you believe the Bible is the inspired, inerrant, infallible Word of God? Or have you taken from it, or added to it?" If the person is using any other source outside the Word of God, the person is one of the devil's dirty birds. It does not matter if the ideas are his own, or a source book written by a man to accompany the Word of God, or even if it is the traditions of man; the source test will help you in your spiritual bird watching.

Next is the savior test. Ask the person what he believes about the Lord and Savior Jesus Christ. If he is wrong about Jesus, it will not matter what he is right about. Ask Him, "What do you believe about Jesus? Do you believe He is the Son of the Most High God?" Many will say, "Yes." Then ask him, "Do you believe He was born of a virgin? Do you believe He is the only begotten Son of God? Do you believe He is 100% man and 100% God?" Anybody who does not believe Jesus is God in human flesh is the devil's dirty bird and "whoever transgresses and does not abide in the doctrine of Christ does not have God. He who abides in the doctrine of Christ has both the Father and the Son" (2 John 1:9 KNJV). Another test is the subject test. Ask, "What do you preach? What is the theme of your message? What are you trying to get across? Is it the gospel of

Jesus Christ? (Make sure they understand what the gospel is.) Do you know the what the gospel is?" You find out what their central message is; if their message is anything other than the gospel of Jesus, he is one of the devil's dirty birds. If his message is something other than, Christ died for our sin; He was buried; and He arose from the grave on the third day according to the Word of God, then it is one of the devil's dirty bird lodging in the branches of apostate Christianity.

The last test is the salvation test. You will want to find out about his own salvation. Here is your opportunity to share the gospel. You ask, "Have you been born again? Are you trusting in the shed blood of Jesus Christ, and God's grace to save you? Or have tried to mix in some of your good works? Do believe it is Jesus plus this, or Jesus plus that?" Ask Him if believes, "For by grace you have been saved through faith, and that not of yourselves; it is the gift of God, not of works, less anyone should boast" (Eph. 2:8-9 NKJV). Ask him, "Have you personally received Christ as your personal Lord and Savior? Would you like to?" If the opportunity presents itself for you to lead someone to salvation do not hesitate to share the gospel and see someone come to know the Lord.

Now, that is a course in bird watching, because we need to be aware the devil, if it were possible would deceive the very children of God. Is it not marvelous how Jesus saw this strange evil tree which would develop in the last days? Is it not amazing as Jesus looked down through the tunnel of time, and knew there would come an evil development like an herb becoming a tree? John tells us what God said we should be doing. "And I heard another voice from heaven saying, "Come out of her, my people, lest you share in her sins, and lest you receive of her plagues" (Rev. 18:4 NKJV). God just wants us to come out from among this evil tree. This parable is God's warning for us not become this evil tree. Thankfully, Jesus gives another future warning we need to take notice.

The Devil's Bakery

"Another parable He spoke to them: "The kingdom of heaven is like leave, which a woman took and hid in three measures of meal till it was all leavened" (Matt. 11:33 NKJV). This parable is one of the most misunderstood parables of all the other parables. Remember, yeast or leaven is what you put into bread to cause it to rise. The normal, usual interpretation of this parable is wrong, it is the total opposite of what the Bible teaches. The normal, usual interpretation is this: the leaven is the gospel, the woman is the church, the three measures of meal is the world, and we are to take the gospel and put it into the world until all the world knows about the Lord Jesus Christ. This interpretation is wrong for obvious reasons. First, the Bible does not teach the whole world is going to be reached with gospel of Jesus Christ. As a matter fact, the Bible does not teach the world is going to get better and better and better. It is going to get worse and worse and worse until Jesus comes. The Bible teaches that in the last days there is going to be much wickedness, much religion, wars, rumors of wars, men's hearts filled with hate, false prophets deceiving many, and having a form of godliness, but denying the power thereof (Matt. 24:3-14; 2 Tim. 3:5). There are three basic things this parable does teach us about the kingdom of heaven.

THE LOAF

First, we want to take notice of what the loaf represents and what does the measure of meal represents. Again, remember the people to whom Jesus is speaking is familiar with the Old Testament. So, the first time you find three measures of meal mentioned in the Bible is in Genesis 18:6. Where Abraham had a visitor from heaven to speak with him and to make a covenant with him. In Genesis 18:6, it says that Sarah took three measures of meal and made some food for them, which was a loaf of bread for them to eat. The word unleavened is not mentioned in that verse, just the mention of the three measures of meal. Then later in the Bible, Gideon, who was a man of valor whom God used to deliver Israel, had an angelic guest in Judges 6:19. In this verse we read were Gideon prepared a meal for them to share and he used three measures of meal or an ephah. The loaf that Gideon served was unleavened bread.

In the Old Testament, in the Levitical law, the Jews made an offering to the Lord; and the offering to the Lord was made of three measures. For example, in Numbers 15:9 it says, "then shall be offered with the young bull a grain offering of three tenths of an ephah of fine flour mixed with half a hin of oil" (NKJV). Oil is an emblem of the Holy Spirit, and they would take three measures mixed with the oil to offer it to the Lord. This loaf would be unleavened bread. Also in Leviticus 2:4-5 it says, "And if you bring as an offering a grain offering baked in the oven, it shall be unleavened cakes of fine flour mixed with oil, or unleavened wafers anointed with oil. But if your offering is a grain offering baked in a pan, it shall be of fine flour, unleavened, mixed with oil" (NKJV). From time centuries old, the breaking of bread together, the sitting down to a meal together, has always been symbolic of the most intimate of fellowship; breaking bread together. Three measures of meal, as we find it in the Bible, symbolizes the fellowship of God with His people, the people with God, and the people with one another. This is how we should behave as a church. John writes, "That which we have seen and heard we declare to you, that you also may have fellowship with us; and truly our fellowship is with the Father and with His Son Jesus Christ" (1 John 1:3 NKJV).

In case you have any doubt about what the Old Testament says the bread represents, we could let the New Testament speak. Paul understood this Old Testament terminology, Paul writes, "For we, though many, are one bread and one body; for we all partake of that one bread" (1 Cor. 10:17 NKJV). Jesus Christ is the bread we all feed on, and we ourselves have been baked into one great big loaf of bread. Do you know how a lot of grains become bread? The grain of wheat goes into the ground and dies, then it sprouts and brings forth more wheat. The wheat is harvested, then ground up, then baked, and then you have a loaf of bread. What are the children of God? God's children are those who have died to themselves, who have been broken, who have been through the fire of judgment and tribulation, and have become one loaf; and therefore, we are all equal. There is no upper crust; we are just a lot of crumbs held together by the Spirit of God. As you trace the idea of three measure down through the Bible, you will find it symbolizes worship and fellowship with God.

THE LEAVEN

Now let us take notice of the leaven which is being put into the loaf. Again, remember leaven is yeast is used to make bread rise. What does this symbolize? Well, yeast may make things taste good. You may like those biscuits and light bread, but in this passage, and through out all the Bible, leaven is always a symbol of evil and sin; something bad, something wicked, and something which corrupts. According to Exodus 12:8, the Hebrews were to celebrate the Feast of Passover with unleavened bread. As a matter of fact, when the Feast of Passover came around, they were to go through the house and cast out all the leaven. Because they did not want even a speak of leaven in the house. They would get all the leaven out of the house because leaven speaks of evil and sin. They would keep the oil because oil is symbolic of the Holy Sprit of God. Leaven is yeast, it would cause fermentation; and fermentation is literally corruption. Leaven speaks of that which corrupts and what is puffed up. When the leaven starts to work, the bread, the dough would just start to rise and get huffy and puffy. Listen, that may be good for bread, but it is not good for Christians. Christians are not supposed to be puffed up. There are three kinds of leaven in which the church and Christians should be aware.

First, is the leaven of the Pharisees found in Mattew 23:13-15. The Pharisees were very religious people. They had their heads full of Scripture, but they had their hearts full of sin. Their religion was external not internal. They had profession, but they did not have possessions. They had laws, but they did not have life. In verse 13, they pretend to be gatekeepers, but what they were really roadblocks. In verse 14, they pretended to be intercessors, but they were extortionists. In verse 15, they pretended to be converters, but they were corrupters. Every one of their converts was doomed. Why? Because they were legalist who were never born again, and the religionist does not think they have a need for Jesus. The hardest people to win to Jesus is those who are like the self-righteous Pharisees. Then, according to Matthrew 23:16-17, the Pharisees pretended to be guides, but they themselves were blind. They pretended to be givers, but in fact were takers. They were selfish, self-centered, devouring widows by taking their houses, and yet they were so careful to tithe. They pretended to cleanse themselves, but they were still dirty. They pretended to be mourners, but they were murderers. Jesus just wants us to beware the leaven of the Pharisees (Matt. 16:11).

Next is the leaven of the Sadducees found in Mattew 16:11. Since the leaven of the Pharisees is legalism, then the leaven of the Sadducees would be liberalism. Liberalism and legalism are heads and tails of the same false religion. "For Sadducees say that there is no resurrection; and no angel or spirit; but the Pharisees confess both" (Acts 23:8 NKJV). The Pharisees were the fundamentalists, while the Sadducees were liberals; but neither one of them had the true Spirit of God in their hearts. The Sadducees were the sophisticated crowd without any hope because of what they believed. Jesus wants us to be aware of this leaven, because not only is legalism going to penetrate God's loaf, but also liberalism. Liberalism will rob you and the church of hope and joy. So, when it comes to liberalism or legalism, I could not tell you which one to be more afraid of, or on guard against because both are deadly.

The last leaven is the leaven of Herod found in Mark 8:15. "Then He charged them, saying, "Take heed, beware of the leaven of the Pharisees and the leaven of Herod" (NKJV). What is the leaven of Herod? The leaven of Herod was depravity. Herod was a pleasure seeking, mad king. He lived in a life of luxury and did not care much about liberalism or legalism. He just thought of himself and living in pleasure. He was a lover of pleasure more than a lover of God (2 Tim. 3:4). So, to behave as a church, we need to "Therefore purge out the old leaven, that you may be a new lump, since you truly are unleavened. For indeed Christ, our Passover, was sacrificed for us" (1 Cor. 5:7 NKJV). Satan has worked hard to introduce these leavens, these false doctrines and false living into the church, into the ministry of sharing the Word of God. Legalism, liberalism, and luxury have been something the church and the true believer have been battling since the early days of the church. It is sad how some churches who were once thought of as those who were true to the Word of God, have turned the truth into fables. To behave as a church we should, "Test all things; hold fast what is good. Abstain from every form of evil" (1 Thess. 5:21-22 NKJV).

THE LADY

The lady in the parable of the Devil's Bakery represents the power of the devil. Let me clarify, a woman in the Bible can represent that which is good or that which is evil. It just so happens in this parable the lady represents the power of the devil. In the other parables of Matthew 13, some of the men represent good and some represent evil. Remember the birds in these parables represent the power of the devil, but a bird does not always have to represent the power of the devil. The Holy Spirit who descended on Jesus was like a dove. What I am getting at is you must see the context in which the author is using the representation. Therefore, the lady represents the power of the devil. Here in this parable, you have a woman out of place in the Bible, a woman who relates to false religion, representing the power of the devil. Think about this comparison, the church is called "the Bride of Christ". There you have a woman who spoken of in the good sense. However, the false church is spoken of as a harlot, who is the devil's bride. Notice what the woman in this parable did.

First, she performs a deliberate act of sabotage. There in Matthew 13:33, we can clearly see the woman is mixing in, hiding to be exact, three measures of meal. She apparently knows exactly what she is doing. She did what she did not by chance, but by a deliberate act of her own choice. The devil knows what he is doing, he is out to sabotage the work of God. Next, she is being deceitful. If you are trying to go unnoticed in something you are going to do, you usually try to be stealthy, or sneaky, or cunning kind of like a snake. This woman is mixing in this meal not out in the open but mixing it in behind the scenes. Jesus done nothing in secret, as matter fact He points this out by saying, "Jesus answered him, "I spoke openly to the world. I always taught in synagogues and in the temple, where the Jews always meet, and in secret I have said nothing" (John 18:20 NKJV). When we behave as a church we are not to go out and hide the gospel in the ground (Matt. 25:14-30). We are not to try to make the leaven in this parable represent the gospel. You cannot make the three measures of meal represent the world. We are not to hide the gospel, instead we are to go out and make the gospel known. Shout it from the rooftops, get into the highways and byways shaking the hedges and compelling them to come in (Luke 14:23). Be alert, Satan is working beneath the surface, and he is the master of deception (1 Pet. 5:8).

One other act that the lady performs is indeed a devilish act. It does not take much to see the power of Satan behind all this evil work of putting leaven into something that is meant to be unleavened. Remember whenever you see a woman in the Bible doing something wrong, something wicked it is speaking about that which is wicked, harmful, and hurtful. Therefore, the Bible calls this type of woman a harlot. "Nevertheless, I have a few things against you, because you allow that woman Jezebel, who calls herself a prophetess, to teach and seduce My servants to commit sexual immorality and eat things sacrificed to idols" (Rev. 2:20 NKJV). In this parable you have a woman, in the kitchen, being a very sneaky housewife, she is the bride of the devil representing the false church not the true bride of Christ. She is representing Satan's work in the last days, infiltrating the church with legalism, liberalism, and luxury.

The parable of the Mustard Seed or the Devil's Dirty birds illustrates for us the false outward expansion of the kingdom. While the leaven in the parable of the Devil's Bakery illustrates the inward development of false doctrine and false living. The kingdom of heaven began with the sowing of the Word of God in the hearts of men. Most of the seeds did not produce any fruit because the devil's dirty birds snatch away the seed. Satan opposed the work of the kingdom by imitating the seed and planting counterfeit Christians. Satan then encouraged false growth by corrupting the seed to become something it is not, like a tree. Satan encourage this false growth by introducing false doctrine by mixing in leaven. Why is the Jesus telling us all of this about the kingdom of heaven, which we can apply to the church? Jesus is showing us, through the parable in Matthew 13, what is going to happen from the time Jesus began to sow the seed unto the end of the world at the final judgment.

According to the Bible these things are just simply signs of the last days. False religion and all these wild and weird cults which are popping up today and add to this is those liberals who deny the Word of God and the deity of Jesus does not disprove the Bible; it confirms the Bible! It is happening exactly as Jesus said it would be. We are on course to fulfill His prophecy. We do not have to worry about false religion, it is coming. Church members tend to be saying, "Oh, the cults are going to overtake us. Apostasy is going to overtake us!" Let me alleviate church members' fears: "You are of God, little children, and have overcome them, because He who is in you is greater that he who is in the world" (1 John 4:4 NKJV). Listen, it is not the false church we must worry about; it is our ignorance and our lethargy and our failure to "go" and "make" disciples (Matt. 28:18-20), our failure to share the Word of God. We must behave as a church because Jesus is greater than all our fears.

CHAPTER TWENTY

What are You Looking At?

*And while they looked steadfastly toward heaven as
He went up, behold, two men stood by them in white
apparel, who also said, "Men of Galilee, why do you
stand gazing up into heaven? This same Jesus, who
was taken up from you into heaven, will so come
in like manner as you saw Him go into heaven."*
(Acts 1:10-11 NKJV)

THE DISCIPLES OF JESUS ARE STANDING THERE ON THE MOUNT OF
Olives, and they are gazing up at the sky watch as Jesus left them
behind to continue His work here on earth. Then two angels appeared
and asked them, "Hey guys, what are you looking at?" The past month
and a half had been a whirlwind for the disciples. Just forty days
earlier they had seen Jesus die on a cross. On that day, all their dreams
and hopes came crashing to the ground. They hid themselves away
in fear of suffering the same fate Jesus had experienced. However,
after three days after Jesus died, He appeared to them alive and well.
Jesus has risen from the grave, and He is Lord! There was hope, and
yet they hesitated. For forty days they were like a roller coaster, they
were up and they were down.

Jesus took His disciples aside and began to teach them some
truths they desperately needed to know. "To whom He also presented
Himself alive after His suffering by many infallible proofs, being seen
by them during forty days and speaking of the things pertaining to

the kingdom of God" (Acts 1:3 NKJV). He tells them He is going away, and He is leaving His work, His ministry in their hands. They needed to know what the Lord expected of them, and He taught them. They needed to know what they were to be doing, and He taught them. They needed to be comfort for their troubled hearts, and He gave it to them. He spent forty days with His men instructing them, comforting them, and spending time with them.

On the fortieth day, Jesus and His disciples went up to the Mount of Olives. While they were there, He gave them some final words of instruction. These words were more than instructions, they were words of prophecy. Here is another account where Jesus gives a prophecy while being on the Mount of Olives. If you will remember, it was a month and a half ago that Jesus and His disciples were leaving the temple and was walking towards the Mount of Olives. While passing by the temple the disciples mentioned the beautiful structure, embellished with its many costly decorations, but Jesus was not impressed by it. He then makes the statement, "These things which you see; the days will come which not one stone shall be left upon another that shall not be thrown down" (Luke 21:6 NKJV). As they arrived at the Mount of Olives, the disciples began asking Him about when all this would come to pass. Jesus replies to all their question by giving what is known as "The Olivet Discourse," the greatest prophetic message Jesus ever preached (Luke 21, Matt. 24-25, Mark 13).

To properly understand The Olivet Discourse, we need to keep a few truths in mind. First, this passage never mentions the church or the rapture. Why? It does not mention because this passage was not written to the church, it was written to the nation of Israel. This is primarily a Jewish prophecy. Still, there are many truths that we can glean from these verses to help us behave as a church. Second, this prophecy covers a tremendous expansion of time. Over three thousand years of human history are in view here. These verses contain prophecies that have been partially fulfilled and will be completely fulfilled in the future. So, as we read them, we are looking backwards and forwards at the same time. Third, as with any prophetic passage of Scripture, we need to move cautiously and with the knowledge that no one person has all the answers. No Bible scholar has ever been able to solve all the theological riddles hidden within The Olivet Discourse. Let us listen in on this conversation between Jesus and His disciples as we look at the account recorded in Mark 13.

A Strange Prediction

"Then as He went out of the temple, one of His disciples said to Him, "Teacher, see what manner of stones and what buildings are here!" And Jesus answered and said to him, "Do you see these great buildings? Not one stone shall be left upon another, that shall not be thrown down" (Mark 13:1-2 NKJV). Jesus is leaving the Temple with His disciples following in behind. It has been an intense time for Jesus and His disciples while they were in the temple. Mark in chapters 11-12, records the encounter they had with the Jewish religious leader there in the temple. His disciples are probably baffled by the actions and words of Jesus while He was in the temple. It is possible they were thinking Jesus would try to win the favor of the Jews and the Jewish leaders. Instead, Jesus did everything in His power to expose them as religious phonies.

Now, their time in the temple is over, and they are heading out of the temple, and one of the disciples tries and lighten the mood. Because after all their negative experience in the temple, it was time for something more positive. He directs Jesus's attention to the temple, with all its elaborate and beautiful construction. The temple in Jerusalem, in those days, was among the most spectacular wonders of the ancient Roman Empire. The original temple, constructed by Solomon, was a magnificent building that took seven years and millions of dollars to build. Solomon's temple was destroyed by Nebuchadnezzar and the Babylonians around 600 B.C. When the Jews returned to their homeland seventy years later, they constructed the second temple. The second temple served the Jews for nearly five hundred years, but it suffered great damage due to passing of time. When King Herod assumed the throne of Israel, he wanted to gain favor with the Jews. So, he offered to rebuild their temple. The accepted and in 18 B.C. work began.

By the time of Jesus, the work had been underway for forty-six years (John 2:20) and would continue for another twenty years. The temple which Jesus and His disciples visited was an amazing building of its time. It sat atop Mount Moriah and literally dominated the skyline of the ancient city. The temple mount covered one-sixth of the land area of Jerusalem. The temple itself was one hundred seventy-two feet long and twenty stories high. It could be seen from many miles away and from anywhere in the city. The disciple, who is trying to lighten the mood, points everyone's attention to the stones and the buildings. The stones which made up Herod's temple were enormous for they were forty feet long, eighteen feet high, and fifteen feet wide. They were cut by hand from pure white limestone and fit tightly and perfectly. So tight in fact, not even a sheet of paper could be inserted between the stones. The doors, walls, and even the floors of the temple were overlaid with pure gold. There were jewels, ornate carvings, and many awe-inspiring sights. It was said that when the sun camp up over Jerusalem, you could not look at the Temple because of the light gleaming from its golden walls. Anything which was not covered with gold was the purest white. Whether the temple was seen during the day or at night, it was a sight no one ever forgot. Like every other Jew, this disciple was impressed by the temple, and he was proud it was a part of his nation and his religion. Therefore, he calls Jesus to look at the building and its wonder.

The response that Jesus makes in Mark 13:2 is somewhat strange to His disciples. Jesus hears the exclamation of this disciple and responds by telling him that the temple he loves so dearly will eventually be dismantled and destroyed. We know from history this prophecy was fulfilled in 70 A.D. when Roman General Titus and his army conquered the city. Titus ordered his men to preserve the temple, but the building was gutted by a fire set by one of his soldiers. As a result, General Titus ordered the destruction of the temple and the city. The Romans dismantled every stone in the building to get to the gold which melted into the cracks during the fire. As of today, there is not a single stone left from the great temple Herod built. However, one day, as prophesied, there will be a new temple built in Jerusalem. During the Tribulation Period, the Jews will build their temple and offer sacrifices once again.

A Startling Panorama

After Jesus makes this statement about the temple, there was probably awkward silence as they walked. The disciple who was hoping to change the mood is probably feeling a little deflated. As they walk, more questions were was stirring up in their minds as to what Jesus meant by His statement. "Now as He sat on the Mount of Olives opposite the temple, Peter, James, John, and Andrew asked Him privately, "Tell us, when will these things be? And what will be the sign when all these things will be fulfilled?"" (Mark 13:3-4 NKJV). The Mount of Olives stood some one hundred fifty feet higher than the city below. If offered a commanding view of the temple and its grounds. As Jesus sat down, the disciples who by now were baffled by what they heard Jesus say about the destruction of the temple, approached Him for an explanation.

These four disciples come asking Jesus about the end times. These same questions are the same questions that people today are still asking. Everyone wants to know "when" it will happen, and "what" will be the signs that the end times are here. All you need to do to guarantee a good crowd in any service is to announce you will be preaching on the end times and people will come to hear that. "And Jesus, answering them, began to say: "Take heed that no one deceives you. For many will come in My name, saying 'I am He,' and will deceive many. But when you hear of wars and rumors of wars, do not be troubled; for such things must happen, but the end is not yet. For nation will rise against nation, and kingdom against kingdom. And there will be earthquakes in various places, and there will be famines and troubles. These are the beginnings of sorrows" (vs. 5-8 NKJV). Jesus answered their last question first, and later in Mark 13 He will answer their first question. Let's examine the explanation of Jesus to His men.

THERE WILL BE FALSE MESSIAHS

The first thing to notice is the potential of deception. Jesus warned His men that they needed to beware of deception. Even the disciples could be drawn away by the things they might hear and see. The potential which Jesus spoke of still exists today. Therefore, we need to behave as a church by being grounded in the Word of God. We need to be familiar with what the Bible says and what we believe (1 Pet. 3:15). We need to have our doctrine nailed down tight in our hearts so when the deceptions come, we can be faithful to stand for the Lord. In Mark 13:6, Jesus said that many false christs would come along and draw many away into deception. By the time of Jesus, several Jews had came claiming to be the Messiah. There were some living even during the time of Christ. Many more have since followed down through history. Over in Acts 5:36-37 it mentions two would-be Messiahs that lived from the time of Jesus. One was named Theudas who claimed he could part the Jordan River. He deceived about four hundred people and led them to their deaths. The other was named Juda the Galilean who was a radical anti-Roman revolutionary, and he founded the Zealot movement in Israel. If you will remember, one of Jesus's disciples was one of his followers named, Simon the Zealot.

After the death and resurrection of the Lord Jesus many more would-be Messiahs came to fame in Israel. One man was named Shimon Bar-Kochba. He started a rebellion that lasted three years and cost thousands of lives in Israel. His revolt led to a harsh Roman crackdown which left Jerusalem in utter ruins (Shimon Bar Kokhba, 1998) Others included Moses of Crete, who claimed that he would part the Mediterranean Sea and lead his followers across dry land from the Island of Crete to Israel. On the appointed day, the false messiah marched towards the sea and commanded them to throw themselves down and the water in the sea would divide before them. Many leapt from the cliffs at his command and were drown in the sea. (Jewish Encyclopedia, 2021) In the 1502, a man by the name of Asher Lemmlein, pretended to be forerunner of the Messiah. While in Venice, Italy he convinced people that the Messiah was coming the next year. He and his followers did much fasting, praying, and giving out assistance that they named the year as the year of penitence. When he disappeared, the disturbance ceased. (Jewish Encyclopedia, 2021) In 1666, Shabbetai Zevi, claimed to have heard the voice of God declaring he was the son of God. He led his followers to the city of Constantinople and was arrested by the Turkish Sultan. The Sultan ordered him to either prove he was the Messiah or be executed. The would-be Messiah promptly converted to Islam. He was later diagnosed with what is now known as severe bipolar disorder (Plen, 2002) Since the Jews rejected their true Messiah, therefore many imposters rose to take His place.

In our own era, there have been many so-called Messiah who have paraded across the stage of history. Moses Guibbory, Menachem Mendel Schneerson, Maria Beulah Woodworth-Etter, Aimee Semple McPhearson, Kathryn Kuhlman, A.A. Allen, William Branham, Jack Coe, Joeseph Smith, Charles Taze Russel, Mary Baker Petterson Glover Eddy, and Sun Myung Moon. As the end of time approaches, there will be more and more people who will step forward claiming to be the savior of the world. Beware that you are not deceived by their slick words and evil deception. The appearance of such people is merely a sign the end is approaching.

THERE WILL BE POLITICAL CONFLICT

Our world has been marked by war since the beginning of time. According to one historian, in the 3,421 years of recorded history, there has only been 268 years of peace (Unknown, 2015) This figure does not consider the wars which were not recorded. The history of our world is one of war. Jesus told His disciples there would be wars and rumors of war and they would increase the closer we got to the end of time (Mark 13:7). We are seeing this proven in our day. Wars ravage our planet, even as man claims to be climbing ever higher on the ladder of intelligence, compassion, and peace. Jesus even cautioned us against getting caught up in the wars we see raging around us. When the United States invaded Iraq, many believed it was the end of time. All those who believed were wrong. God is using the tragedy of war to shape the world for the coming of His Son. God uses the wrath of men for His pieces into place for the end game.

In the first part of verse 8, we are told there will be strife among nations. We should not be overly concerned about this aspect either. Again, it is merely a sovereign God preparing the world for the appearance of His Son. Yet, when we hear the saber rattling of Iran, Russia, China, and North Korea it tends to make us a little afraid. We start thinking about the end of time because of all the things going on in our world. We can also apply to what Jesus is saying to the political realm. We do not need to be disturbed by political conflict within a country's government, including the United States. From history we can see, the Roman Empire had enjoyed a measure of peace for many years, but it would not last. As the empire decayed and nationalism developed from within, it was inevitable the Roman nation would collapse. Of course, this is the fulfillment of Daniel's prophecy interpretation of Nebuchadnezzar's dream (Dan. 2). Daniel had told King Nebuchadnezzar the image in his dream represented another nation succeeding the previous nation. When Daniel gets to the toes of the image, Daniel tells the king that all these gentile nations will not last. Daniel said, "You watched while a stone was cut out without hands, which struck the image on its feet of iron and clay and broke them in pieces. Then the iron, the clay, the bronze, the silver, and the gold were crushed together, and became like chaff from the summer threshing floors; the wind carried them away so that no trace of them were found. And the stone that struck the image became a great mountain and filled the whole earth" (Dan. 2:34-35 NKJV). Daniel interprets this by saying, "And in the days of these kings the God of heaven will set up a kingdom which shall never be destroyed; and the kingdom shall not be left to other people; it shall break in pieces and consume all these kingdoms, and it shall stand forever" (vs. 44 NKJV). As the end approaches, we will see an increase in this kind of activity we must not allow these things to disturb us. Paul told Timothy, "For God has not given us a spirit of fear, but of power and of love and of a sound mind" (2 Tim. 1:7 NKJV).

THERE WILL BE NATURAL DISASTERS

We are told from the rest of Mark 13:8, there will be earthquakes, famines, and troubles. This world is no stranger to earthquakes. Some earthquakes are evidence of God's wrath (Rev. 6:12; 8:5; 11:13;

16:18). Scientists tell us more than thirteen million people have died in earthquakes over the past 4,000 years. Earthquakes can even happen in various places. For example, in December of 2003 a major earthquake occurred in the Pacific Ocean. The earthquake spawned a tsunami which killed 300,000 people. Another example, among the locals of Northeast Arkansas and the Boot-hill of Missouri, there is a story about a series of earthquakes that took place in 1811-1812. The story goes, there was a series of earthquakes which rearranged the landscape of the area. It was said, the earthquake caused the Mississippi River to flow backwards and change path from its original journey. The sky was filled with dirt and ask, and the earthquake even started many forest fires. Earthquakes are increasing in their frequency and their intensity. They will continue to do so as end of time approaches but take heart Jesus told us it would be this way!

Did you know the devastating result which typically follows wars? Wars often leaves famine in its wake (2 Kings 25:2-3). Famine can be caused by man's abuse of the environment, or it was sent by God. According to World Vision, hunger is worsening. There is about ten percent of the global population that goes to bed regularly without food. This is due to factors like the economy, weather, or wars like the one in the Ukraine or the one in Israel. Since 2022, the number of countries facing food insecurities is 58 and that number continues to grow. The lingering effect of Covid contributes to these insecurities. The war in the Ukraine has impacted one-fifth of the global population due to rising food prices. Families who do not have enough money have to choose which could endanger their children. Their children are acceptable to situations like child marriages or child labor just so the family will have enough to eat. Most children under the age of five are malnourished (Omer, 2023) Famines devastate the poor nations around the world, and we are just one bad harvest away from starvation here in America. Famines will also increase as the ends nears Do not be disturbed by these things, because Jesus said it would be this way!

THERE WILL BE DISEASES OF EVERY KIND

In Matthew's account of this conversation, he uses the world "pestilences" (Matt. 24:7 NKJV) instead of the word "troubles" (Mark

13:8 NKJV). The world "pestilence" means "a contagious or infectious epidemic disease that is virulent and devastating" (Concise Oxford English Dictionary Eleventh Edition, 2004) What this means is there will be an upsurge in diseases and plagues as the end of time approaches. Growing up we learned in school about Medieval Europe and how it was affected by the plague known as "Black Death." Whole villages were destroyed by the plague. We also learned how other plagues would sweep through other cities and nations throughout history leaving millions of dead in their wake. There was this one outbreak known as the Spanish Influenza that occurred during World War I. Some Americans even called it the "purple death". During 1918, there were twenty-five million people who would die from the flu in the world. Which means there were more people who from the flu than those who died in battle. Before 2020, we were thinking nothing like that could ever happen in our day and age. Yet, Covid-19 did happen, and what we have forgotten is that we have also been through the AIDS epidemic, SARS, Bird Flu, and Swine Flu. What about the horrors of viruses like Ebola? Please understand, there are killer diseases out there just waiting for an opportunity to devastate the human race no matter where it originates from. An outbreak of deadly disease in our world has the potential to kill hundreds of millions of people in just a few short weeks. An outbreak like that would shut down the entire world as we know it; and it would be worse than Covid. But we must not allow this kind of information to fill us with fear. Jesus said that we would see diseases and pestilence and trouble of every kind increase as the end approached.

A Sobering Promise

After telling His men some of the things which will cause the people to believe the end is near, Jesus lets them know they cannot really know when the end will come. He tells them when they see these things, they will know it is the beginning of sorrows. These men are looking for signs. What Jesus gave them were not signs at all; they non-signs. The phrase "the beginning of sorrows" means "the beginning of the birth pangs" (Holman Illustrated Bible Dictionary, 2003) meaning they are just an indicator of a long, hard time ahead.

That was his promise while He was here as stated in John 14:1-3. That was the promise of the angel when He ascended to Heaven in Acts 1:3-14. After spending forty days with Jesus after His resurrection, the disciples are standing with Him on the Mount of Olives. As Jesus is giving His disciples some final instructions with prophecy, His Olivet Discourse should still be fresh on their minds as they listen to His words. Then as they were still listening and watching, He begins to rise from off the ground, and ascends into the heavens. Suddenly, He is gone and taken from their presence. They stand their bewildered on that mountain without Him. In that moment, the disciples are filled with more questions than answers. Their minds are doubtless filled with many confusing thoughts.

While they are standing there looking up into the sky, two men in white apparel appears to them. The angel says, "Men of Galilee, why do you stand gazing up into heaven?" (Acts 1:10 NKJV). Basically, what is being said is, "What are you looking at?" That is a sobering question, when we have a sobering promise from Jesus (John 14:1-3). The same confusing thoughts the disciples had the day Jesus ascended, is the same typical thought which are on the minds of many of God's children which can hinder us from behaving like a church.

A CONFUSING FUTURE

For the disciples, the ascension of the Lord back into heaven changed everything. For the last three years these men had spent nearly every moment with Jesus. They had left their families, friends, and businesses to follow him. Now, He is gone, and they do not know what to do. "Therefore, when they had come together, they asked Him, saying, "Lord, will You at this time restore the kingdom to Israel?" And He said to them, "It is not for you to know times or seasons which the Father has put in His own authority" (Acts 1:6-7 NKJV). With Jesus going away, the disciples are concerned about what the future holds both for them, and the work of the Lord. They ask Jesus about the future, and about when they can expect Him to establish the kingdom of God. They want to know if the time has come, or if they must wait. The answer Jesus gives them is anything but clear. Jesus tells them, essentially, such matters are not their business, but they belong to the secret, providential workings of the Lord. "The secret things belong to the Lord our God, but those things which are revealed belong to us and to our children forever, that we may do all the words of the law" (Deut. 29:29 NKJV).

The future is a secret thing, which man is prevented from knowing. No so-called psychic, medium, soothsayer, or prophet can tell you what will happen tomorrow. Only God knows what the future holds or when Jesus will come for His people. Anyone who says different is deceiving you. While no human may know what the future holds, we do know Who holds the future. Our Heaven Father stands outside of time and transcends the boundaries of time and space. While we cannot see the future, the Lord is already in all our tomorrows. He has prepared our way and ordered our steps (Ps. 37:23; Prov. 16:9). To me that is a comforting thought, because our world is filled with pain, sorrow, and heartache. None of us know whether tomorrow will be better or worse than today. Regardless of what the path of life holds for us, our Heavenly Trinity not only walks with us (Heb. 13:5), but He also walks ahead of us to secure our future. Tomorrow is a confusing mystery to us mortals. Think about this, today we are here, tomorrow we may be in eternity. Today the winds be blowing around us, tomorrow we could be in the middle of a storm. While the future may be shrouded in mystery, we have the Lord's blessed assurance He is already there, and He has the future well in hand.

The disciples were concerned about the future, but they had no need to be. The Father had the future well in hand. How about you? Are concerned about tomorrow? Do worries, fears, and doubts about tomorrow trouble you? Are you behaving as a church that believes, trust God whole holds the future in His hands?

A CHALLENGING TASK

Jesus gives them an assignment there on the Mount of Olives before He ascends to heaven. This assignment has been passed down from believer to believer, from church to church. It is an assignment which is be ongoing until Jesus returns. The church is to behave as a church by behaving as fishers of men. Here is the assignment, "But you shall receive power when the Holy Spirit has come upon you;

and you shall be witnesses to Me in Jerusalem, and in all Judea and Samaria, and to the end of the earth" (Acts 1:8 NKJV). Matthew records this assignment in Matthew 28:18-20, and Mark records it as well in Mark 16:15. Luke records the word witness for us in Acts 1:8. We are to be Jesus' witnesses to the world. The disciples were to begin a Jerusalem, then they were to take the message to Judea, then to Samaria, and finally to the uttermost parts of the world. They were given the task of sharing the Gospel with all people in all places. Their mandate was to preach to every creature. They were to go and teach all nations. These men had a message to tell, and the Lord sent them out to spread that message. This message must have been front and center in their minds as they watched Jesus depart from the world and disappear into the glory cloud.

For the last three years the disciples watched the Lord Jesus do what He was sending them out to do. They had heard Him preach, watched Him love the lost, and seen Him cross all social and religious barriers to reach sinners. They even got a little practice in while He was here. He sent them out two by two to preach, however they were comforted by the fact He would be there when they came back in. Now, He is going away, and they are left behind to carry on without Him. Surely the task they faced filled them with fear. How would they carry on without Him? How would they accomplish God's work if He was not here physically to help them? This why Jesus told them, before He gave them the assignment, even though He is going away, He is not leaving them here alone to do this assignment alone. Notice how it all went down, "And being assembled together with them, He commanded them not to depart from Jerusalem, but to wait for the Promise of the Father, "which" He said, "you have heard from ME; for John truly baptized with water, but you shall be baptized with the Holy Spirit not many days from now" (Acts 1:4-5 NKJV). The promise was fulfilled ten days later, on the Day of Pentecost, when the Spirit of God came in like a mighty rushing wind and filled the church with His power and presence (Acts 2).

Reminds me of Ezekiel's dream in Ezekiel 37:9-14. When God told him to speak to the wind and command it to breathe upon the dead bodies. The wind came and breathed upon the dead bodies, and they came to life. Yes, the message of Ezekiel was to the nation of Israel, however, the promise Jesus gave to the disciples the night before He died, was a promise to them and to us, that He would send Someone to help them (John 14:16-18). In Acts 1:8, Jesus reminds the disciples of the promise of the Comforter. The Holy Spirt will empower them and give them the ability to carry out the mission God is leaving them here to do. They will not have to do God's work alone! They are promised His power, His touch, and His blessing as they carry the gospel to the ends of the earth. On the Day of Pentecost, the Holy Spirit came in breathed on them and the church was born and given life, power, and the ability to carry out the mission. They turned the world upside down.

Here we are today, the church is still here, and God has not changed His mind. Do you know why you are still in this world? Do you know why the church is still here? You are here because the Lord Jesus is not through with you yet! Jesus is not through with the church yet. One reason He leaves us here in this world, with all its sin, its problems, and its pain, is o we might be witnesses to His saving grace to a world which is trapped in sin. He leaves you here so the world might see Jesus in you. He leaves the church here so we might behave as a church telling the lost that Jesus saves! I have heard people say, "O how we need a fresh anointing of the Holy Spirit." Or "O we need to ask the Holy Spirit to breathe on us, to revive us, and renew us." I'm thinking, "No we don't! We need to repent of our sin of apathy, complacency, bitterness…we just need to repent period!" "If My people who are called by My name will humble themselves, and pray and seek My face, and turn from their wicked ways, then I will hear from heaven, and will forgive their sin and heal their land" (2 Chron. 7:14). We need to get up out of our pews and get on our knees and seek the face of God for forgiveness. The Holy Spirit has already come, and He is still here. He never left us, but we left Him! We need to quit quenching the Holy Spirit and let Him loose in our lives and in the church. He has already breathed upon us the moment we asked Him to come into our hearts, at the moment of salvation. Therefore, we need to behave as a church empowered by the Holy Spirit to take the gospel and spread it to every creature (1 Pet. 3:15).

A COMFORTING PROMISE

The minds of the disciples are filled with many thoughts. They have been given an assignment which far exceeds their abilities. They face a future which is unknown and probably a little more than frightening to them. To top it all off, they have just watched as their Savior, their Lord, the One they have left everything behind to follow, disappeared into a cloud of glory. They are terrified and filled with many questions about today and about all tomorrows which lie ahead.

They are so captivated by the sight of Jesus going up into heaven, they are oblivious to the two strangers who appear on the mountain with them (Acts 1:10). These two men turn out to be angels, who have come to speak comfort to the confused disciples. These are the angels, "who also said, "Men of Galilee, why do you stand gazing up into heaven? This same Jesus, who was taken up from you into heaven, will so come in like manner as you saw Him go into heaven" (Acts 1:11 NKJV). The implication is clear, why sit around doing nothing and waiting on the Lord to return, when you could be doing something. We need to behave as a church and be about the business, the assignment, Jesus has left for us to do. Working and serving Him with a sense of urgency knowing full well there is coming a day when He will return. What are you looking at today? What has your attention? What are occupied with which might keep you from behaving as a church? Are you confused about the turn of life? Are you actively serving the Lord by sharing the gospel? Jesus wants His people to know He is coming back. But He does not want us to get caught up in speculating when that day will be. He wants us to live our lives as if He is never coming or He is coming at any second. He does not want us guessing when He will appear and we are not to be looking for signs, but the Savior! Jesus is coming! But things are likely to get tough for His people before He does. Let us not be deceived by the signs of the times. Let us be determined in our hearts we will obey His Word, live for Him, and behave as a church.

CHAPTER TWENTY-ONE

Why Going to Church
Should Make Us Glad

*I was glad when they said to me, "Let us
go into the house of the Lord."
(Psalm 122:1 NKJV)*

THERE WAS A PASTOR WHO HAD COME HOME FROM THE OFFICE ONE day, to find his daughter arguing with her friends in the bedroom. From the front hallway he could hear them yelling and calling each other names. So, he quickly made way up the stairs to see what was going on. When he gets to the bedroom door he asks, "What is going on in here?" His five-year-old looks up at him, smiles, and replies, "It's okay, daddy. We are just playing church!" You know we laugh at this story, but it is much darker and far more serious than we often realize. The sad but true fact is the church is often thought of as being out of touch and insensitive to what is going on in the world. Often, the church is seen as being so wrapped up within itself it seems as though it has no compassion, nor time for a world which is perishing. In fact, there are many outside the church who would rather turn anywhere else for help but to the church.

One theologian tells the story of a homeless shelter worker who worked with the homeless in Chicago. "There was a woman this shelter worker was trying to help who was addicted to cocaine. She was so desperate she would rent her two-year-old daughter to men so they could have sex with her. The woman would get $100 per man which would be just enough for another fix. She was homeless, in bad health, and no one cared for her. One day the homeless lady poured her heart out to the shelter worker, who was a Christian minister, and he was overwhelmed and amazed at her story. At the end of their counseling session, he said to her, "As you went through all this, did you ever think about going to a church for help?" What the homeless woman said next took him by surprise. With a naïve shocked expression upon her face she said, "Church! Why would I ever go there? I was already feeling bad enough; they would just make me feel even worse!" (Unknown, 2015)

Why do people have this perception of the church? Where did we go wrong? I believe the honest answer is we are not behaving as a church because we have forgotten why going to church should make us glad. Jesus said, "The thief does not come except to steal, and to kill, and to destroy. I have come that they may have life, and that they may have it more abundantly" (John 10:10 NKJV). Let me ask you, "How do you behave when you get ready to go to church?" When you get up on a typical Sunday morning, what is the focus of getting ready for church? "Your attitude is like the aroma of your heart. If your attitude stinks your heart is not right." (Kendrick, 2006) When you get up and get ready to go to church for worship, your heart should be glad because you are going to worship in the presence of the Lord Jesus. Take for instance Psalms 120-134. These psalms were what the Jewish Pilgrims were sing as they made their way to Jerusalem to observe the mandatory feasts given in the Law of Moses. They would sing them to get their hearts right as they made their way to the holy place of worship. These psalms ascend the heights of the glory and majesty of God. They were designed to glorify the Lord and help prepare the hearts of the saints of God for worship in the tabernacle and later the temple. Psalm 122 talks about the place of worship which is Jerusalem; it talks about the purpose of worship, and the power of worship and how worship brings gladness to the hearts of the worshipers.

David writes, "I was glad when they said to me, "Let us go into the house of the Lord." (Ps. 122:1 NKJV). The word "glad" means "to cause to rejoice" (Dictionary, 1828) In Psalm 122, David gives us the reasons he has found for being glad when he goes into the house of the Lord. These reasons should be what causes us to behave as a church and be glad.

The Purpose for Going

David says, "Where the tribes go up, the tribes of the Lord, to the Testimony of Israel, to give thanks to the name of the Lord" (Ps. 122:4 NKJV). David mentioned the testimony of Israel. By doing so he is referencing God's command for Israel to gather at the tabernacle, later it would be the temple, for three important Jewish feasts. They are: The Feast of Unleavened Bread, The Feast of Pentecost, and the Feast of Tabernacles. The Jews made their pilgrimage to the place of worship because doing so honored the Word of the Lord. One of the primary reasons we gather in the place of worship, the church, is to hear and to heed God's Word. When you go and study how the tabernacle was designed by God in the book of Exodus, you will see how this portable tent was intended for the purpose of worshipping Jehovah. Every piece of cloth, every board, every piece of furniture, every item in the tabernacle was commissioned, developed, and designed for the use in the worship of Almighty God.

Everything which was part of the tabernacle was a picture of or pointed to Jesus Christ in some form or another. The tabernacle was called the tent of meeting. It was here Israel met with God, offered their sacrifices unto Him, where daily worship was conducted, and where atonement offering was made for the sins of the people of Israel. When Israel would make camp, God gave them a special designed way for each tribe to set their camp as they were moving through the wilderness. God's special design would have them to set up camp in four surrounding directions with the tabernacle being in the center of the camp. This reminded them the worship of God was to be at the center of their lives. The tabernacle and later the temple was the most important place in Jewish social and religious life.

In the same way the Word of God should be at the heart of everything we do as well! Every service, ministry, missions, and event the church has should be and must be centered on the Word of God. Every worship service we have is a God given opportunity to open His book and share the gospel. The place of preaching and proclaiming should start at the house of God. Paul writes, "For since, in the wisdom of God, the world through wisdom did not know God, it pleased God through the foolishness of the message preached to save those who believe" (1 Cor. 1:21 NKJV). "How then shall they call on Hin to who they have not believed? And how shall they believe in Him of who they have not heard? And how shall they hear without a preacher? And how shall they preach unless they are sent? As it is written: "How beautiful are the feet of those who preach the gospel of peace who bring glad tidings of good things!" But they have not all obeyed the gospel. For Isaiah says, "Lord, who has believed our report?" So, then faith comes by hearing, and hearing by the word of God" (Rom. 10:14-17 NKJV). Going to hear a Spirit-filled, Bible-centered message should thrill the heart of the saint of God. When you hear the great precepts and doctrines of the Bible preached, it should cause us to behave because hearts are glad, and our souls are moved by the Word of God!

David then tells us the Jewish Pilgrims were going to the place of worship for the purpose of giving thanks unto the name of the Lord. The ancient Jews made their way to the tabernacle at great personal cost and difficulty to offer their praises to the Lord. The would be even more significant when Israel settled in their Promised Land and then would have to travel to Jerusalem for worship. However, they believed He was worthy to be praised for His grace in their lives, so they paid the price, stood before His designated place and they praised His name! What is interesting today is the fact not everyone shares the same excitement about going to the house of the Lord as the Jews did. Because if we did, His house would be full every time the doors were opened for worship! Some are glad, some are mad, some are sad, some can be bad, and some even feel like they have been had when they go to church. However, when you get down to it and think, in our day it does not take much effort for church members or visitors to go to church. No one needs to walk a hundred miles in their sandals to go to the house of the Lord. No one had to ride on the back of a donkey. No one had to contend with dust, dirt, nor danger to go to church. It is true some families rush around the house to get ready to go to church. There are some days when you might leave a warm house to brave the cold to get to your car, which might not have been warmed up yet, to go to church. It is possible you might have given up watching your favorite TV program or decided not to go shopping or dining out to go to church, but going to church does not cost you. The ancient Jews remembered what God had done for their forefathers. They knew what He had done for them, and this gave them ample reason to praise the Lord. So, they did! How much more do we have today to praise Him for? Just stop to consider everything He has done for you: there is salvation, His provisions, protection, grace, mercy, love, etc. Then add to the fact we are commanded to praise Him, and you should come to the realization that we are behind in the praising of the Lord department. "Oh, clap your hands, all you peoples! Shout to God with the voice of triumph!" (Ps. 47:1 NKJV). "Therefore, let us go forth to Him, outside the camp, bearing His reproach. For here we have no continuing city, but we seek the one to come. Therefore, by Him let us continually offer the sacrifice of praise to God, that is, the fruit of our lips, giving thanks to His name" (Heb. 13:13-15 NKJV). I cannot speak fore you, but I would be ashamed to got to church where the Word of God was not preached and where the name of the Lord was not praised!

The People Who Gather There

David found gladness in the people who he would meet him at the house of the Lord. David said, "Let us go into the house of the Lord" (Ps. 122:1b NKJV). He adds, "Where the tribes go up, the tribes of the Lord to the Testimony of Israel, to give thanks to the name of the Lord" (vs. NKJV). When David went to the tabernacle to worship, he knew the people who gathered there would be united in fellowship. The Jews saw their time at the tabernacle as a time when they would come together ("let us") on common ground, for a common purpose. All their petty disputes and family disagreements were put aside so they could worship the Lord together. We could learn a lot from those ancient worshipers. When you look at the people who attend church with you what do you see. You see people who are all different than you. We come from different families, different points of views, different backgrounds, different temperaments, different interests (outside of church), different cultures (in some cases), and even somewhat different belief systems. Yet, we are all commanded to gather to worship the Lord (Heb. 10:25).

From what David was saying in Psalm 122:4, for us to behave as a church we need to behave as a family. The ancient Jews were a people connected by blood. They were a family. When they came together for worship, it was a family affair. It was a time to renew acquaintances, to catch up on family news, and meet the new members of the family. It was a family reunion every time they met. The church today should behave as a church in the same manner. When we come together, the family is coming together. All the redeemed are united by the precious blood of Jesus. When we come together, whether it is to worship, to fellowship, or just to pray, we should use this opportunity to strengthen our family bonds. One of the reasons we offer so many opportunities for fellowship is important to a healthy family spirit in the church. The church who will not fellowship together lacks unity and harmony! Imagine if a family never shared a meal or got to know one another; this kind of family would be dysfunctional at best and a family with serious problems at worse. We need to ensure we behave as a church giving of the sweet aroma as the church in the book of Acts did. They were enjoying one another's company, praying, preaching, praising, and worshiping the Lord Jesus Christ.

THE MATERIALS IN THE INCENSE

When I think of a church that is behaving and giving off a sweet aroma to the Lord, I think of the incense that burned in the tabernacle. Exodus 30:34-38 deals with the incense which burned in the tabernacle. Incense speaks of Jesus Christ and His worship. When the incense burned, the smoke ascended towards heaven. Its scent, aroma, came up before the Lord and He was pleased. When the incense was burned, its fragrance filled the tabernacle, and everyone knew worship was taking place. This was what happened when Mary broke her alabaster box of ointment and anointed the head of Jesus. John tells us, "the house was filled with the fragrance of the oil" (John 12:3 NKJV). Real worship has a way of making its presence known. When real worship takes place, it leaves its scent behind. Therefore, your behavior is like the aroma of your heart. When you are out of fellowship with your church family, you are out of fellowship with God and your aroma stinks.

In Exodus 30:34, God was very specific when He gave Moses the ingredients that were used in the incense, because these ingredients teach us about Jesus and why He is worthy of our worship as family. The four ingredients listed in Exodus 30:34 remind us why He is worthy of our worship. The first ingredient is stacte, which speaks of His proclamations. Stacte is an aromatic gum the comes from a certain shrub. The word stacte means "to drop" (Wood, Marshall, & Millard, 1996) for the stacte was collected a drop at a time from the plant. This substance speaks to us about the Words of our Lord. Like the stacte dropped from the plant, the precious Word of God is dropped a word at a time from our Savior's lips. John reminds us that Jesus is the living word in John 1:1, 14. He also gives us the written inspired word which is pure (Ps. 19:8; 30:5; Jam. 3:17; 2 Tim. 3:16-17). Praise God for His word, because His word speaks to fallen men, it reveals Himself to man, and it gives His gospel plan of salvation. His word is health for the soul, food for the journey, strength for the battle, light for the darkness, and hope for every tomorrow. We ought to behave as a church by giving thanks for His Holy Word.

The next ingredient is onycha, which speaks of His person. This ingredient was found in certain species of shellfish which are only found in the Red Sea. The word "onycha" comes from the Hebrew root word for "lion" (Strong's Concordance, 1984) This ingredient reminds us He is a King Who is to be revered, honored, served, loved, obeyed, and worshiped. Jesus is the King of kings and the Lord of lords (Rev. 19:16). He is the Lion of the tribe of Judah (Rev. 5:5). He is the fulfillment of all the Old Testament prophecies said would come (Jer. 23:5; Gen. 49:10). He came into this world through a virgin birth, He lived a sinless life, died on the cross, rose from the dead, and ascended back to heaven. He is the One Who is coming back for His church (1 Thess. 4:17). He is the Judge we, Christians, will face at the judgment seat of Christ (2 Cor. 5:10; 1 Cor. 3:10-15). He is going to come again in power and glory to rule and reign during the millennium (Rev. 19:11-16). He is the Judge sinners will face as Judge on the Great White Throne of judgment (Rev. 20:11-15). He is the One Who will be worshiped in heaven for all eternity!

The next ingredient is galbanum which speaks of His pain. The word "galbanum" means "cutting" (Holman Illustrated Bible Dictionary, 2003) because the resin was obtained from a certain plant by cutting it open. After the cut was made the resin could run out and be collected. This cutting of this plant to gain this ingredient should remind us of Jesus' suffering and pain He endured upon the cross. It should remind us of His death on the cross which He gave His life to redeem His bride from her sins. Here is a list of His pain and suffering: Beating (Luke 22:63-64; Ps. 129:3); Scourging (Matt. 27:26); Spitting (Matt. 27:30); Mockery (Matt. 27:26-29); Beard plucked from His face (Isa. 50:6); Stripped naked (Matt. 27:35 and the soldiers gambled for His garments); Nailed to the cross (Matt. 27:38). The crucifixion itself, a death on a cross, is the most horrible form of execution know to mankind. We derive our word "excruciating" from the word crucifixion and means "out of the cross" (Strong's Concordance, 1984) Jesus suffered pain at the hand of a Sovereign God. Jesus literally became sin on the cross for us (2 Cor. 5:21). God judged Jesus in the place of sinners. God poured out His undiluted wrath into the body of His Son. Jesus is to be worshiped for His sufferings. He is to be worshiped for His sacrifice. He is to be worshiped for the salvation He provided through His death.

The last ingredient is frankincense which speaks of His purity. Frankincense is another resin taken from a tree. When this resin was burned, it gave off a pure white smoke. Jesus is the sinless Son of God because He was born without the taint of human sin. As He lived here upon earth, He never committed a single sin. In fact, since He was fully God in human form it was impossible for Him to sin (Heb. 7:26; 1 Pet. 2:22; 2 Cor. 5:21; 1 John 3:5). Jesus was and is the pure sinless Son of God. He came into this world to give His life a ransom for the guilty, by dying on the cross, therefore He is to be worshiped for His sinless nature.

THE MIXING OF THE INCENSE

Not only does Exodus 30:34-38 speak about the ingredients in the incense, but these verses tell us how the incense was to be mixed together. As we are thinking about how to behave as a church, keep in mind the ingredients speak about why Jesus deserves to be worship and the mixing together of the ingredients teach how we are to come together as we approach Him in worship. The first way to approach Him talked about in these verses is the personal aspect of worship. When we come together before the Lord in worship, there are two ways. One way we are to approach Him in the personal aspect of worship is by being holy. Verse 35 says the incense is to be "salted, pure and holy" (vs. 35 NKJV). Jesus said, "You are the salt of the earth; but if the salt loses its flavor, how shall it be seasoned? It is then good for nothing but to be thrown out and trampled underfoot by men" (Matt. 5:13 NKJV). Salt in the Bible is a picture of purity. What Moses and Jesus is implying is the condition of your heart and your behavior of your worship when you come before His presence. If you are not in a right relationship, if your heart is not right, even if we as a church do not behave as a church, then we cannot approach Him in worship. It is as if our worship is good for nothing, except for the praise of men who trample it under their feet. "If I regard iniquity in my heart the Lord will not hear" (Ps. 66:18 NKJV). "But your iniquities have separated you from your God; and your sins have hidden His face from you, so that He will not hear" (Isa. 59:2 NKJV). The personal aspect of worship is we must come before Him with holy hearts!

We must also come before in the personal aspect of worship in humbleness. Exodus 30:36 says they were to take some of the incense "and you shall beat some of it very fine" (vs. 36 NKJV). In other words, take the ingredients and reduce them into a powder. This speaks to the fact we cannot approach the Lord with pride or pretense in our hearts. Pretense means "to cover the real motive and present others with a false idea" (Wood, Marshall, & Millard, 1996) We cannot approach Him boasting in ourselves and our abilities. We must come to him with a sense of our weakness by recognizing His power. We must come before Him remembering without Him we can do nothing (John 15:5). We must be contrite, broken before Him in worship.

Another way the ingredients teach us how we are to come together is through the perpetual aspect of worship. According to Exodus 30:36, after they had prepared the incense, they were to take it and place it before the Ark of the Covenant in the Holy of Holies. Above the Ark, over the Mercy Seat, was where God met with His people in the tabernacle or temple. The incense before the Ark was symbol their worship was to be continual and perpetual. Paul says, "Rejoice always" (1 Thess. 5:16 NKJV). The incense was always to be there ready to be offered in worship before the Lord. In other words, worship was to be the defining behavior of the people God. Worship is how we are to behave as a church. The people of God today, are to be marked by perpetual, continual worship. We are to worship at every opportunity for personal, public, corporate worship (Heb. 10:25). Jesus said, "But the hour is coming, and now is, when the true worshippers will worship the Father in spirit and truth; for the Father is seeking such to worship Him. God is Spirit, and those who worship Him must worship in spirit and truth" (John 4:23-24 NKJV). We are to behave as a church who worship. Something is wrong with a person's walk who does not possess a desire to worship the Lord. Something is wrong when there is no desire for prayer, for Bible reading, for singing praises to Him, and to worship His holy name. Every day of our lives should be spent in the worship of the Lord who redeemed us by His grace. "Praise the Lord! Praise, O servants of the Lord, Praise the name of the Lord! Blessed be the name of the Lord from this time forth and forevermore! From the rising of the sun to its going down the Lord's name is to be praised" (Ps. 113:1-3 NKJV). "Therefore, whether you eat or drink, or whatever you do, do all to the glory of God" (1 Cor. 10:31 NKJV).

The last way the ingredients teach us how we are to come together is through proportional aspect of worship. The phrase in verse 34 "there shall be equal amounts of each" (Ex. 30:34 NKJV). God has gifted every child of God, through the Holy Spirit, spiritual gifts which are to be used to behave as a church. We are to come and use those gifts with equal mixtures with other believers as we behave as a church member blended in worship. Our worship as a church should be balanced and proportional. What this means is we are not to go off in a tangent in our worship services. There are some churches who emphasize the life of Christ while they make very little of His death. Others focus on His death and exclude His life. Each aspect of His life, ministry, and death is equally important. His life means nothing if He did not die. His death means nothing if He did not live a sinless life. His sinless nature means nothing if He did not suffer for our sins. His Word means nothing if He did not fulfill every aspect of His promises. Every part of His life and ministry is vitally important and He is to be worshiped in the fullness of His glory.

THE MINISTRY OF THE INCENSE

Once the incense was prepared, it was to be employed in the worship of the Lord. The means we are to be in the active business of, or given to, the worship of God alone every day. No person, possession, nor pastime deserves more worship than God. "I will bless the Lord at all times; His praise shall continually be in my mouth" (Ps. 34:1 NKJV). "Therefore, by Him let us continually offer the sacrifice of praise to God, that is, the fruit of our lips, giving thanks to His name" (Heb. 13:15 NKJV). The incense had a definite job to do, it was to be "holy for the Lord" (Ex. 30:37 NKJV). This incense was to be used for no other purpose than for the worship of the Almighty God. We live in an age where God receives very little genuine, biblical worship. The fact is most people tend to be worshiping the god of self these days. With the dawning of technology and social media platforms, people tend to be bowing down to idols and false gods because the are more wrapped up in what is being posted over the internet. Money, pleasure, memes, blogs, funny videos, sports, TikTok, FaceBook, Twitter, politics, among others seem to be what is occupying people's minds and hearts. This even incudes Christians who succumb to this fiery dart. We need to behave as a church, followers of Christ, and church members by being aware of the fact: "What people live for are the things they worship." In essence those things, including self, become their gods. True worship belongs to God! He is to be loved, served, shared, and exalted. He is to be honored with every moment of our lives (1 Cor. 10:31). We are to honor Him with every available resource and every ounce of energy. Yes, He demands, but it is more than a command, He deserves it!

God tells us, "Whoever makes any like it, to smell it, he shall be cut off from his people" (Ex. 30:38 NKJV). In other words, if the incense was used for anything other than the worship of God, it would bring His judgment upon the guilty person. This is what happened to Aaron's sons, Nadab and Abihu. These two sons came before the Lord and brought the incense in, but they also brought a "strange fire." They went against the Lord's command concerning His worship; therefore, God killed them (Lev. 10:1-2). This should serve as a warning; false worship always leads to destruction. If you want to invite the judgment of God into your life, just give your worship to other gods. Just offer the holy incense of worship to things other than Him. There are a lot of God's children who are giving their attention and affection to things other than the Lord. It is an unlawful use of worship, and it will not go unpunished. May the Lord help us to search our hearts and see where we are offering "strange fire and incense" before the Lord. He is a jealous God and He will not allow His worship to be given to another.

The Person They Glorify There

When the church family gathers in His house, Jesus is to be the central focus of all worship. Four times in Psalm 122 David mentions the "Lord" (Ps. 122: 1, 4, 9). Jehovah God was at the heart of all the Jews did. Every moment and event of life for the Jews revolved around the Lord and His worship. He was the centerpiece of everything. When David calls God, "the Lord", he is using the most common name of God in the Bible. The word He used here in Psalm 122 is "Yahweh" or "Jehovah" (Strong's Concordance, 1984) This name for God appears over 6,800 times in the Old Testament. It identifies God as the eternal, self-existent One. This should remind us God had no beginning and He will have not ending (Rev. 22:13). This is the name God used to make Himself know to Moses (Ex. 3:14), "And God said

313

to Moses, "I Am Who I Am." And He said, "Thus you shall say to the children of Israel, 'I Am has sent your'" (NKJV). The name also identifies God as the covenant-keeping One. He is a God who makes covenants with His people, and He never breaks our faith in Him. He is a God Who keeps every promise He makes. He keeps every soul He saves; therefore, His name is worthy of our praise and worship.

RECOGNIZE A GOOD PLACE

When it comes to glorifying God in His house, I think about what went on at the Mount of Transfiguration. In Matthew 17, Peter makes a statement after seeing wash was happening around him. However, he did not really understand what was going on at the time, but he did know enough to know he was in a good place. Here is what transpired to show us how we can recognize a good place, and it is all because of Who we glorify there. "Then Peter answered and said to Jesus, "Lord, it is good for us to be here; if You wish, let us make here three tabernacles: one for You, one for Moses, and one for Elijah" (Matt. 17:4 NKJV).

As you and I travel through life, we find ourselves in all kinds of places. Some are okay and some are not okay for us to be in. There are valley times and there are mountaintop times and times which fall everywhere in between. You can be in a good place and not recognize it. You could be in a valley, but that valley might just be a good place fro the moment. You might be in a time of physical pain, emotional trouble, financial turmoil, or any other different kinds of trial and tribulations; however, you still might be in a good place. There are three things in which you can know you are in a good place as you glorify God.

First, you know you are in a good place to glorify God, when you can examine His glory. Matthew 17:1 tells us Jesus only took three of His men with Him to the Mountain of Transfiguration. He took Peter, James, and John. This is not the only time Jesus selected these men for a special ministry. He took these three with Him when He went to raise Jairus's daughter from the dead (Mark 5:37). These are the three who would go a litter deeper into Gethsemane to pray (Mark 14:33). While it is true God is not a respecter person (Rom. 2:11), however, it is also true some people are closer to Him than are others. This does not mean He loves them more than others. It means some people are more responsive to His love than others. You are as close to God as you want to be (Jam. 4:8). By the way, those who are open to all God has for them are more likely to see Him move in glory and power than those who tend to stay farther away from the Lord.

We are told the three men went to the mountain top with Jesus, or "high mountain" (Matt. 17:1 NKJV). For Peter, the mountaintop became a holy place and even John referred to this event (1 John 1:1-3). Peter wanted to settle down and stay right there (Matt. 17:4). When you find a church home where you can examine the glory of God and a place where you can glorify God you have found a good place. Yes, it is true when you come to the house of the Lord and worship Him, for a moment of your week, day, hour, you can leave behind, at the altar, your burdens. However, when you go out the doors, you are faced with new burdens. Those three men when they came down off the mountain, were hit square in the face with the pressures and burdens of life (vs. 14-27). They would have to deal with a demonic spirit and would have to pay their taxes. But they carried that worship service in their hearts (Mark 9:10). Here is the point, if you really know the Lord, there will be some mountain top times with Jesus. There will be times when His presence is real, and His glory is clear to see. When you are in one of those moments, enjoy it for all it is worth, because you will soon be back in the valley. Praise God, the mountaintop experience will sustain you through many long and difficult valleys!

Matthew 17:2 tells us, Jesus was transfigured. This word is translated from the same word which gives us "metamorphosis" (Wood, Marshall, & Millard, 1996) Nearly anyone who has ever taken biology know what metamorphosis is: "a change of form or appearance" (Dictionary, 1828) The term is used to refer to what happens to transform a caterpillar into a butterfly. The caterpillar encloses itself within a cocoon and goes through a metamorphosis. It goes in a worm and comes out a butterfly. It goes in having to crawl and comes out able to fly. This is what happened to the Lord Jesus on this day. Up until that moment, He had appeared to be just another Jewish man, who did some remarkable things (Isa. 53:2-3). But on the mountain, the glory which was concealed inside His human body burst forth. However, this is not the first time Jesus experience a metamorphosis. The first time was when He was placed within the womb of a virgin named Mary and was born into this world. Jesus existed before Bethlehem; He merely concealed His heavenly glory within the earthly frame (Phil. 2:5-8). On the mountain, the glory on the inside was visible on the outside and Peter decided that seeing Jesus in His glory was a good thing. Every not and then as we pass through this life, we are privileged to catch a glimpse of His glory. I have never seen His back parts like Moses did (Ex. 33:23). I have never heard Him speak in an audible voice like Abraham, Jacob, Moses, Elijah, and others did. I have never been within the veil in the Holy of Holies and been enveloped in His glory cloud. But I have seen a time or two when Heaven brushed up next to earth and things got a little foggy. There have been times when He pulled back the veil and let me catch a little glimpse of Him in His glory. When this happens, it is a good place to be in and you can glorify Jesus there.

Second, you know you are in a good place to glorify God, when you can exalt His greatness. While Jesus and His three disciples were on the mount, Jesus was visited by two prominent Hebrew ancestors, Moses, and Elijah. The appearance of these two men teaches us many lessons. For instance, Moses had been dead for 1,500 years when this even took place, but there he stands with Jesus and Elijah alive and well! This serves to remind us of the fact the redeemed do not go to the grave to wait a resurrection, but the pass from this life and are immediately in the presence of Jesus (2 Cor. 5:8; Phil. 1:23). Another lesson is this: Moses died on a mountain in the embrace of God. God conducted his funeral and carried his spirit home to glory. Moses represents those believers who die in faith. Since Elijah did not die but was carried off to heaven on a chariot of fire, he represents those saints of God who will one day be gathered up in the rapture and taken to glory. While the lessons are great, the question is what were they talking about? According to Luke 9:31 they were talking with Jesus about His "decease" (NKJV). The word "decease" means "exodus" (Strong's Concordance, 1984) Which means they were talking about His upcoming death on the cross. Here is another reason why going to church should make us glad about the one we come to glorify there: Moses and Elijah represent the Prophets, the Law, and every sacrifice described in the Law. All these points ahead to Jesus, the perfect fulfillment of the Law. The Prophets spoke of One Who was to come as a perfect sacrifice and redeemer. The bottom line here is Moses and Elijah came to exalt the greatness of Jesus and to reveal to the disciples He was Who He claimed to be.

Now why didn't Peter, James, and John ever mention in their writing the moment Moses and Elijah appeared? Why couldn't they tell it what it was like to seem two people materialize before their eyes? It was because the three disciples were fast asleep (Luke 9:32). It was only when they awoke, did they see Moses and Elijah. As usual Peter just had to say something and did, but according to Mark 9:6 "he did not know what to say, for they were greatly afraid" (NKJV). Peter had the same problem many people have; every time he opened his mouth it was just to change feet. In other words, he put his mouth in motion before he got his brain in gear. So, Peter wants to build three booths or tabernacles there on the mountain for Jesus, Moses, and Elijah. On the surface, this seems fine, but when Peter's statement is examined, it is clear he is placing Jesus on the same level as Moses and Elijah. If we are going to behave as a church, we need to stop placing Jesus on the same level as anyone else. Jesus is the only One to be glorified in His house. This is why a seventh person shows up on the mountain. God reminds everyone on the mountain that Jesus is far greater than Moses (the Law) and Elijah (the prophets). You are in a good place or church when you have arrived at the place where only Jesus has your attention. Who or what has your worship?

Finally, you know you are in a good place to glorify Christ, when you can experience His grace. When the three disciples hear the voice of God, they realize the scope of what is happening upon the mountain, this caused them to bow down in fear before the Lord (Matt. 17:6-8). Jesus, as was His custom, walked over to them and touched them and spoke peace to them. We are to behave as a church because when you are in His presence glorifying Him, there should be this sense of a touch from the Master's hand. Whether He touches you through peace in the heart, through the song service, the message of the pastor, prayer time, the reading of God's Word, or He even send His voice to speak to you; it is a great day when you can partake in the grace and peace of the Lord. Praise God for those times when His presence is real! His presence, His touch can drive away the icy fingers of fear and replace it with the warmth of His peace (Phil. 4:6-7). His touch can unlock the bars of worry and liberate the troubled soul! God's grace is sufficient for you and for me in every need of life (2 Cor. 12:9). You know you are in a good place when you can go to church and Jesus blesses you. As you go through life there is one constant we can always count on, regardless of what life throws at us: Jesus Christ will never change (Heb. 13:8), and He will never leave us (Heb. 13:5; Matt. 28:20). He will always be there!

In the final analysis, Jesus is the reason we come to church. When you consider everything, David said about his reason for being glad to go to the house of the Lord, you can agree to his reason to go to church should make us glad. When we behave as a church, there is ample reason to rejoice in the Lord. When we behave as a church, we bring glory to His holy name. May the Lord Jesus Christ bless and keep His bride as we behave as a church.

REFERENCES

Coca-Cola Company. (2012, January 1). *Chronicles of Coca Cola.* Retrieved from The Coca-Cola Company: https://www.coca-colacompany.com

Concise Oxford English Dictionary Eleventh Edition. (2004). New York: Oxford University Press.

Crosby, F. J. (1873). Blessed Assurance, Jesus is Mine.

Dictionary, M.-W. (1828). Merriam-Webster Dictionary. In *Merriam-Webster Dictionary.* Merriam-Webster Dictionary.

Flyod, R. (2018, July 8). *William Borden: A Life Without Regret.* Retrieved from Outreach Magazine: https://outreachmagazine.com/features/discipleship/31313-william-borden-life-without-regret.html

Friedrich Nietzsche. (2022). Retrieved from Standford Encyclopedia of Philosophy: https://plato.stanford.edu/entries/nietzsche/

Holman Illustrated Bible Dictionary. (2003). Nashville: Holman Bible Publishers.

Jewish Encyclopedia. (2021). Retrieved from Moses of Crete: https://www.jewishencyclopedia.com/articles/11071-moses-of-crete

Jewish Encyclopedia. (2021). Retrieved from LEMMLEIN (LÄMMLIN), ASHER: https://www.jewishencyclopedia.com/articles/9597-lammlein

Kendrick, A. (2006, September 29). Facing the Giants. *Facing the Giants.* Georgia: Sherwood Pictures.

Maraniss, D. (1999). When Pride Still Matter. In D. Maraniss, *When Pride Still Matter.* New York: Touchstone.

Mayo Clinic Staff. (2021, July 29). *Healthy Lifestyle.* Retrieved from Mayo Clinic: https://www.mayoclinic.org/healthy-lifestyle/stress-management/in-depth/stress-relief/art-20044456

Omer, S. (2023, August 28). *10 world hunger facts you need to know.* Retrieved from World Vision: https://www.worldvision.org/hunger-news-stories/world-hunger-facts

Plen, M. (2002). *My Jewish Learning.* Retrieved from My Jewish Learning: https://www.myjewishlearning.com/article/shabbetai-zevi/

Powers, D. C. (2021). *Behave as a Fisher of Men.* Bloomington: WestBow Press.

Powers, D. C. (2021). *Behave as a Follower of Christ.* Maitland: Xulon Press.

Powers, D. C. (2023). *Behave as a Church Member.* Westbow Press.

Rodriguez, T. (2016, September 1). *Laugh Lots, Live Longer.* Retrieved from Schientific American: https://www.scientificamerican.com/article/laugh-lots-live-longer/

Shimon Bar Kokhba. (1998). Retrieved from Jewish Virtual Library: https://www.jewishvirtuallibrary.org/shimon-bar-kokhba

Smith, G. (1887). *The Life of William Carey, Shoemaker and Missionary.* London: Murray.

Spurgeon, C. (1864, July 16). The Metropolitan Tabernacle Pulpit, Vol. X. *The Restoration and Conversion of the Jews*, p. 426

Stetzer, E. (2017, February 16). *Dropout and Disciples: How Many Students are Really Leaving the Church?* Retrieved from Christianity Today: http://www.christianitytoday.com

Storms, D. E. (1978). Standing on the Promises. *Content Magazine*, 13-14.

Strong's Concordance. (1984). Nashville: Thomas Nelson Publishers.

Twenty Five things Church Members Fight Over. (2022). Retrieved from Church Answers: https://churchanswers.com/blog/twenty-five-silly-things-church-members-fight-over/

Unknown. (2015).

Wood, D., Marshall, I. H., & Millard, A. (1996). *The New Bible Dictionary, Third Edition.* Intervarsity Press.

Printed in the United States
by Baker & Taylor Publisher Services